NICK HILL lives in Devizes, not far from the Ridgeway. As part of the Trailblazer team he is author, illustrator and cartographer, drawing many of the maps for the guides.

After completing a design degree at university, he set off into Asia having planned a short trip; several enthralling years later he'd crossed the continent overland four times. He settled temporarily in Thailand, his four years in Bangkok punctuated by periods in Siberia, China, India and Pakistan.

Nick has updated new editions of several other Trailblazer guides including the *Trans-Siberian Handbook* and the *South Downs Way* and is co-author of the forth-coming *Indian Rail Handbook* and *China Rail Handbook*.

The Ridgeway
First edition: 2006; this third edition 2012

Publisher
Trailblazer Publications
The Old Manse, Tower Rd, Hindhead, Surrey, GU26 6SU, UK
Fax (+44) 01428 607571, info@trailblazer-guides.com
www.trailblazer-guides.com

British Library Cataloguing in Publication Data
A catalogue record for this book is available from the British Library

ISBN 978-1-905864-40-9

© **Trailblazer** 2006, 2009, 2012
Text and maps

Editor and layout: Anna Jacomb-Hood
Proof-reading: Nicky Slade
Illustrations: © Nick Hill (pp59-60)
Photographs: cover © Nick Hill
flora section: C1 – Row 1, left; Row 3, middle & right: © Tricia Hayne
all other flora photographs © Bryn Thomas
all other photographs © Nick Hill
Cartography: Nick Hill
Index: Anna Jacomb-Hood

Warning: long-distance walking can be dangerous
Please read the notes on when to go (pp23-5) and health and safety (pp52-3).
Every effort has been made by the author and publisher to ensure that the information
contained herein is as accurate and up to date as possible. However, they are unable
to accept responsibility for any inconvenience, loss or injury sustained by anyone
as a result of the advice and information given in this guide.

Printed on chlorine-free paper by
D'Print (☎ +65-6581 3832), Singapore

The Ridgeway

AVEBURY TO IVINGHOE BEACON
planning, places to stay, places to eat,
includes 53 large-scale walking maps
and GPS waypoints

NICK HILL

TRAILBLAZER PUBLICATIONS

Acknowledgements

Many thanks to my walking companions, Ms Gift and Soph, for their company and help on various stages of the Ridgeway. Thanks also to Bill and Jenny Hill for the lift back from East Ilsley.

I am also grateful to the readers of the second edition who kindly wrote in with comments and new information: Michael Batty, Deborah Bennett, Tony Bird, Richard Butler, Timothy Cook, Emma Dann, Peter Davis, Martin Hockey, Marie Jones, Chris & Jenny Sharpe, Carol & Bill Tweedie, Neil Wolfenden and Alex Wright.

At Trailblazer, many thanks to Anna for all her advice and hard work on the text, Nicky Slade for proof-reading and also to Bryn for giving me this opportunity again.

A request

The author and publisher have tried to ensure that this guide is as accurate and up to date as possible. Nevertheless things change. If you notice any changes or omissions that should be included in the next edition of this book, please write to Trailblazer (address on p2) or email us at 🖳 info@trailblazer-guides.com. A free copy of the next edition will be sent to persons making a significant contribution.

Updated information will be available on:
🖳 **www.trailblazer-guides.com**

Front cover: By the White Horse near Uffington. (Photo © Nick Hill).

CONTENTS

INTRODUCTION

The Ridgeway stretches 87 miles (139km) across five counties, starting at Overton Hill near Avebury in Wiltshire and passing through Oxfordshire, Berkshire and Hertfordshire and ending at Ivinghoe Beacon in Buckinghamshire. Part of a network of tracks that from time immemorial naturally evolved all over the country, the Ridgeway was used by travellers, traders and drovers. Nowadays it is used only by travellers, most of them walking for pleasure. It is easily accessible from major cities such as Swindon, Oxford, Reading and London making it an ideal place to ramble, yet few seem to take the opportunity.

From its starting point at Overton Hill in Wiltshire, the trail immediately takes you up onto high ground with views of the countryside which change with the light and reach endlessly to the horizon. This stretch is open to the elements but it is exhilarating; on sunny days the air is wonderful, filling you with energy and physical well-being. It is also one of the most enjoyable sections of the Ridgeway; in blissful solitude you can look down at the towns and villages far below. Walking up here you're unlikely to meet many people and you are soon back in the distant past with the huge Iron Age forts of Barbury Castle and Liddington Castle. More ancient remains are at Wayland's Smithy, a Neolithic long barrow, before you reach the magnificent Uffington White Horse.

After the village of East Ilsley human habitation becomes more frequent and the path's character changes completely. A gradual descent brings you to the village of Streatley, on the banks of the Thames, and the bridge crossing into the neighbouring town of Goring. From here an easy trail runs along the tranquil banks of the Thames for several miles, passing through the attractive villages of South Stoke and North Stoke, then turns eastwards just before the towns of Wallingford and Crowmarsh Gifford.

The path now follows an ancient earthwork, Grim's Ditch, for several miles until it reaches Nuffield where the Ridgeway crosses a golf course. From here on the woodlands become a frequent companion with many ascents and descents before you can visit some of the old market towns just off the official route, such as Watlington, Chinnor and Princes Risborough. The trail continues through some fine beech woods; from the occasional clearings you look down on the landscape far below. The route then goes through the Chequers Estate, traditional country home of the prime minister. Later it passes close to small, picturesque villages, such as Wigginton and Aldbury, after which it climbs steadily as it enters the final section of woodland. When the trees thin out you can see your goal up ahead in the distance, several more hills away. At the end of the path, at Ivinghoe Beacon, you may be tired but you'll be rewarded by some spectacular, panoramic views of the countryside below.

Walking the Ridgeway is not difficult. It can be done in five days but this won't leave much time for relaxation or for enjoying the countryside you are walking through. You should also allow time to explore some of the towns along the way.

About this book

This guidebook is as practically useful, comprehensive and up to date as humanly possible. It is the **only** book you need; no phoning around for tourist brochures. You can find here everything for planning your trip including:

● All standards of accommodation from campsites to luxurious hotels
● Walking companies' details if you want an organised tour
● Suggested itineraries for all types of walkers
● Answers to all your questions: when to go, degree of difficulty, what to pack and the approximate cost of the whole walking holiday.

We also give comprehensive information to get you to and from the Ridgeway and 53 detailed maps (1:20,000) and 21 town plans to help you find your way along it. The route guide section includes:

● Walking times in both directions
● Reviews of campsites, hostels, pubs, B&Bs, guesthouses and hotels
● Cafés, pubs, teashops, takeaways and restaurants as well as shops for supplies
● Rail, bus and taxi information for all the villages and towns along the path
● Street plans of the main towns and villages along the route
● Historical, cultural and geographical background information.

Minimum impact for maximum insight

Nature's peace will flow into you as the sunshine flows into trees. The winds will blow their freshness into you and storms their energy, while cares will drop off like autumn leaves. **John Muir** (one of the world's earliest and most influential environmentalists, born in 1838)

It is no surprise that, since the time of John Muir, walkers and adventurers have been concerned about the natural environment; this book seeks to continue that tradition. By developing a deeper ecological awareness through a better understanding of nature and by supporting rural economies, local businesses, sensitive forms of transport and low-impact methods of farming and land-use we can all do our bit for a brighter future.

As we work harder and live our lives at an ever faster pace a walking holiday is a chance to escape from the daily grind and the natural pace gives us time to think and relax. This can have a positive impact not only on our own well-being but also on that of the area we pass through. There can be few activities as 'environmentally friendly' as walking.

PLANNING YOUR WALK

1

About the Ridgeway

HISTORY

The Ridgeway is very ancient. It's often described as 'the oldest road in Britain' and it's clear that parts of the route were in use 5000 years ago or more. The Ridgeway, as we know it today, is in fact the middle section of the Greater Ridgeway (see p183), an ancient system of tracks that stretches from Lyme Regis on the Dorset coast up to Hunstanton on the Norfolk coast. These tracks evolved over centuries as people chose the driest and most suitable paths across the countryside for themselves and their animals.

During your walk you will still be able to see and touch stone structures dating back to the prehistoric days of the Ridgeway; the burial mound known as Wayland's Smithy (see box p106) dates back to around 4000BC. Bronze Age stone structures also still stand, with the Avebury stone circle (see box pp72-3) and West Kennet Avenue (see box p75) being by far the most famous and accessible of these. Additionally, you can see numerous Bronze Age burial mounds dotted along the Ridgeway.

From the Iron Age there are several important hill forts to investigate including Barbury Castle (see p92) and Uffington Castle (see p108) plus earthworks such as Grim's Ditch (see box p142) also dating from this time. During the Dark Ages the Ridgeway was used as a major transport route for invading Danish Viking armies. By the late 9th century they had conquered most of Saxon England and had turned their attention to the kingdom of Wessex. In 871 they marched west along the Ridgeway from their base by the Thames at Reading only to be defeated by King Alfred at the Battle of Ashdown which some think took place in the area around White Horse Hill.

Up until the 18th century the Ridgeway still consisted of a broad network of routes across the country but then the Enclosures Acts were passed by parliament and these initiated the division of previously communal open land into privately owned fields. These fields were then hedged in to protect them from passing livestock and as a result the Ridgeway was forced to follow a single, defined route.

As coaching routes to London developed they avoided the actual course of the Ridgeway so it was left largely neglected – although several towns on the path, such as Marlborough and Wendover, were important rest-stops. The main users of the path, therefore, for several hundred years were drovers transporting their sheep from the West Country, and even Wales, to the large sheep fairs at East Ilsley (see p125). The width of the Ridgeway in this area, sometimes up to 20 metres, gives an idea of just how much livestock was transported on this route. At their peak the fairs held auctions for up to 80,000 sheep a day though by the early 20th century these fairs were in decline: the last one was held in 1934. From then on the path was used mainly by farmers for access to their land.

This was especially the case during World War II when many of the hillsides around the Ridgeway saw a change in use from sheep-grazed areas to cultivated fields. This was the result of a government-initiated effort to provide sufficient food for the population as imports were threatened owing to the fighting. This not only changed the visual landscape of many areas of the Ridgeway but also damaged the indigenous wildlife as powerful chemical fertilisers were used to improve the poor soil.

The first calls for the Ridgeway to be recognised as a long-distance walking trail were made in 1947 by the National Parks Committee and in the 1950s the Ramblers' Association (now Ramblers; see box p36) joined the appeal. However, it wasn't until 1973 that it was officially opened as a National Trail, since when, the most common use for the path has been for recreation. Only minor alterations have been made to its course since then which enables everyone to make their way along the 87-mile (139km) trail in the footsteps of the first Ridgeway pioneers from thousands of years ago.

HOW DIFFICULT IS THE RIDGEWAY?

If you are reasonably fit you won't encounter any problems walking the Ridgeway. There are no sections that are technically difficult and despite having a couple of steep climbs during each day's walking, it's nothing like as demanding as many other National Trails. The most important thing to do is plan your walking based on your own abilities. If you try to walk too far in one day, not only will you lose the chance to really enjoy the countryside you are walking through, but you will end up exhausted and won't feel much like walking the next day.

If anything, the western section of the Ridgeway, up to Streatley, could be considered more difficult than the eastern section owing to its remote and exposed conditions that become very apparent during bad weather. From

Streatley onwards the Ridgeway is often in woodland or passing through fields and goes through, or near to, numerous towns and villages.

Route finding

You shouldn't have any problems staying on the Ridgeway. At nearly all the junctions there are special 'Ridgeway' signposts clearly showing the direction of the trail and other branching paths. For many stretches you barely even need these signposts as the path is clear and well-trodden. However, it is always worth checking them as at some junctions the Ridgeway does veer off from what you'd consider the 'obvious' path. All path junctions are included on the maps in this book along with relevant notes.

GPS waypoints

If you have a handheld **GPS receiver** you will be able to take advantage of the waypoints marked on the maps, and listed on pp184-6 of this book.

Essentially a GPS will calculate your position on earth using a number of satellites and this will be accurate to a few metres. You might say that if this is possible, what is the point of taking paper maps and a compass with you? The answer is that if the batteries go flat, or the machine malfunctions, you'll have only your sense of direction to fall back on. Depending on how good that is, you might, or might not, be left wondering exactly where you are.

Having said this, it is **by no means compulsory** that you use a GPS in conjunction with this guide and you should-be able to get by with simply the signposts on the trail and the maps in this book. However, a GPS can be useful if for some reason you do get lost, or if you decide to explore off the trail and can't find your way back. It can also prove handy if you find yourself on the trail after dark when you can't see further than your torch beam.

If you do decide to use a GPS unit in conjunction with this book don't feel you need to be ticking off every waypoint as you reach it; you'll soon get bored and should get by without turning on your GPS for most of the trail. But if at any point you are **unsure of your position**, or wonder which way you should be headed, your GPS can give a quick and reassuring answer.

You can manually key the nearest presumed waypoint from the list in this book into your unit as and when the need arises. Or, much less laboriously and with less margin for keystroke error, you can download the complete list (but not the descriptions) for free as a GPS-readable file from the Trailblazer website. You'll need the correct cable and adequate memory in your unit. This file, as well as instructions on how to interpret an OS grid reference, can be found in the updates section of the Ridgeway text on the Trailblazer website (🖳 www.trailblazer-guides.com).

HOW LONG DO YOU NEED?

This depends on your fitness and experience. Do not try to do too much in one day if you are new to long-distance walking. Most people find that eight days is enough to complete the walk and still have time to look around the villages and enjoy the views along the way. Alternatively, the entire path can be done in five days if you are fit enough, but you won't see much of the surrounding countryside.

If you're camping don't underestimate how much a heavy pack laden with camping gear will slow you down. It is also worth bearing in mind that those who take it easy on the Ridgeway see a lot more than those who sweat out long days and tend to only ever see the path in front of them. If you are walking on your own you can dictate the pace, but when walking with someone else you need to take their abilities into account and take time to enjoy their company – this may slow you down. If you don't take time to do this, you might as well be walking separately and simply meet up at the end of the day.

On all sections, but particularly the western section, you'll also need to consider how far off the path your accommodation is and build that distance into your daily total. Although some B&Bs will collect you from the Ridgeway and drop you back the next morning, not all offer this service so you do need to check when reserving a room. On p28 there are some suggested itineraries covering different walking speeds that will give you an idea of what you can expect to achieve each day.

If you only have a few days it makes sense to concentrate on the 'best' parts of the Ridgeway; there is a list of recommended day/two-day walks on p29.

Practical information for the walker

ACCOMMODATION

There is plenty of accommodation along the Ridgeway and if you plan ahead you shouldn't encounter any problems finding somewhere to stay. However, most accommodation falls into the B&B category: there are a number of campsites but only one YHA hostel and one bunkhouse on/near the path.

On the western section, up to Streatley, there is virtually no accommodation on the Ridgeway itself and the nearest place to stay might be a mile or two off the path: for this reason, you really should book ahead otherwise you might find yourself very tired and without a bed for the night.

Camping

Wild camping (see also pp48-9) is not strictly allowed on the Ridgeway: it's private land and although it's a public right of way this does not entitle you to stop and camp. However, if you pitch your tent on the path and move on the next morning leaving no trace of yourself, you shouldn't have any problems. In many places the path is wide enough to pitch a tent and leave room for anyone else passing by. Unless you have personally asked permission from the land-owner, do not pitch your tent in fields or woods next to the Ridgeway.

There are a number of official campsites with basic facilities such as toilets and the all-important showers with prices around £5 per person which makes this the cheapest accommodation option. The campsites aren't usually open in the winter (October to March), which is a strong hint that camping at this time of year really isn't much fun.

There simply aren't enough official campsites along the Ridgeway for you to stay at one every night of your walk so sometimes you'll have to engage in a spot of wild camping or splash out on a B&B.

YHA hostels and bunkhouses

YHA hostels and bunkhouses are cheap and allow you to travel on a budget without having to carry cumbersome camping equipment. They are also good places to meet fellow walkers and in many cases are just as comfortable as B&Bs. However, there is now only one YHA hostel actually on the Ridgeway – at Streatley – and one independent bunkhouse, at Court Hill.

Both Streatley (see p130) and Court Hill (see p116) provide bedding so there is no need to carry a sleeping bag if you are expecting to be in B&Bs most other nights. Additionally both have a self-catering kitchen and provide meals.

YHA hostels are, despite their name, for anyone of any age. You can join the **Youth Hostels Association of England and Wales** (YHA; ☎ 01629 592700, 🖳 www.yha.org.uk) on arrival at any hostel, or over the phone or on the internet, for £15.95 per year. However, if you are not a member and are only planning to stay in Streatley for one night it is cheaper to pay the non-member rate, an additional £3 per adult.

Bed and breakfast

Anyone who has not stayed in a bed and breakfast (B&B) has missed out on something very British. They usually consist of a bed in someone's house and a big cooked breakfast (see p14) in the morning. For visitors from outside Britain it can provide an interesting insight into the way of life here as you often feel like a guest of the family.

What to expect The B&Bs in this guide are included primarily due to their proximity to the Ridgeway. They basically all offer the same thing but can vary greatly in terms of quality, style and price.

Many B&Bs offer en suite rooms but often this can mean a shower and toilet have been squeezed into a corner of the room. For a few pounds less you can usually get a standard room and it's rarely far to the bathroom, which may have the choice of a bath or a shower, though admittedly you might have to share with other guests. At the end of a long day's walking some people prefer to stretch out in a bath rather than squash into a shower.

A **single** room has one bed in it, though not all B&Bs have a single room so if you are walking alone you might have to book a twin or double room and pay a supplement (see p14). **Twin** rooms and **double** rooms are often confused but a twin room comprises two single beds (which may be pushed together or left separate) while a double room has one double bed. **Family** rooms are for three or more people: they often have one double bed and one or two single beds but sometimes these are bunk beds.

If you think you would like an **evening meal** ask when you are booking as most B&Bs require advance warning. Alternatively, the owner may give you a lift to and from the nearest eating place if there isn't a pub or restaurant within walking distance. Some proprietors will make a **packed lunch** as long as you request it by the night before.

B&B owners may also provide a **pick-up service** from the Ridgeway and drop you off there the next morning, which can be a great help; offering to pay something towards the petrol would definitely be appreciated.

PLANNING YOUR WALK

Rates Some places charge a rate per room based on two people sharing, others charge per person. Many places do not have single rooms; if the rate is charged per room there may be a discount for single occupancy but if the rate is per person a supplement may be payable; in both cases this will be about £10-15. For further details see p23.

Booking You should always book your accommodation in advance. In summer, at weekends and on public holidays there can be stiff competition for beds and in winter there's the distinct possibility that the place could be closed.

Some B&Bs have their own website and offer online/email booking but for the majority you will need to phone. Most places ask for a deposit (about 50%) which is generally non-refundable if you cancel at short notice. Some places may charge 100% if the booking is for one night only. Always let the owner know as soon as possible if you have to cancel your booking so they can offer the bed to someone else.

Larger places take credit or debit cards. Most smaller B&Bs accept only cheques by post or payments by bank transfer for the deposit; the balance can be settled with cash or a cheque.

Guesthouses, pubs, inns and hotels
Guesthouses are usually more sophisticated than B&Bs and offer evening meals and a lounge for guests. Some **pubs** and **inns** offer accommodation; these have the added advantage of having a bar downstairs so it's not far to stagger up to bed. However, the noise from tipsy punters might prove a nuisance if you want an early night. **Hotels** are usually aimed more at the motoring tourist rather than the muddy walker and the tariff is likely to put off the budget traveller. You'll probably arrive there in the late afternoon and leave fairly early the next morning so it's hard to justify the price. However, if you want a few more luxuries in your room, or room service, it may be worth considering a hotel.

FOOD AND DRINK

Breakfast and lunch
Almost everywhere you stay, other than if camping, you'll be offered a full English cooked **breakfast**. A cooked breakfast includes some or all of the following: fried bacon, eggs, sausages, tomatoes, mushrooms, baked beans and fried bread – in addition to cereal and toast, washed down with a fruit juice and tea or coffee. This will certainly be enough to set you up for a day's walking – if you are thinking about calories, you'll probably want to spend the day trying to walk it off – but it may be more than you are used to or even want. If so, ask for a continental breakfast. If you want an early start or would prefer to skip breakfast it might be worth asking if you could have a packed lunch instead.

Many places to stay can also provide you with a packed **lunch** for an additional cost. Alternatively, packed lunches (and indeed breakfast) can be bought and made yourself. In most towns and villages you should be able to find at least one shop selling sandwiches and usually a café. If you are lucky you may be in town when there is a farmers' market (see box opposite).

❏ **Farmers' markets along the Ridgeway**

If you happen to be in town when a farmers' market is on you should definitely try to have a look at what's for sale. The general rule of these types of markets is that whatever is being sold must have been produced locally and by the people selling it. Not only do these markets offer an outlet for farmers to sell their produce direct to the public but you will also see many other small producers of high-quality niche foods selling too. Although these markets are becoming more commercial, the vendors are still usually from around the surrounding area, so you should get to try some local specialities.

Products that you are likely to find are seasonal fruit and vegetables; meat, poultry and game; dairy products such as local cheeses and yoghurt; eggs from hens, ducks and geese; sausages and pies; soups; farmed fish such as trout, and preserves like chutney and jam. Many of these are likely to be organic.

Few markets are held weekly or throughout the year owing to a current lack of demand and the stallholders need time to work their way round the other markets in the area too. Below is a list of farmers' markets in towns along the Ridgeway, though more are likely to be established as their popularity grows (see 🖳 www.farmersmarkets.net).

● **Marlborough** (see p67) Second Saturday (9am-1pm, Town Hall) and last Sunday (9am-1.30pm, High St) of every month.
● **Wantage** (see p118) Last Saturday of every month (8.30am-1pm), Market Place.
● **Wallingford** (see p139) Third Tuesday and fifth Saturday (when there is one) of every month (8.30am-1pm), Market Place.
● **Princes Risborough** (see p161) Third Thursday of every month (9am-1pm), High St.
● **Wendover** (see p168) Third Saturday of every month (9am-1pm), off the High St.
● **Tring** (see p174) Every other Saturday (9am-12.15pm), The Marketplace, off Brook St (🖳 www.tringfarmersmarket.co.uk).

Remember that certain stretches of the walk are devoid of anywhere to eat so look at the town and village facilities table (pp26-7) and check the information in Part 4 to make sure you don't go hungry.

Evening meals

There are some lovely **pubs** and **inns** on the Ridgeway but none directly on the path before Streatley. Although there are fewer freehouses than there used to be you can still sample some excellent beers (see box pp16-17) during or after a day's walking. Most pubs also serve food (at lunchtime and in the evenings, though not always daily) and this ranges from standard 'pub grub' to restaurant quality fare. There will usually be at least one vegetarian option. A popular lunchtime option in a pub is a 'ploughman's lunch'. This is a cold meal traditionally comprising a thick slice of cheese, bread and butter, salad, some pickles and possibly an apple, though there are many variations.

There are some quality **restaurants** in the larger towns. Additionally, most towns and some of the larger villages are riddled with cheap **takeaway** joints offering kebabs, pizzas, Chinese, Indian and fish 'n' chips; they can come in handy if you finish your walk late in the day, since they usually stay open until at least 11pm.

PLANNING YOUR WALK

Buying camping supplies

If you are camping, fuel for your stove, outdoor equipment and food supplies are important considerations. Plan your journey carefully as, particularly on the first half of the Ridgeway, there aren't many opportunities to stock up without embarking on a fair trek to the nearest shop and back.

Drinking water

Depending on the weather you will need to drink as much as two to four litres of water a day. If you're feeling lethargic it may well be that you haven't drunk enough, even if you're not particularly thirsty.

Drinking directly from streams and rivers is tempting, but is not a good idea. Streams that cross the path tend to have flowed across farmland where you can be pretty sure any number of farm animals have relieved themselves. Combined with the probable presence of farm pesticides and other delights it is best to avoid drinking from these streams.

There are drinking **water taps** at some points along the Ridgeway and these are marked on the maps. Where these are thin on the ground you can usually ask a friendly shopkeeper or pub staff to fill your bottle or pouch for you – from a tap, of course.

❏ Real ales along the Ridgeway

Among the many pleasures of strolling on the Ridgeway is coming across country pubs and inns that you would never otherwise have visited. As you'll discover, they all have their own character and you'll end up with some very fond memories of your time spent at some of them. You'll usually have the chance to try some real ales that you might not have tried before. There are too many ales to list here and many pubs change their beers on a regular basis, but below is a selection of real ales that you are almost guaranteed to see in the course of your walk. (ABV means 'alcohol by volume' and is expressed as a percentage of how much alcohol a drink contains).

● **Ridgeway Brewing**   Perhaps the most apt beers for Ridgeway walkers are those produced by Ridgeway Brewing, based in South Stoke in Oxfordshire. Their ales have only been brewed under contract by other breweries since 2003 but already have a good reputation. **Ridgeway Bitter** (ABV 4%) is their standard brew, but if you have time to linger you might like to try their stronger premium bitter, **Ridgeway Blue** (5%). Stronger still is their **Ridgeway IPA** (5.5%) and there is also **Ridgeway Ivanhoe** (5.2%). These are all available in bottles and sometimes on draught, though from personal experience they can be quite elusive; if you do see any of them, grab the opportunity!

● **White Horse Brewery**   Also very fitting for walkers of the Ridgeway, this company has been brewing since 2004. They produce three ales year round and various seasonal beers throughout the year. You are most likely to encounter their **Bitter** (3.7%), which is perfect if you're stopping off for a few. Their excellent **Wayland Smithy** (4.4%), is tastier though has the potential to stop you in your tracks. You might also like to try a pint of their **Village Idiot** (4.1%).

● **Wadworth**   Mainly around the beginning of the Ridgeway, but even as far as Tring, you will find Wadworth ales. The best known of these is **6X** (4.3%); this has been brewed in Wadworth's Devizes brewery since 1921 and has a fruity, malty taste and a copper colour.

When you are filling your bottle have a good drink from it then fill it again so you leave the tap with a full bottle and don't feel like drinking half of it 100 metres down the path. When you reach a water tap, remember to check that is working before you drink your remaining water.

MONEY

As there are no banks and few post offices on the first half of the Ridgeway, you should take plenty of **cash** with you when you set out. You'll find a bank and an ATM in Goring but after that, unless you leave the Ridgeway, you'll have to wait until Princes Risborough. Increasingly in towns where there is no bank there will be an ATM in a garage or at a newsagent but be aware that many of these charge £1.25-1.95 whatever amount you withdraw.

Small independent shops rarely accept payment by debit/credit card and require you to pay in cash, as will most B&Bs and campsites. Shops that do take cards, such as supermarkets, will sometimes advance cash against a card (cash-back) as long as you buy something (usually at least £5) at the same time, but these are few and far between on the Ridgeway. See also p35 and the town and village facilities table, pp26-7.

- **Arkell's** brewery in Swindon produces mainly **2B** (3.2%) and **3B** (4%), which you'll see in any of the pubs they own.
- **Brakspear** You'll certainly come across Brakspear ales, especially during the middle sections. The most common is **Brakspear Bitter** which is easy enough for anyone to drink, being only 3.4%. It has an amber colour and a mild taste. It's a good beer for more prolonged rest stops and has won many national awards. In March you'll also see **Brakspear Special** which at 4.3% is more like it for a quick lunchtime stop-off. This pint is a golden-brown colour with more bitterness than the normal Brakspear Bitter. Their **Oxford Gold** (4%) is brewed year-round and has a light, golden colour and fruity flavour.
- **Greene King** There are plenty of Greene King pubs on the east of the Ridgeway. The beers are all produced in its brewery in Bury St Edmunds, Suffolk, with **Abbott Ale** and **Greene King IPA** the most common sights on bars along the Ridgeway. Abbott Ale is fairly strong at 5% and has a very full flavour. It has been brewed since the 1950s and is one of the most esteemed ales in the country. Greene King IPA isn't quite as strong (3.6%) and its more subdued flavours make it popular as a session beer.
- **Timothy Taylor** Another real ale that you are likely to see is the famous **Landlord** (4.3%), brewed in West Yorkshire by Timothy Taylor. At the time of writing it had won CAMRA's Beer of the year award four times.
- **Hop Back Brewery** This brewery is in Downton, near Salisbury. Among the range of ales they produce is one that could be of particular interest to Ridgeway walkers, namely **Crop Circle**. Its ABV of 4.2% accompanied by its crisp and thirst-quenching qualities make it an ideal mid-walk drink. You might find this pint hard to find on the Ridgeway but it's available in pubs around the south-west of England.

For more information about real ales look at the website for **CAMRA** (Campaign for Real Ale) at ⌨ www.camra.org.uk.

Using the Post Office for banking Several banks in Britain have agreements with the Post Office allowing customers to make cash withdrawals using a debit card (with a PIN number) at branches throughout the country.

As many towns along the Ridgeway have a Post Office this can be a very useful service. However, check with the Post Office Helpline (☎ 08457-223344, 🖥 www.postoffice.co.uk) that the post offices en route are still open and that your bank has an agreement with the post office. If using the website click on Counter services, then Counter money services, then Pay in and withdraw money under Use your bank account for a full list of banks offering withdrawal facilities through post office branches and for a list of the branches with an ATM.

❏ **Information for foreign visitors**

● **Currency** The British pound (£) comes in notes of £100, £50, £20, £10 and £5, and coins of £2 and £1. The pound is divided into 100 pence (usually referred to as 'p', pronounced 'pee') which comes in silver coins of 50p, 20p, 10p, and 5p and copper coins of 2p and 1p.

● **Rates of exchange** Up-to-date rates of exchange can be found on 🖥 www.xe.com/ucc; alternatively ask at banks, post offices or travel agencies.

● **Business hours** Most **shops** and main **post offices** are open at least from Monday to Friday 9am-5pm and Saturday 9am-12.30pm but many shops choose longer hours and some open on Sunday as well. Occasionally, especially in rural areas, you'll come across a local shop that closes at lunchtime during the week, usually a Wednesday or Thursday. Many **supermarkets** are open 12 hours a day. **Banks** typically open at 9.30am Monday to Friday and close at 3.30pm or 4pm though in some places they may open only two or three days a week and/or in the morning only; ATM (cash) machines though are open all the time as long as they are not in a place that has limited opening hours. **Pub** hours are less predictable; although many open Mon-Sat 11am-11pm and Sun to 10.30pm, often in rural areas opening hours, particularly in the winter months, are Mon-Sat 11am-3pm & 6-11pm, Sun 11am/noon-3pm & 7-11pm.

● **National (bank/public) holidays** Most businesses are shut on 1 January, Good Friday (March/April), Easter Monday (March/April), first and last Monday in May, last Monday in August, 25 December and 26 December.

● **School holidays** State-school holidays in England are generally as follows: a one-week break late October, two weeks over Christmas and the New Year, a week mid-February, two weeks around Easter, one week at the end of May/early June (to coincide with the bank holiday at the end of May) and five to six weeks from late July to early September. State school holidays in Scotland are basically the same apart from the summer when terms ends late June/early July and starts again in mid-August. Private-school holidays fall at the same time, but tend to be slightly longer.

● **EHICs and travel insurance** Although Britain's National Health Service (NHS) is free at the point of use, that is only the case for residents. All visitors to Britain should be properly insured, including comprehensive health coverage. The European Health Insurance Card (EHIC) entitles EU nationals (on production of the EHIC card so ensure you bring it with you) to necessary medical treatment under the NHS while on a temporary visit here. For details, contact your national social security institution. However, this is not a substitute for proper medical cover on your travel insurance for unforeseen bills and for getting you home should that be necessary.

OTHER SERVICES

On the first half of the Ridgeway, services are a bit scant, but on the second half most villages and all the towns have at least one public **telephone**, a small **shop** and a **post office**. Apart from getting cash, post offices can be used for sending home unnecessary equipment that may be weighing you down.

In Part 4 special mention is given to other services that may be of use to the walker such as: **laundrettes**, **internet access**, **pharmacies** and **tourist information centres** – the latter can be used for finding and booking accommodation among other things.

Also consider cover for loss and theft of personal belongings, especially if you are camping or staying in hostels, as there may be times when you'll have to leave your belongings unattended, though you should always keep important things, such as your passport, with you.

● **Weights and measures** The European Commission is no longer attempting to ban the pint or the mile: so, in Britain, milk can be sold in pints (1 pint = 568ml), as can beer in pubs, though most other liquid including petrol (gasoline) and diesel is sold in litres. Distances on road and path signs will continue to be given in miles (1 mile = 1.6km) rather than kilometres, and yards (1yd = 0.9m) rather than metres. The population remains divided between those who still use inches (1 inch = 2.5cm), feet (1ft = 0.3m) and yards and those who are happy with millimetres, centimetres and metres; you'll often be told that 'it's only a hundred yards or so' to somewhere, rather than a hundred metres or so. Most food is sold in metric weights (g and kg) but the imperial weights of pounds (lb: 1lb = 453g) and ounces (oz: 1oz = 28g) are frequently displayed too. The weather – a frequent topic of conversation – is also an issue: while most forecasts predict temperatures in Celsius (C), many people continue to think in terms of Fahrenheit (F; see the temperature charts on p24 for conversions).

● **Smoking** The ban on smoking in public places relates not only to pubs and restaurants, but also to B&Bs, hostels and hotels. These latter have the right to designate one or more bedrooms where the occupants can smoke, but the ban is in force in all enclosed areas open to the public – even if they are in a private home such as a B&B. Should you be foolhardy enough to light up in a no-smoking area, which includes pretty well any indoor public place, you could be fined £50, but it's the owners of the premises who take the blame if they fail to stop you, with a potential fine of £2500.

● **Time** During the winter the whole of Britain is on Greenwich Meantime (GMT). The clocks move one hour forward on the last Sunday in March, remaining on British Summer Time (BST) until the last Sunday in October.

● **Telephone** From outside Britain the international country access code for Britain is ☎ 44 followed by the area code minus the first 0, and then the number you require. Within Britain, to call a landline number from a landline phone in the same telephone code area, the code can be omitted: dial the number only. If you're using a **mobile (cell) phone** that is registered overseas, consider buying a local SIM card to keep costs down. Mobile phone reception is quite reliable along the Ridgeway.

● **Emergency services** For police, ambulance, fire and mountain rescue dial ☎ 999 or the EU standard number ☎ 112.

WALKING COMPANIES & LUGGAGE TRANSFER

Several UK-based companies offer self-guided holidays on the Ridgeway but none, at the time of writing, offered a fully guided walk.

Self-guided holidays

Self-guided holidays usually include detailed advice and notes on itineraries and routes, maps, accommodation including breakfast, daily baggage transfer and transport arrangements at the start and end of your walk.

● **British & Irish Walks** (☎ 01242 254353, 💻 www.britishandirishwalks.com, Cheltenham) Offer walks along the southern section of the way.

● **Celtic Trails** (☎ 01291 689774, 💻 www.celtic-trails.com, Chepstow) Have two itineraries covering the whole walk and will also tailor-make walks.

● **Contours Walking Holidays** (☎ 01629 821900 💻 www.contours.co.uk, Derbyshire) Operate two itineraries covering the whole route and two offering just part of the route: Avebury to Goring, and Goring to Ivinghoe Beacon.

● **Discovery Travel** (☎ 01904 632226, 💻 www.discoverytravel.co.uk, York) Offer a seven night itinerary but it is flexible to suit requirements.

● **Explore Britain** (☎ 01740 650900, 💻 www.explorebritain.com, Durham) Operate two itineraries: the first half of the route and the whole route.

● **Footpath Holidays** (☎ 01985 840049, 💻 www.footpath-holidays.com, Wiltshire) Offer itineraries for the whole way or part of it.

● **Freedom Walking Holidays** (☎ 01491 871111; 💻 www.freedomwalking holidays.co.uk, Goring-on-Thames)   Can accommodate a variety of requirements within your holiday package. See also Carrier Bags below.

● **Macs Adventure** (☎ 0141 530 8886, 💻 www.macsadventure.com, Glasgow) Operate a number of self-guided walks lasting four to nine nights.

Luggage transfer

Carrier Bags (☎ 01491 871111, 💻 www.ridgewaytransportation.co.uk), part of Freedom Walking Holidays, see above) provides a luggage-transportation service (£7 per bag per stage, two bags minimum, max 20kg) along the Ridgeway.

Some of the B&Bs listed in this guide (see Part 4) will also take your luggage on to your next overnight stop if you are staying with them. Local taxi companies can also provide this service but may be more expensive.

DISABLED ACCESS

There are no officially recognised stretches of the Ridgeway open for wheelchair users, though that doesn't mean it isn't possible to use some stretches of the path. Particularly on the first half there are no stiles and only a handful of gates, none of which would prove problematic for a wheelchair user. On the downside though, the route on this section often consists of rutted tracks that can also be very muddy after rain. One area on this first half that is accessible is around Barbury Castle (see p92). There is a car park here and although the castle itself would prove very difficult for a wheelchair user, the area around it is beautiful and provides excellent views over the surrounding countryside. The second half of the Ridgeway is less isolated and the route passes through several towns that could make good starting points. The path heading east from Wendover (see p170) is accessible, but not particularly exciting.

Where the Ridgeway crosses a road there is often a car park and driving to one of these enables you to get into the open countryside quickly with little effort.

There is an ongoing project by National Trails to remove kissing gates and stiles and install wide gates in their place; this programme has been particularly successful on the first half of the trail. They also improve the surface of the trail in areas where it has become damaged.

MOUNTAIN BIKING

The Ridgeway and trails leading off it are very popular with mountain bikers. However, not all of it is open to them. The western section from Avebury to Streatley is totally open and has only a short section of road and relatively few gates compared to the eastern section. The paths along this portion are generally wide and shouldn't present a problem for mountain bikers. From Streatley heading east most sections of the Ridgeway are closed to cyclists except for an eight-mile stretch from Britwell Hill (near Watlington) to Wainhill (near Bledlow). This, of course, doesn't deter some cyclists who do use the designated footpaths despite doing so illegally.

Conditions on the Ridgeway during the summer months are pretty good for cyclists though some sections of heavily rutted path might cause problems. Also be aware of flint on some sections of the path as it can cause punctures.

MOTOR VEHICLES

Despite many people's opposition, motor vehicles are allowed to use selected stretches of the Ridgeway. Since 2006 only five short sections have been open to cars and motorcycles. The total length of these sections is about 17 miles and all but one mile of that is before the Thames. Of the five sections that are open, four can only be used between May and September.

Although you will rarely come across a car or 4x4 on the Ridgeway you are far more likely to be overtaken by motorcyclists, often riding in groups, which you'll hear coming from a long way off.

It's obvious that motor vehicles do serious damage to the Ridgeway tracks that they use and the effects of this damage are most keenly felt by walkers. It's not much fun walking on a deeply rutted, muddy track for several miles.

HORSE RIDERS

The same sections of the Ridgeway that are open to cyclists are also open to horse riders. In practice, most horse riders only use short sections of the path which link into many other bridleways. Deeply rutted tracks can be problematic for horses and you should also be aware of the flinty sections of path that can injure horses' hooves.

TAKING DOGS ALONG THE RIDGEWAY

You are allowed to take your dog on all sections of the Ridgeway. Indeed, the majority of people you meet will be accompanied by at least one dog. Although I've personally never met anyone on the trail who was walking the whole path with their dog, I have received a letter from a walker whose dog, Lottie, has completed the entire route in stages.

As the owner, you are fully responsible for your dog's behaviour. Dogs should always be kept on leads while around livestock (see box p51). Having said this, if you are harassed by cattle because of your dog, the Ramblers/NFU recommend letting the dog off the lead. Dog excrement should be cleaned up and not left to foul the boots of other walkers. Where there are water taps along the Ridgeway, there is often a trough for your dog to drink from but this is not always the case. You should take a bowl for your dog that you can fill from a water tap.

Remember, if you do plan to walk the whole path, or even a section of it, you will need to check if your dog will be welcome wherever you plan to stay. Places that accept dogs in the accommodation are identified in the route guide by the symbol 🐕; some charge extra (£5-10) for a dog.

Budgeting

The amount of money you need to take with you depends on your accommodation plans and how you're going to eat. If you camp and cook your own meals your expenses can be very low but most people prefer to have at least some of their meals cooked for them and even the hardiest camper may be tempted into the occasional B&B when the rain is falling.

Also, don't forget all those little things that inevitably push up your daily bill: postcards, stamps, cream teas, ice-creams, beer, buses here, buses there and more beer; it all adds up! Budget on an extra £50-100 per person for your trip.

CAMPING

You can survive on as little as £15 per person if you use the cheapest sites and cook all your own food from staple ingredients. Nevertheless, most people find that the best-laid plans to survive on the bare minimum soon fall flat after a couple of hard days' trekking. Always budget for unforeseen expenses and, of course, the end-of-day pint of beer which costs around £3. Assuming such liquid treats and the occasional takeaway or pub meal a budget of £20-25 per day is far more realistic.

HOSTELS AND BUNKHOUSES

Since there is only one YHA hostel and one bunkhouse on/near the path using only this kind of accommodation is not feasible for this walk. Accommodation costs from £12 per night and both places offer meals: breakfast costs about £5 and an evening meal about £9. Both places also have a self-catering kitchen. For further details see p130 and p116.

B&B-STYLE ACCOMMODATION

Rates can be as little as £50 per night for two people sharing a room but are more often £60-70, particularly for guesthouses and hotels, and can even be over £100 for the most luxurious places. Add on the price of lunch (though if you have had a cooked breakfast you may not want much), an evening meal, beer and other expenses and you can expect to need at least £55-75 per person per day. However, rates can be substantially less if you are planning to stay for three or more nights and are also usually lower during the winter months. If you are on a budget you could always ask to go without breakfast which will probably result in a reduction. See also p14.

When to go

SEASONS

The western half of the Ridgeway follows the high ground and is very exposed so if it rains you'll certainly know about it. Likewise, if it is sunny, you'll get very hot. To compound this there is very little in the way of shelter on the western section. The eastern section, on the whole, follows lower ground and is often in sheltered woodland. You are also far closer to human habitation on this section should the weather turn really bad. The **main walking season** is from Easter (March/April) to the end of September.

The biggest attraction of walking the Ridgeway in the **spring** is to see the wild flowers in bloom, especially the carpets of bluebells in the woods. You'll also get good walking weather at this time but there will be a risk of showers and thick fog can obscure pretty much everything in the early to mid-morning. Unsurprisingly, the Easter holiday is a busy time.

Obviously **summer** is the busiest season for walkers on the Ridgeway owing to fact that it is the main holiday period and the weather should be good. You probably still won't see many people on the western section, but the eastern section is very popular with dog-walkers and day-trippers. If you are walking on your own it can be nice to stop and chat to other walkers every once in a while. Although summer is your best bet, the weather in England is not always good at this time. Look at the forecast before you go and be prepared.

Autumn can be one of the best times of year to walk the Ridgeway. Most walkers have finished their holidays but you can still have good, clear weather and the sections of woodland walking are especially colourful. The western section is less inviting at this time owing to its exposed conditions.

The cold and often unpredictable weather in the **winter** makes walking the Ridgeway low on most people's lists of priorities. It certainly wouldn't be much

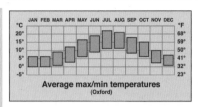

Average max/min temperatures
(Oxford)

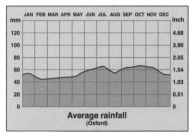

Average rainfall
(Oxford)

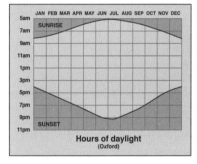

Hours of daylight
(Oxford)

fun on some of the open western sections but there is still plenty of opportunity for some good day walks on other sections if the weather is clear.

TEMPERATURES & RAINFALL

As the English climate is temperate, walking can be enjoyed at most times of the year. However, there will be plenty of days in the winter where it will be too cold for comfortable walking but equally in the summer it can sometimes be too hot. The air **temperature** will generally be fine, it's the rain you need to watch out for. On average it rains on about one day in three in England, though more often in the winter.

Rainfall in July can be as little as half that of January in the Ridgeway area, but that's not much consolation if you are caught in a summer downpour.

DAYLIGHT HOURS

If walking in autumn, winter and early spring, you must take account of how far you can walk in the available light. It may not be possible to cover as many miles as you would in summer. The sunrise and sunset times in the table (see above) are based on information for Oxford on the first of each month. This gives a rough picture for the Ridgeway. Also bear in mind that you will get a further 30-45 minutes of usable light before sunrise and after sunset depending on the weather.

FESTIVALS AND EVENTS

The main events along the Ridgeway are:
● **Organised events along the Ridgeway** The National Trails Office (🖥 www.nationaltrail.co.uk/ridgeway) organises walks and activities along the Ridgeway **year-round**. Most weekends there will be something going on, be it a walk along a particularly interesting section accompanied by a knowledgeable guide, a focus on specific wildlife, or a class in navigating skills. Visit the website for details of events.

● **Sarsen Trail** (Wiltshire Wildlife Trust, 🖳 www.wiltshirewildlife.org) This sponsored walk in aid of the Wiltshire Wildlife Trust covers a 26-mile route from Avebury to Stonehenge. It's held on the first Bank Holiday weekend in **May**. The route is dotted with checkpoints and there is a free coach service between the start and finish points. The event attracts more than 2000 walkers and you must register in advance.

● **The Ridgeway 40** (🖳 http://ridgeway40.org.uk) This is a 40-mile walk along the Ridgeway from its start at Overton Hill to the YHA hostel at Streatley. You are expected to complete the walk in one day and there are checkpoints along the route to keep you on track. There is also a separate event for people wishing to run the route. Walkers and runners must register in advance. The Ridgeway 40 is held annually on a weekend in **May**.

● **Marlborough Jazz** (🖳 www.marlboroughjazz.co.uk) This three-day festival features around 60 artists, performing all genres of jazz music, and attracts more than 5000 visitors. The festival takes place **early to mid-July**.

● **Goring & Streatley Regatta** (🖳 www.goringgapbc.org.uk) This regatta, held in **mid-July**, is organised by Goring Gap Boat Club. The focus is on providing a family day out with a funfair, live entertainment and food and drink stalls, in addition to the boat races on the Thames.

● **Uffington White Horse Show** (🖳 www.whitehorseshow.co.uk) This traditional country show, held on ground between Uffington and Kingston Lisle villages, is a well-organised event attracting over 10,000 visitors. Past attractions have included a fly-past by a Vulcan Bomber, stunt horses, ferret racing, morris dancing, a heavy horse show and a falconry display. This event is held on the Bank Holiday weekend at the end of **August**.

● **Morris dancing** During the **summer months** you can see Morris groups performing at festivals and pubs along the first half of the Ridgeway. Most performances are arranged well in advance which allows you to plan your trip to coincide with them if you so desire. See box p112 for more information about the Morris dancing tradition.

Itineraries

This guidebook has not been divided up into rigid daily stages. Instead, it's structured to make it easy for you to plan your own itinerary. If you have a week to spare you can walk the Ridgeway in one go. However, many people decide to walk it in sections over a longer period. Or you might simply want to pick out the best parts for a series of day walks.

To help you plan your walk look at the **planning map** (see opposite inside back cover) and the **table of village & town facilities**, see pp26-7, which gives a rundown on the essential information you need regarding accommodation possibilities and services. Alternatively, you could follow one of the suggested **itineraries**, see p28, that are based on walking speed. *(continued on p28)*

PLANNING YOUR WALK

				VILLAGE AND
Place name (places in brackets are a short walk off the Ridgeway)	**Distance from previous place** approx miles/km (Distances in brackets indicate how far the place is from the nearest point on the Ridgeway)	**ATM** (**cash machine) or bank**	**Post office** (✔) means limited opening hours	**Tourist Information Centre (TIC) Visitor Centre (VC)**
(Marlborough)		ATM+bank	✔	
(Avebury)		ATM only	(✔)	
(West Overton)				
(East Kennet)				
Overton Hill	0			
(Ogbourne St George)	9/14.5 (+0.6/1)			
(Liddington)	6.5/10.5 (+0.6/1)			
Foxhill	1/1.5			
(Bishopstone)	1.2/2 (+0.6/1)			
(Ashbury)	1.5/2.5 (+0.6/1)		(✔)	
(Woolstone)	2/3 (+1.2/2)			
(Uffington)	0 (+1.7/2.5)		✔	
(Down Barn Farm)	2.5/4 (+0.6/1)			
(Sparsholt)	0 (+1.5/2.5)			
(Letcombe Regis)	3.9/6 (+1.5/2.5)			
(Court Hill)	0.6/1 (+0.3/0.5)			
(Wantage)	0 (+2/3)	ATM+bank	✔	VC
(East Ilsley)	8.2/13 (+1/1.5)			
(Compton)	0 (+1.5/2.5)		✔	
(Aldworth)	2.7/4.5 (+1.2/2)			
Streatley	3/5			
Goring	0.3/0.5	ATM+bank	✔	
South Stoke	1.5/2.5			
North Stoke	2.5/4			
(Wallingford)	1.2/2 (+1.2/2)	ATM+bank	✔	TIC
(Crowmarsh Gifford)	0 (+0.7/1.2)			
Nuffield	4/6.5			
(Watlington)	5.5/9 (+0.6/1)	ATM+bank	✔	
(Lewknor)	2.5/4 (+0.5/0.8)			
(Kingston Blount)	1.7/2.5 (+0.6/1)			
(Chinnor)	1.5/2.5 (+0.3/0.5)	ATM only	✔	
Princes Risborough	5.3/8.5 (+0.2/0.3)	ATM+bank	✔	TIC
Wendover	6.2/10	ATM+bank	✔	TIC
Wigginton	6.2/10			
(Tring)	0 (+1/1.5)	ATM+bank	✔	TIC
(Aldbury)	2/3 (0.6/1)	ATM only	✔	
Ivinghoe Beacon	3.1/5			
(Ivinghoe)	3.4/5.5 (+1.2/2)		✔	

TOTAL DISTANCE 87 miles/139km

TOWN FACILITIES

Eating place ✓=one ✔✔=two ✔✔✔=3+	Food store	Campsite	Hostel/ bunk- house	B&B-style accommodation ✓=one ✔✔=two ✔✔✔=three+	Place name (places in brackets are a short walk off the Ridgeway; see opposite for distances)
✔✔✔	✓			✔✔✔	(Marlborough)
✔✔	✓			✔✔✔	(Avebury)
✓					(West Overton)
				✓	(East Kennet)
					Overton Hill
✔✔		✓		✔✔✔	(Ogbourne St George)
✓					(Liddington)
✓					Foxhill
✓				✔✔	(Bishopstone)
✓				✓	(Ashbury)
✓				✓	(Woolstone)
✓	✓			✔✔	(Uffington)
		✓		✓	(Down Barn Farm)
✓				✓	(Sparsholt)
✓				✓	(Letcombe Regis)
✓		✓	B		(Court Hill)
✔✔✔	✓			✔✔✔	(Wantage)
✔✔				✔✔	(East Ilsley)
✓	✓			✓	(Compton)
✓				✓	(Aldworth)
✓			YHA	✔✔✔	Streatley
✔✔✔	✓			✔✔✔	Goring
✓				✔✔	South Stoke
				✓	North Stoke
✔✔✔	✓			✔✔✔	(Wallingford)
✔✔	✓	✓		✓	(Crowmarsh Gifford)
				✓	Nuffield
✔✔✔	✓	✓		✔✔	(Watlington)
✓				✓	(Lewknor)
✓				✔✔	(Kingston Blount)
✔✔✔	✓				(Chinnor)
✔✔✔	✓			✔✔✔	Princes Risborough
✔✔✔	✓			✔✔	Wendover
✓				✓	Wigginton
✔✔✔	✓			✔✔	(Tring)
✔✔	✓			✓	(Aldbury)
					Ivinghoe Beacon
✔✔	✓	✓		✓	(Ivinghoe)

YHA = YHA hostel   B = Bunkhouse

PLANNING YOUR WALK

(continued from p25) There is also a list of recommended linear day and two-day (weekend) walks (see opposite) that cover the highlights of the Ridgeway.

The **public transport map** and the table of **bus services** are on pp42-5.

SUGGESTED ITINERARIES

CAMPING

Night	Relaxed pace Place	Approx Distance miles/km	Medium pace Place	Approx Distance miles/km	Fast pace Place	Approx Distance miles/km
0	Overton Hill		Overton Hill		Overton Hill	
1	Ogbourne St G	9/14.5	Ogbourne St G	9/14.5	Ogbourne St G	9/14.5
2	Down Barn Farm	14.5/23	Down Barn Farm	14.5/23	Court Hill	19/30.5
3	Court Hill	4.5/7	Court Hill	4.5/7	Streatley*	14/22.5
4	Streatley*	14/22.5	Streatley*	14/22.5	Watlington	15/24
5	Crowmarsh Gifford	7.3/12	Crowmarsh Gifford	7.3/12	Princes Risborough	11/18
6	Watlington	9.6/15	Nuffield*	4/6.5	Ivinghoe Beacon	17.5/28
7	Princes Risborough	11/18	Princes Risborough	16.5/26		
8	Wigginton*	12.4/20	Ivinghoe Beacon	17.5/28		
9	Ivinghoe Beacon	5.1/8				

*No campsites but alternative accommodation is available

STAYING IN B&B-STYLE ACCOMMODATION

Night	Relaxed pace Place	Approx Distance miles/km	Medium pace Place	Approx Distance miles/km	Fast pace Place	Approx Distance miles/km
0	Overton Hill		Overton Hill		Overton Hill	
1	Ogbourne St G	9/14.5	Bishopstone	17.7/28.5	Bishopstone	17.7/28.5
2	Bishopstone	8.7/14	Letcombe Rgs	9.9/15.5	East Ilsley	18.7/30
3	Letcombe Rgs	9.9/15.5	Goring	14.8/23.5	Nuffield	15.2/24
4	Goring	14.8/23.5	Watlington	14.7/23.5	Princes Risborough	16.5/26
5	Nuffield	9.2/14.5	Princes Risborough	11/18	Ivinghoe Beacon	17.5/28
6	Kingston Blount	10.3/16.5	Wigginton	12.4/20		
7	Wendover	13.6/24.5	Ivinghoe Beacon	5.1/8		
8	Wigginton	6.2/10				
9	Ivinghoe Beacon	5.1/8				

The best day and two-day walks   29

Once you have an idea of your approach turn to **Part 4** for detailed information on accommodation, places to eat and drink, as well as other services in each village and town on the route. Also in Part 4 you will find summaries of the route to accompany the detailed trail maps.

PLANNING YOUR WALK

❏ THE BEST DAY AND TWO-DAY WALKS

The desire of most walkers is to tackle the whole Ridgeway in one go but sometimes this isn't possible. Spare time, good weather, transport and money all need to be found at the same time. For this reason many walkers choose to walk the Ridgeway in separate sections, maybe over a series of summer weekends. Other walkers might not be so concerned about walking every inch of the official path and might only want to walk the best bits. Simply getting out and walking any part of the Ridgeway will be rewarding, but listed below are some especially enjoyable parts. If you're feeling ambitious and the weather is on your side, you could try completing a weekend walk in one day.

For details of public transport services to/from the places listed below see pp41-5.

Day walks
● **Avebury to Ogbourne St George** 9¹/₂ miles/15km (see pp88-97) This path starts at Avebury stone circle and walks the quiet high ridge to the Iron Age fort of Barbury Castle where there are magnificent views northwards; it then goes onto Smeathe's Ridge and finally down into the pleasant village of Ogbourne St George where there is a pub to relax in.
● **Foxhill to White Horse Hill** 5 miles/8km (see pp101-9) Start outside The Burj restaurant at the Foxhill crossroads and quickly climb up onto the open high ground for stunning views, visit the ancient burial site at Wayland's Smithy and finish at White Horse Hill, the site of an Iron Age hill fort, Dragon Hill, and the original white horse.
● **White Horse Hill to East Ilsley** 15 miles/24km (see pp109-26) If you fancy a bit of time on your own, this is the most isolated section of the Ridgeway path. It keeps to the high ground with only a few road crossings and a handful of farms on the entire stretch. Make sure you choose decent weather for this walk as there is virtually no shelter.
● **Streatley to Wallingford** 7 miles/11.5km (see pp130-42) Begin in the Thames-side village of Streatley and walk into Goring before following the bank of the Thames northwards through the delightful villages of South and North Stoke. The path then heads into the old town of Wallingford.
● **Wendover to Ivinghoe Beacon** 10 miles/16km (see pp165-82) From the attractive town of Wendover the path takes you through the best woodland walking on the Ridgeway, coming close to the village of Wigginton should you choose to stop off for lunch. The final section takes on Ivinghoe Beacon, a long, steep climb through woodland and finally some excellent open walking with increasingly fantastic views.

Two-day (weekend) walks
● **Avebury to White Horse Hill** 22 miles/35.5km (see pp41-109) This walk takes in many of the most interesting ancient sites along the Ridgeway. The walking is mainly along broad, grassy tracks with few steep climbs. There is no accommodation near the middle of this walk so you'll either have a short first day and long second, or vice versa depending on where you decide to stay.
● **East Ilsley to Watlington** 22 miles/35.5km (see pp125-51) This walk takes in a bit of each of the Ridgeway's main attractions – first, isolated walking, then, the path along the Thames and finally, some fine woodland walking. You can stay in Wallingford to divide the journey neatly into two days.

WHICH DIRECTION?

The generally accepted way to walk the Ridgeway is from west to east though it really doesn't matter. As the two halves are very different you might base your decision on what type of scenery and terrain you'd like to tackle first. Neither section is particularly demanding but the western section is far more isolated and really isn't much fun in bad weather. The eastern section, being in woodlands for much of the time, is far more sheltered and relaxing.

Availability of public transport heading in either direction along the Ridgeway is similar so this shouldn't have much bearing on which direction you choose to walk in.

Although the maps in Part 4 of this book follow the Ridgeway from west to east, there are timings on all the maps for walking in either direction.

SUGGESTED ITINERARIES

The itineraries in the box on p28 are based on different accommodation types: one is for those who prefer to camp or stay in hostels/bunkhouses; the other is for those who choose to stay in B&B-style accommodation. Each is divided into three alternatives based on walking speeds. They are only suggestions so feel free to adapt them to your needs. **Don't forget** to add your travelling time before and after the walk.

SIDE TRIPS

There are plenty of good circular and linear walks from the Ridgeway. Listed on p29 are just a selection of them, starting from the western end of the trail and heading east. Detailed information about all these routes can be obtained from local tourist information centres (see box p36) or from the relevant county/district councils (see box p56).

● **Aldbourne Circular Route** This is a 12-mile (19.5km) route which for several miles uses the Ridgeway. It takes in Aldbourne village, several Bronze Age burial mounds, the deserted village of Snap (see p97), Liddington Castle (see p97) and Sugar Hill. The trail is waymarked with discs and it's also marked on OS Explorer maps 157 and 170.

● **Ashbury Circular Walk** This 10-mile (16km) walk from the village of Ashbury (see p105) takes the walker through some beautiful countryside once the initial steep climb has been completed. The path crosses the Ridgeway and heads to Alfred's Castle, an Iron Age hillfort, before reaching Ashdown House, a 17th-century Dutch-style property owned by the National Trust. From here it returns to the Ridgeway via a different route and takes in Wayland's Smithy (see box p106), before heading back down the hill to Ashbury. The trail is waymarked with discs and although the paths are marked on OS Explorer map 170, they aren't labelled.

● **Lambourn Valley Way** This 20-mile (32km) route starts at Uffington White Horse and leads down into the valley to reach the village of Lambourn. It then broadly follows the River Lambourn along the valley to its end in Newbury.

This is a very peaceful walk passing through several small villages with only the crossing of the M4 to spoil the atmosphere. The route is waymarked with discs and fingerposts and is also marked on OS Explorer maps 170 and 158.

● **East/West Ilsley Circular Route** This 6-mile (9.5km) walk is best started and finished in one of the pubs in East Ilsley. The path takes a wayward route to West Ilsley before heading up to the Ridgeway and following it for just over a mile then turning back to East Ilsley. Much of this path is on broad tracks that often run close to racehorse gallops. The route is waymarked with discs and the paths are marked on OS Explorer map 170.

● **The Chiltern Link** This 8-mile (13km) linear walk starts on Wendover High St and meanders through woods and open countryside to the town of Chesham where you can pick up the Chess Valley Walk. Several miles into the walk you reach The Lee, a tiny village with a popular pub – The Cock and Rabbit Inn – that is well worth visiting. The route is waymarked with discs and fingerposts and is also marked on OS Explorer map 181.

● **Beacon View Walk** This 5-mile (8km) circular walk is usually started and finished at The Greyhound in Wigginton (see p173) and follows the course of the Ridgeway for about two miles from Hastoe Cross to the bridge over the Grand Union Canal. The route then follows the canal to Cow Roast (a village!) before heading back to Wigginton. The paths comprising the route are marked with standard signs and all paths appear on OS Explorer map 181.

● **The Ashridge Drovers' Walk** This 6-mile (9.5km) circular walk starts and finishes at Tring Station (see Map 47, p179). From there it makes for Aldbury (see p178) then up to the Bridgewater Monument where there is a visitor centre and tea shop. The route then follows the high ground to join the Ridgeway which it follows down to the railway station. The walk often follows wide, sunken lanes used in the past for droving (moving livestock). The paths comprising the route are marked with standard signs and all paths appear on OS Explorer map 181.

● **Two Ridges Link** This 8-mile (13km) linear walk runs from Ivinghoe Beacon, the very end of the Ridgeway, to Leighton Buzzard at the start of the Greensand Ridge Walk. The walk takes you first through the villages of Ivinghoe Aston and Slapton before joining the Grand Union Canal. The trail is fully waymarked with dedicated Two Ridges Walk signs and it's also marked on OS Explorer maps 181 and 192.

● **Ridgeway Link Walk** This 7½-mile (12km) linear walk was officially opened in June 2007. It follows the Icknield Way from Chilterns Gateway Centre, on Dunstable Downs, to Ivinghoe Beacon (see Map 48, p181). Of course, walking the path in reverse might be more practical for Ridgeway walkers, especially if you are heading to Dunstable for transport connections. The walk passes through Whipsnade and Dagnall, both of which have a pub. Chilterns Gateway Centre is open all year and has a café, shop and toilets and there is also a car park. Although the route is well waymarked with Ridgeway Link discs some of the paths can get rather muddy after rain. The entire route is marked as the Icknield Way on OS Explorer map 181.

What to take

Deciding how much to take with you can be difficult. Experienced walkers know that you really should take only the bare essentials but at the same time you need to ensure you have all the equipment necessary to make the trip safe and comfortable.

KEEP IT LIGHT

Carrying a heavy rucksack really can ruin your enjoyment of a good walk and can also slow you down, turning an easy seven-mile day into an interminable slog. Be ruthless when you pack and leave behind all those little home comforts that you tell yourself don't weigh that much really. This advice is even more pertinent to campers who have added weight to carry.

HOW TO CARRY IT

The size of your **rucksack** depends on where you are planning to stay and how you are planning to eat. If you are camping and cooking for yourself you will probably need a 65- to 75-litre rucksack which can hold the tent, sleeping bag, cooking equipment and food. Make sure your rucksack has a stiffened back and can be adjusted to fit your own back comfortably. This will make carrying the weight much easier.

When packing the rucksack make sure you have all the things you are likely to need during the day near the top or in the side pockets. This includes map, water bottle or pouch, packed lunch, waterproofs and this guidebook, of course. Make sure the hip belt and chest strap (if there is one) are fastened tightly as this helps distribute the weight with most of it being carried on your hips. Rucksacks are decorated with seemingly pointless straps but if you adjust them correctly it can make a big difference to your personal comfort while walking.

If you plan to stay in B&B-style accommodation a 30- to 40-litre pack should be more than enough to carry everything you need.

Consider taking a small **bum bag** or **day pack** for your camera, guidebook and other essentials for when you go sightseeing or for a day walk.

A good habit to establish is to always put things in the same place in your rucksack and memorise where they are. There is nothing more annoying than having to pull everything out of your pack to find that lost banana when you're starving, or scrambling for your camera when there is a rare opportunity to photograph an owl perched on a fencepost. It's also a good idea to keep everything in **canoe bags**, **waterproof rucksack liners** or strong plastic bags. If you don't, it's bound to rain.

FOOTWEAR

Your **boots** are the single most important item of gear that can affect the enjoyment of your trek. In the summer you can use a light pair of trail shoes if you're only carrying a small pack. Make sure they have a Gore-Tex lining otherwise you could end up with wet, cold feet if there is any rain. Although the Ridgeway isn't particularly strenuous, some of the terrain can be quite rough so a good pair of walking boots is a safer bet. They must fit well and be properly broken in. It is no good discovering that your boots are slowly murdering your feet two days into a week-long trek. See p52 for more blister-avoidance advice.

The traditional wearing of a thin liner **sock** under a thicker wool sock is no longer necessary if you choose a high-quality sock specially designed for walking. A high proportion of natural fibres makes them much more comfortable. Three pairs are ample. Some walkers like to have a **second pair of shoes** to wear when they are not on the trail. Trainers, sport sandals or flip-flops are all suitable as long as they are light.

CLOTHES

Experienced walkers know the importance of wearing the right clothes. Especially up on the western part of the Ridgeway the wind, rain and sun can all be fierce and there's often no shelter if you are caught out. Modern technology in outdoor attire can seem baffling but it comes down to: a base layer to transport sweat away from your skin; a mid-layer or two to keep you warm; and an outer layer or 'shell' to protect you from the wind and rain.

Base layer
Cotton absorbs sweat, trapping it next to the skin which will chill you rapidly when you stop exercising. A thin lightweight **thermal top** made from synthetic material is better as it draws moisture away, keeping you dry. It will be cool if worn on its own in hot weather and warm when worn under other clothes in cooler conditions. A spare would be sensible. You may also like to bring a **shirt** for wearing in the evening.

Mid-layers
In the summer a woollen jumper or mid-weight polyester **fleece** will suffice. For the rest of the year you will need an extra layer to keep you warm. Both wool and fleece, unlike cotton, have the ability to stay reasonably warm when wet.

Outer layer
A **waterproof jacket** is essential year-round and will be much more comfortable (but also more expensive) if it's also 'breathable' to prevent the build up of condensation on the inside. This layer can also be worn to keep out the wind.

Leg wear
Whatever you wear on your legs it should be light, quick drying and not restricting. Many British walkers find polyester tracksuit bottoms comfortable. Poly-

cotton or microfibre trousers are also excellent. Denim jeans should never be worn; if they get wet they become heavy, cold and bind to your legs. A pair of **shorts** is nice to have on sunny days. Thermal **longjohns** or thick tights are cosy if you're camping but are probably unnecessary even in winter. **Waterproof trousers** are necessary most of the year. In summer a pair of windproof and quick-drying trousers are useful in showery weather. **Gaiters** are not really necessary but may come in useful in wet weather when the vegetation around your legs is dripping wet.

Underwear
Three changes of what you normally wear is fine. Women may find a **sports bra** more comfortable because pack straps can cause bra straps to dig into your shoulders.

Other clothes
A **warm** hat and **gloves** should always be kept in your rucksack, year-round. You never know when you might need them. In summer you should also carry a **sun hat** with you, preferably one that also covers the back of your neck. Also consider a small **towel**, especially if you are camping.

TOILETRIES

Only take the minimum: a small bar of **soap** in a plastic container (unless staying in B&B-style accommodation) which can also be used instead of shaving cream and for washing clothes; a tiny tube of **toothpaste** and a **toothbrush**; one roll of **loo paper** in a plastic bag. If you are planning to defecate outdoors you will also need a lightweight **trowel** for burying the evidence (see p48 for further tips). A **razor**, **deodorant**, **tampons/sanitary towels** and a high-factor **sun screen** should cover all your needs.

FIRST-AID KIT

There is a pharmacy in many towns and villages along the route so you only need a small kit to cover common problems and emergencies: pack it in a waterproof container.

A basic kit will contain **aspirin** or **paracetamol** for treating mild to moderate pain and fever; **plasters/Band Aids** for minor cuts; **Moleskin**, **Compeed**, or **Second skin** for blisters; a **bandage** for holding dressings, splints or limbs in place and for supporting a sprained ankle or a weak knee; a small selection of different-sized **sterile dressings** for wounds; **porous adhesive tape**, **antiseptic wipes**, **antiseptic cream**, **safety pins**, **tweezers** and **scissors**.

GENERAL ITEMS

Essential
The following should be in everyone's rucksack: a one-litre **water bottle** or **pouch**; a **torch** (flashlight) with spare bulb and batteries in case you end up

walking after dark; **emergency food** (see pp51-2) which your body can quickly convert into energy; a **penknife**; a **watch** with an alarm; and a suitable **bag** for packing out any rubbish you accumulate.

A **whistle** is also worth taking. It can fit in a pocket and although you are very unlikely to need it you may be grateful for it in the unlikely event of an emergency (see p51 and p53). Although the path is easy to follow, a 'Silva' type **compass** and knowing how to use it is a good idea in case you need to leave the trail when there is heavy fog.

Useful

Many would list a **camera** as essential but it can be liberating to travel without one once in a while; a **notebook** can be a more accurate way of recording your impressions. A **book** helps to pass the time on train and bus journeys and for comfort, particularly in the summer, you may wish to take a pair of **sunglasses**. Also useful are **binoculars** for observing wildlife, a **walking stick** or pole to take the shock off your knees, a **vacuum flask** for carrying hot drinks and a **mobile phone** (reception is quite reliable along the Ridgeway).

CAMPING GEAR

Campers will need a **tent** (or bivvy bag if you enjoy travelling light) which is able to withstand wet and windy weather. You should find that a two- to three-season **sleeping bag** is sufficient, but obviously in winter a warmer bag is a good idea. You will also need a **sleeping mat**, a **stove** and **fuel**, a **pan** with a lid that can double as a frying pan/plate (this is fine for two people), a **pan handle**, a **mug**, a **spoon** and a wire/plastic **scrubber** for washing up.

MONEY

There are no banks along the first half of the Ridgeway so you will have to carry most of your money as **cash**. From Streatley onwards most towns have at least one **ATM**. A **debit card** is the easiest way to withdraw money from banks, ATMs or post offices (see pp17-18) and debit/credit cards can be used to pay in larger shops, restaurants and hotels.

MAPS

The hand-drawn maps in this book cover the trail at a scale of 1:20,000; they provide plenty of detail and information to keep you on the right track. If you are only walking on the Ridgeway, you shouldn't need any other maps but for side trips you will need an Ordnance Survey map (☎ 08456 050505, 💻 www. ordnancesurvey.co.uk).

The entire Ridgeway route is covered on four OS Explorer/Active maps at a scale of 1:25,000. The numbers of these maps are 157 (Marlborough & Savernake Forest), 170 (Abingdon, Wantage & Vale of White Horse), 171 (Chiltern Hills West, Henley-on-Thames & Wallingford), and 181 (Chiltern Hills North, Aylesbury, Berkhamsted & Chesham). The Explorer maps cost

❏ SOURCES OF FURTHER INFORMATION

Trail information

The Ridgeway National Trails Office (☎ 01865 810224, 🖳 www.nationaltrail.co.uk/ridgeway) The National Trails website has up-to-date information concerning all aspects – history, wildlife, events, future projects – of the Ridgeway. If you need further information you can call the office and leave a message.

Tourist information

● **Tourist Information Centres (TICs)** TICs or tourist information points (TIPs; usually only leaflets) are based in towns throughout Britain and provide locally specific information.

The centres/points relevant to the Ridgeway: **Wallingford** (see p139), **Princes Risborough** (see p161), **Wendover** (see p168) and **Tring** (see p174).

● **English Tourist Board** (🖳 www.enjoyengland.com) The tourist board oversees all the local tourist information centres. It's a good place to find general information about the country and details about outdoor activities and local events. They can also help with arranging holidays and accommodation.

● **County/district councils** The websites for the county/district councils for the area covering the route can also be a useful source of tourist information. See box p56 for council contact details.

Organisations for walkers

● **Backpackers' Club** (🖳 www.backpackersclub.co.uk) A club for people who are involved or interested in lightweight camping through walking, cycling, skiing or canoeing. They produce a quarterly magazine and provide members with a comprehensive advisory and information service on all aspects of backpacking, as well as discounts on maps and at outdoor stores. They also organise weekend trips and publish a farm-pitch directory. Membership is £12 per year and £15 for a family.

● **The Long Distance Walkers Association** (LDWA; 🖳 www.ldwa.org.uk) An association of people with the common interest of long-distance walking. Membership includes a copy of their journal *Strider* three times per year giving details of challenge events and local group walks as well as articles on the subject. Members also receive a discount on maps and also on the *UK Trailwalker's Handbook* which details 730 trails across the UK. Membership is £13 per year or £19.50 for a family.

● **Ramblers** (formerly Ramblers' Association; 🖳 www.ramblers.org.uk) Looks after the interests of walkers throughout Britain. They publish a large amount of useful information including their quarterly *Walk* magazine (£3.60 to non-members). The website also has a discussion forum. Membership costs £31/41/19.50 individual/joint/concessionary.

£7.99 each and the Active series (which are covered in laminated plastic) are £13.99 each; these maps are widely available in bookshops or can be ordered from the Ordnance Survey website.

A very useful service which can ease the significant cost of purchasing maps for a walk is provided by Ramblers (see box above). Their library allows members to borrow up to ten maps for a period of four weeks at 50p per paper map and £1 per weatherproof map. Alternatively, members of the Backpackers' and LDWA clubs (see box above) are entitled to a discount on maps.

RECOMMENDED READING

Most of the following books can be found in the tourist information centres.

The Ridgeway, John Cleare, Frances Lincoln 2011; hardback; includes a history of the trail but most of the book is filled with beautiful colour photographs.

The National Trails Office publishes a *Ridgeway Information Pack* for £3.30, covering the history and natural history of the Ridgeway and also a *Walks Around The Ridgeway Pack* for £4.70 detailing circular walks from the Ridgeway.

Of course if you are a seasoned long-distance walker or even if you are new to the game and like what you see, check out the ever-growing list of titles in the Trailblazer series (see pp190-2).

Flora and fauna field guides

The *Ridgeway Information Pack* (see above) includes separate leaflets on the wild flowers, birds and animals you might encounter.

Dorling Kindersley's *RSPB Birds of Britain and Europe* at £16.99 is one of many excellent bird guides though is a little bulky for carrying with you on the trail. The extensive but pocket-sized *Wild Flowers* published by Collins is well worth £4.99; they also produce *Butterflies*, for the same price. The Field Studies Council (www.field-studies-council.org) publishes a series of inexpensive *Identification Guides* (fold out charts) which are also practical.

There are also several fieldguide apps for the iPhone, including those that can aid in identifying birds by their song as well as by their appearance.

Getting to and from the Ridgeway

Both the start and finish of the Ridgeway are easily reached by public transport or car and its convenient location in the centre of southern England means that it's one of the most accessible long-distance trails in the country.

The obvious advantages of travelling to the Ridgeway by public transport are that you don't have to go back and collect your car at the end of the walk (in fact, you can't leave your car at the start point of the Ridgeway for more than a day) and you don't need to worry about the safety aspect of leaving your car unattended for a long period of time.

If you are walking the Ridgeway from one end to the other, in one go, you shouldn't need public transport at any point along the trail. If, however, you are just walking one section, or want to skip a certain stretch and move on to the next, you will. For short distances between towns you will be using the bus.

On the whole there are plenty of services throughout the day to the majority of towns and villages but on Sundays and public holidays there is often just a limited service, or none at all. Even during the week, getting from one place to another isn't always straightforward; you often need to get a bus to a town

❏ GETTING TO BRITAIN

● **By air** Most airlines serve London Heathrow (🖥 www.heathrowairport.com) or London Gatwick (🖥 www.gatwickairport.com). In addition a number of budget companies fly from Europe's major cities to the other London terminals at Stansted (🖥 www.stanstedairport.com) and Luton (🖥 www.london-luton.co.uk); the latter is the most convenient airport for the end of the walk (or the start if you choose to walk east to west). There are also flights to Bristol (🖥 www.bristolairport.co.uk), which is far closer to the start of the Ridgeway than London Heathrow.

For details of the airlines using these airports and the destinations served visit the relevant airport's website.

● **From Europe by train** Eurostar (🖥 www.eurostar.com) operates the high-speed passenger service via the Channel Tunnel between Paris/Brussels (and other cities) and London. The Eurostar terminal in London is St Pancras International at St Pancras station; there are connections from King's Cross St Pancras station on the London Underground to all the other main railway stations in London. Paddington is the main station for trains to Swindon; services to Tring go from Euston (see box opposite).

For more information about rail services from Europe contact your rail service provider or Railteam (🖥 www.railteam.eu).

● **From Europe by coach** Eurolines (🖥 www.eurolines.com) have a huge network of long-distance bus services, connecting over 500 cities in 25 European countries to London. Check carefully, as some expenses, such as food for the journey, are taken into consideration it often does not work out much cheaper than taking a flight, particularly when compared to the prices of some of the budget airlines.

● **From Europe by car** Ferries operate between Calais and Dover, Santander and Roscoff to Plymouth as well as from Cherbourg to Poole and Portsmouth and from Caen to Portsmouth. There are also services on routes between mainland Europe and ports on Britain's eastern coast. Look at 🖥 www.ferrysavers.com or 🖥 www.direct ferries.com for a full list of operating companies, routes and services.

Eurotunnel (🖥 www.eurotunnel.com) operates a shuttle train service for vehicles via the Channel Tunnel between Calais and Folkestone taking just 35 mins.

from where you can then catch a bus to your destination. This can mean that you might have to finish walking early to ensure you get your bus connections.

From nearly any given town or village on the Ridgeway it is fairly easy to get to a large town that has connections to the national public transport network. So, if you decide to walk only a certain section, you shouldn't have any problems getting back home, even if it does take some time and a series of buses.

NATIONAL TRANSPORT

By rail   [see box opposite]

The most convenient railway station for Overton Hill at the start of the Ridgeway is Swindon (12½ miles/20km away). Swindon is on the main line from London Paddington to Bristol; it takes about an hour from London to Swindon and about half an hour from Bristol to Swindon (services are operated by First Great Western). From Swindon you'll need to take one of the regular local bus services (see box pp42-3) in the direction of Marlborough and get off at the West Kennet stop, just a few hundred metres from Overton Hill.

In the middle of the Ridgeway, First Great Western has services to Goring & Streatley on the London Paddington to Oxford line.

The nearest railway station to the eastern end of the path at Ivinghoe Beacon is at Tring (3³/₄ miles/6km away). You will already have walked past this station on your way up to the Beacon. Tring is on London Midland's London Euston to Northampton line via Hemel Hempstead, Berkhamsted and Milton Keynes. Euston to Tring takes about 40 minutes.

Chiltern Railways operate services from London Marylebone to Birmingham – via High Wycombe, Princes Risborough (on the Ridgeway) and Banbury – and to Aylesbury via Wendover (on the Ridgeway). There are also services from London Marylebone to Little Kimble and Saunderton, both of which are fairly close to the Ridgeway.

All timetable and fare information can be found at **National Rail Enquiries** (☎ 08457 484950, 🖳 www.nationalrail.co.uk). You can also purchase tickets

---

❏ RAIL SERVICES

Chiltern Railways (🖳 www.chilternrailways.co.uk)
● London Marylebone to Birmingham via High Wycombe, **Princes Risborough**, Aylesbury & Banbury, daily 1/hr
● London Marylebone to Aylesbury via **Wendover**, Mon-Sat 1-2/hr, Sun 1/hr
● There are also services from London Marylebone to Saunderton, daily 1/hr; plus to Little Kimble and Monks Risborough, Mon-Fri 6/day, Sat 5/day, Sun 1/hr

London Midland (🖳 www.londonmidland.com)
● London Euston to Birmingham via Hemel Hempstead, Berkhamsted, **Tring**, Milton Keynes & Northampton, Mon-Sat 2/hr, Sun 1/hr
● London Euston to Cheddington via Watford Junction, Hemel Hempstead, Berkhamsted & **Tring**, daily 1/hr

First Great Western (🖳 www.firstgreatwestern.co.uk)
● London Paddington to Swindon via Reading and Didcot Parkway, Mon-Sat 3-4/hr, Sun 1-2/hr (Services from London Paddington to Swansea, Cheltenham and Oxford generally stop at Swindon, Reading and Didcot Parkway)
● London Paddington to Hereford via **Goring & Streatley**, Cholsey, Didcot Parkway & Oxford, Mon-Sat 1-2/hr, Sun 1/hr
● London Paddington to Henley-on-Thames via Reading & Twyford, daily 1-2/hr
● London Paddington to Swansea via Reading, Swindon, Bristol Parkway & Cardiff, daily 1/hr
● London Paddington to Exeter St David's/Plymouth via Reading, Newbury (not all services), Pewsey (not all services) Mon-Sat 1/hr, Sun 5/day
● Reading to Bedwyn via Newbury & Hungerford, Mon-Sat 1/hr, Sun one every two hours
● Bristol Parkway/Bristol Temple Meads to Swindon, Mon-Sat 2/hr, Sun 1/hr

Cholsey and Wallingford Railway See p139.
Chinnor and Princes Risborough Railway See p156.

PLANNING YOUR WALK

over the phone through the relevant train operating company or online at ⌨ www.
thetrainline.com and ⌨ www.qjump.co.uk. It is often possible now to buy a
train ticket that includes bus travel at your destination. For further information
visit the Plusbus website (⌨ www.plusbus.info).

If you think you may want to book a taxi when you arrive visit ⌨ www.
traintaxi.co.uk for details of taxi companies operating at rail stations throughout
England.

By coach   [see box below]

National Express is the principal coach (long-distance bus) operator in Britain.
Coach travel is generally cheaper but takes longer than travel by train.

Marlborough, which is just 4 miles (7km) from Overton Hill and the start
of the Ridgeway, is conveniently located on National Express's NX402 route.
From Marlborough it's a local bus ride (services are frequent and quick) to the
West Kennet bus stop, just a few hundred metres from Overton Hill.

Alternatively, several National Express services stop in Swindon from
where you can take a local bus to Marlborough (see box pp42-3).

Most of the **Oxford Tube** bus services between London and Oxford call at
Lewknor, a good starting point for a walk to Princes Risborough or Wendover.
If you are planning to walk from Wantage ask for a connector ticket from
London rather than a single/return ticket as there will then be no additional

---

❏ **COACH SERVICES**
National Express (☎ 0871 781 8178, lines open 8am-10pm daily, ⌨ www.national
express.com)

NX402	London–Frome via Heathrow, Newbury, Hungerford, **Marlborough**, Beckhampton, Devizes, Melksham & Trowbridge, 1/day
NX403	London–Bath via Heathrow Airport, 10/day: some services call at **Swindon**, Calne, Chippenham, Corsham, Rudloe, Box and/or Batheaston
NX302	Bristol–Northampton via Bath, Corsham, Chippenham, **Swindon** & Oxford, 1/day
NX222	Heathrow Airport–Gloucester via **Swindon**, Cirencester, and Cheltenham, 10/day
NX335	Poole–Halifax via Bournemouth, Salisbury, **Marlborough**, **Swindon**, Cirencester, Gloucester, Cheltenham, Leicester and Huddersfield, 1/day (note: not all stops are listed)
JL737	Stansted Airport to Oxford via Hatfield, Luton Airport, **Hemel Hempstead**, High Wycombe & Stokenchurch, 8/day
JL787	Heathrow Airport to Cambridge via **Hemel Hempstead**, Luton, Hitchin, Letchworth, Baldock, Royston & Harston, 5/day

Oxford Tube (operated by Stagecoach; customer services ☎ 01865 772250, ⌨ www.
oxfordtube.com)
    London to Oxford via **Lewknor**, daily 4/hr

Green Line (☎ 0844 801 7261, ⌨ www.greenline.co.uk)
758/768 London to **Hemel Hempstead**, Mon-Fri 15/day, Sat 9/day

charge for the journey from Oxford to Wantage on Stagecoach's X30 (see box p43). The Oxford Tube operates on a first-come-first-served basis and tickets can be bought online or on the bus but with cash only for the latter.

The nearest place to Ivinghoe Beacon at which National Express coaches stop is Hemel Hempstead (10 miles/17km) from where you can get a local bus to Tring (see box pp42-3). **Green Line** also operates services to Hemel Hempstead from London Victoria.

By car

The Ridgeway is very easily accessed by car. From junction 15 of the M4 motorway it's a short drive down the A345 to Marlborough, then onto the A4 to the start at Overton Hill. You can't, however, leave your car for more than a day in the small car parking area at Overton Hill so you should find somewhere to leave it in Marlborough or maybe Avebury, though even this could be tricky.

The Ivinghoe Beacon end of the Ridgeway is best reached from junction 11 (Dunstable) of the M40 or via Aylesbury along the A41. There is a National Trust car park for Ivinghoe Beacon about half a mile (1km) south of the B489 on the minor road to Ringshall.

However, overall it's probably easier and cheaper (with the rising petrol prices) and certainly better for the environment to use public transport.

By air

The nearest airport to the start of the path is at Bristol but it is so far from the start of the Ridgeway as to make flying there, particularly for domestic travellers, fairly pointless. At the other end of the path Luton airport is much closer, but in most cases it would still be easier to head into London by train or bus and travel on from there. Air travel really is not the best way to get to the Ridgeway.

LOCAL TRANSPORT

There are few useful train services along the Ridgeway so you will have to rely on the public bus services. These bus services, although extensive, aren't always frequent, especially at weekends.

Buses on the western half of the Ridgeway connect more of the places you might need whereas trying to get from one place to another on the eastern section can involve travelling first to a larger town, then changing buses and continuing from there. Obviously this can be quite time consuming and if you don't want to end up paying out for a taxi this is certainly one aspect of your trip that you will need to plan. Services to smaller towns and villages tend to finish by mid-afternoon.

The public transport map on pp44-5 gives an overview of the most useful bus and train routes. The bus services table on pp42-3 gives route operators, their contact details and service numbers as well as the days and approximate

PLANNING YOUR WALK

frequency of services in both directions. The details given are for summer services, though some of those listed operate year-round. It is essential to check the latest details before travelling: you can pick up bus timetables for free at any of the tourist information centres along the route.

❏ LOCAL BUS SERVICES

Note: The services listed below were correct at the time of publication but may change so check before you travel.

● **Arriva The Shires/South-East** (🖥 www.arrivabus.co.uk)
30   Aldbury to Berkhamsted via Tring Station, Mon-Sat 3/day
40   High Wycombe to Thame via Stokenchurch, Kingston Blount & Chinnor, Mon-Sat 1/hr
50   Aylesbury to Wendover, Mon-Sat 2/hr
61   Aylesbury to Luton via Tring, Ivinghoe & Dunstable, Mon-Sat 1/hr (most services go to Luton Airport as well)
300   Aylesbury to High Wycombe via Princes Risborough, Mon-Fri 3/hr, Sat 2/hr, Sun 1/hr
500   Aylesbury to Watford via Tring, Berkhamsted & Hemel Hempstead, Mon-Sat 2/hr
501   Aylesbury to Watford via Tring, Berkhamsted & Hemel Hempstead, Sun 1/hr

● **Connect2Wiltshire (bookings Mon-Sat 6.30am-6.30pm; ☎ 08456 525255, 🖥 www. bookaride.co.uk)**
Note: Stops other than Marlborough, Avebury and West Kennet are request only so it is essential to call Connect2Wiltshire (choose option 1 for a bus service) to book a seat: call at least two hours before you plan to travel. The stop names and code are given below to make booking simpler.
Line 4 Calne (The Strand 10201) to Marlborough (High St 10074) via Avebury (Red Lion 10207, Trusloe 10206), Beckhampton (Race Stables 10260, Waggon & Horses 10261), West Kennet (telephone box 10264), East Kennet (Church Lane 10265, The Manor 10266) & West Overton (Church Hill 10269, Southfield 10268, West Overton Stores 10267), Mon-Sat 6-8/day

● **Heyfordian Travel** (☎ 01869 241500, 🖥 www.heyfordian.travel)
134   Wallingford to Goring circular route via North Stoke, South Stoke, Goring, Streatley, Moulsford & Cholsey, Mon-Fri 6/day, Sat 3/day
135   Wallingford to Goring circular route via Cholsey, Moulsford, Streatley, Goring, South Stoke & North Stoke, Mon-Sat 3/day

● **Newbury & District/Reading Buses (☎ 01189 594000, 🖥 www.newburyanddis trict.co.uk) (Newbury & District operate the services on behalf of Reading Buses)**
6   Newbury circular route via Chievely, West Ilsley, East Ilsley & Compton, Mon-Sat 4/day
6a   Newbury circular route via Compton, East Ilsley & Chievely, Mon-Fri 4/day (1/day goes via West Ilsley)

● **Redline Buses (☎ 01296 426786, 🖥 www.redlinebuses.com)**
50   Aylesbury to Ivinghoe via Wendover & Tring, Sun 3/day
164   Aylesbury to Leighton Buzzard via Tring, Mon-Sat 3/day, via Pitstone & Ivinghoe 1/day

If the contact details in the box below prove unsatisfactory, you can contact **traveline** (☎ 0871 200 2233, daily 8am-8pm; 🖥 www.traveline.info) which has public transport information for the whole of the UK. Alternatively contact the public transport department of the relevant county council (see box p56).

Redline Buses (*continued*)
320   Chinnor to Princes Risborough, Mon-Fri 7-9/day (connects at Princes
       Risborough with trains to/from London)

● **Red Rose Travel** (☎ 01296 747926, 🖥 www.redrosetravel.co.uk)
387   Tring to Wigginton, Mon-Fri 5/day, Sat 4/day; Tring to Aldbury, Mon-Fri 8/day,
       Sat 6/day

● **RH Buses** (☎ 01993 869100, 🖥 www.rhbuses.com)
67   Wantage to Faringdon via Letcombe Regis, Letcombe Bassett, Sparsholt,
       Kingston Lisle & Uffington, Mon-Sat 1-2/day, but only 1/day via Letcombe
       Regis & Letcombe Bassett
X47   Wantage to Swindon via Letcombe Regis, Letcombe Bassett, Sparsholt,
       Kingston Lisle, Uffington, Woolstone, Ashbury, Idstone, Bishopstone,
       Hinton Parva, Foxhill & Liddington, Sat 3/day

● **Stagecoach** (🖥 www.stagecoachbus.com)
70   Swindon to Marlborough via Ogbourne St George, Mon-Sat 1/hr
49   Swindon to Trowbridge (The Trans Wilts Express) via Avebury, Beckhampton
       & Devizes, Mon-Sat 1/hr, Swindon to Devizes, Sun 6/day
31   Oxford to Wantage via Abingdon, daily 1/hr
X30   Oxford to Wantage, Mon-Sat 2/hr

● **Thamesdown Transport** (🖥 www.thamesdown-transport.co.uk)
46   Swindon to Hungerford via Liddington, Foxhill, Aldbourne & Ramsbury,
       Mon-Sat 2/day
47   Swindon to Lambourn via Bishopstone & Ashbury, Mon-Sat 6/day
48   Swindon to Marlborough via Liddington, Foxhill, Aldbourne & Ramsbury,
       Mon-Sat 5-6/day

● **Thames Travel/Go Ahead** (🖥 www.thames-travel.co.uk)
32   Abingdon to Wantage via Didcot Parkway, Mon-Sat about 1/hr
32A   Wantage to Didcot, Sun 5/day
36/X36 Didcot to Wantage, Mon-Fri 9/day
106   Oxford to Watlington, Mon-Sat 1/hr
130   Didcot to Wallingford, Mon-Sat 1/hr, Sun 3/day
133   Goring to Reading via Streatley & Pangborne, Mon-Fri 4/day plus 1/day
       Streatley to Reading, Sat 4/day
139   Henley to Wallingford via Crowmarsh Gifford & Huntercombe (Nuffield),
       Mon-Sat 1/hr, Sun 5/day
X39   Reading to Oxford via Wallingford & Crowmarsh Gifford, Mon-Sat 1/hr
X40   Reading to Oxford via Woodcote, Wallingford & Crowmarsh Gifford, daily 1/hr

● **Wilts & Dorset** (🖥 www.wdbus.co.uk)
X5   Swindon to Salisbury via Ogbourne St George, Marlborough & Pewsey,
       Mon-Sat 1/hr, Sun 2/hr

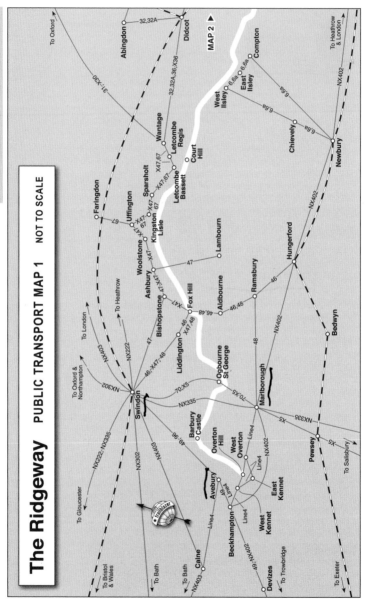

The Ridgeway PUBLIC TRANSPORT MAP 1 NOT TO SCALE

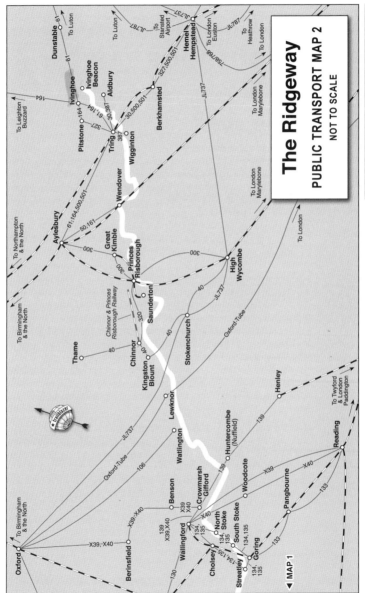

The Ridgeway
PUBLIC TRANSPORT MAP 2
NOT TO SCALE

Dunstable
To Luton
To Luton
61
61
To Stansted Airport
Hemel Hempstead
JL737
To London Euston
JL787
To Heathrow
To London
Ivinghoe
Ivinghoe Beacon
Aldbury
Berkhamsted
30,387
30,500,501
387,500,501
To Leighton Buzzard
164
Pitstone
Tring
Wigginton
61,164
30,500,501
387
327
JL737
To London Marylebone
To London
Wendover
50,161
61,164,500,501
Aylesbury
To Northampton & the North
Great Kimble
Princes Risborough
300
High Wycombe
300
To London Marylebone
To London
Chinnor & Princes Risborough Railway
300
300
Saunderton
Thame
Chinnor
40
JL737
40
Stokenchurch
To Birmingham & the North
320
40
Kingston Blount
40
Oxford Tube
Lewknor
trailblazer
Henley
139
To Twyford & London Paddington
Oxford Tube
JL737
Watlington
Huntercombe (Nuffield)
139
106
Benson
X39 X40
Crowmarsh Gifford
X40
Woodcote
X39
Reading
To Birmingham & the North
139 X39,X40
Wallingford
134, 135
North Stoke
X40
X39
Berinsfield
X39, X40
134, 135
South Stoke
Pangbourne
X40
134,135
133
130
Cholsey
134, 135
Streatley
Goring
133
Oxford
134, 135
133
MAP 1

MINIMUM IMPACT & OUTDOOR SAFETY

Minimum impact walking

ECONOMIC IMPACT

Support local businesses

Rural businesses and communities in Britain have been hit hard in recent years by a seemingly endless series of crises. In light of the economic pressures that many businesses are under there is something you can do to help: buy local.

Look and ask for local produce to buy and eat. Not only does this cut down on the amount of pollution and congestion that the transportation of food creates (the so-called 'food miles'), but also ensures that you are supporting local farmers and producers; the very people who have moulded the countryside you have come to see and who are in the best position to protect it. If you can find local food which is also organic so much the better.

It's a fact of life that money spent at local level – perhaps in a market, or at the greengrocer, or in an independent pub – has a far greater impact for good on that community than the equivalent spent in a branch of a national chain store or restaurant. While no-one would advocate that walkers should boycott the larger supermarkets, which after all do provide local employment, it's worth remembering that businesses in rural communities rely heavily on visitors for their very existence. If we want to keep these shops and post offices, we need to use them.

Encourage local cultural traditions and skills

No two parts of the countryside look the same. Buildings, food, skills and language evolve out of the landscape and are moulded over hundreds of years to suit the locality. Discovering these cultural differences is part of the pleasure of walking in new places. Visitors' enthusiasm for local traditions and skills brings awareness and pride, nurturing a sense of place; an increasingly important role in a world where economic globalisation continues to undermine the very things that provide security and a feeling of belonging.

ENVIRONMENTAL IMPACT

A walking holiday in itself is an environmentally friendly approach to tourism. The following are some ideas on how you can go a few steps further in helping to minimise your impact on the natural environment while walking the Ridgeway.

Use public transport whenever possible

By using the local bus you will help to keep it in service. Although the bus routes along the Ridgeway aren't always convenient for walkers, if fewer people use them they are more likely to disappear altogether. Public transport is always preferable to using private cars as it benefits everyone: visitors, locals and the environment.

Never leave litter

Leaving litter shows a total disrespect for the natural world and others coming after you. As well as being unsightly, litter kills wildlife, pollutes the environment and can be dangerous to farm animals. If you've carried everything at the start of the day you can probably carry whatever remains until you reach a rubbish bin. Put all your rubbish in a biodegradable bag so you can dispose of it in a bin in the next village. It would be very helpful if you could pick up litter left by other people too.

Is it OK if it's biodegradable?   Not really. Apple cores, banana skins, orange peel and the like are unsightly, encourage flies, ants and wasps and ruin a picnic spot for others. Using the excuse that they are natural and biodegradable just doesn't cut any ice. When was the last time you saw a banana tree in England?

The lasting impact of litter A piece of orange peel left on the ground takes six months to decompose, silver foil takes 18 months, a plastic bag 10 years, clothes 15 years and an aluminium can 85 years.

Erosion
Stay on the main trail The effect of your footsteps may seem minuscule but when they are multiplied by several thousand walkers each year they become rather more significant. Avoid taking shortcuts, widening the trail or taking more than one path; your boots will be followed by many others.

Consider walking out of season Maximum disturbance by walkers coincides with the time of year when nature wants to do most of its growth and repair. In high-use areas, like that along much of the eastern section of the Ridgeway, the trail never recovers. Walking at less busy times eases this pressure while also generating year-round income for the local economy. Not only that, but it may make the walk a more relaxing experience with fewer people on the path and less competition for accommodation.

Respect all wildlife

Care for all wildlife you come across along the Ridgeway: it has as much right to be there as you. Tempting as it may be to pick wild flowers, leave them so the next people who pass can enjoy them too. Don't break branches off or damage trees in any way.

If you come across wildlife, keep your distance and don't watch for too long. Your presence can cause considerable stress, particularly if the adults are with young, or in winter when the weather is harsh and food is scarce. Young animals are rarely abandoned. If you come across young birds keep away so that their mother can return.

The code of the outdoor loo
'Going' in the outdoors is a lost art worth re-learning, for your sake and every-one else's. As more and more people discover the joys of the outdoors this is becoming an important issue.

In some parts of the world where visitor pressure is higher than in Britain walkers and climbers are required to pack out their excrement. This could soon be necessary here. Human excrement is not only offensive to our senses but, more importantly, can infect water sources.

Where to go Wherever possible use a toilet. Public toilets are marked on the trail maps in this guide and you will also find facilities in pubs, cafés and camp-sites along the Ridgeway.

If you do have to go outdoors choose a site at least 30 metres away from running water and also away from any site of historic or archaeological interest. Carry a small trowel and dig a hole about 15cm (6") deep in which to bury your excrement. It decomposes quicker when in contact with the top layer of soil or leaf mould. Use a stick to stir loose soil into your deposit as well as this speeds up decomposition even more. Do not squash it under rocks as this slows down the composting process. If you have to use rocks to cover it make sure they are not in contact with your faeces.

Toilet paper and tampons Toilet paper takes a long time to decompose whether buried or not. It is easily dug up by animals and may then blow into water sources or onto the path. The best method for dealing with it is to pack it out. Put the used paper inside a paper bag which you then place inside a biode-gradable bag (or two). Then simply empty the contents of the paper bag at the next toilet you come across and throw the bag away. You should also pack out tampons and sanitary towels in a similar way: they take years to decompose and may be dug up and scattered about by animals.

Wild camping
Unfortunately, wild camping is not allowed along the Ridgeway, but it is gener-ally tolerated if you leave no trace of yourself on the ground when you leave the next morning. Wild camping is an altogether more fulfilling experience than camping on a designated site. Living in the outdoors without any facilities pro-vides a valuable lesson in simple, sustainable living where the results of all your actions, from going to the loo to washing your plates, can be seen.

If you do insist on wild camping on land off the Ridgeway path always ask the landowner for permission. Follow these suggestions for minimising your impact and encourage others to do likewise.

Be discreet Camp alone or in small groups, spend only one night in each place and pitch your tent late and move off early.

Never light a fire The deep burn caused by camp fires, no matter how small, damages the turf which can take years to recover. Cook on a camp stove instead.

Don't use soap or detergent There is no need to use soap: even biodegradable soaps and detergents pollute streams. You won't be away from a shower for more than a day or so. Wash up without detergent: use a plastic or metal scourer, or failing that, a handful of fine pebbles or even some bracken or grass.

Leave no trace Learn the skill of moving on without leaving any sign of having been there: no moved boulders, ripped up vegetation or dug drainage ditches. Make a final check of your campsite before departing: pick up any litter that you or anyone else has left, so leaving the place in a better state than you found it.

ACCESS

Britain is a crowded cluster of islands with few places where you can wander as you please. Most of the land is a patchwork of fields and agricultural land and the area around the Ridgeway is no different. However, there are countless public rights of way, in addition to the official Ridgeway path, that criss-cross the land; so, what happens if you feel a little more adventurous and want to explore the downs, woodland and hills that can be found around the Ridgeway?

Rights of way

As a designated **National Trail** the Ridgeway is a **public right of way**. A public right of way is either a footpath, a bridleway or a byway: the Ridgeway is made up of all three of these.

Rights of way are theoretically established because the owner has dedicated them to public use. However, very few rights of way are formally dedicated in this way. If members of the public have been using a path without interference for 20 years or more the law assumes the owner has intended to dedicate it as a right of way. If a path has been unused for 20 years it does not cease to exist; the guiding principle is 'once a highway, always a highway'.

On a public right of way you have the right to 'pass and repass along the way' which includes stopping to rest or admire the view, or to consume refreshments. You can also take with you a 'natural accompaniment' which includes a dog but obviously could also be a horse on bridleways and byways. All 'natural accompaniments' must be kept under close control (see p50).

Farmers and land managers must ensure that paths are not blocked by crops or other vegetation, or otherwise obstructed, that the route is identifiable and the surface is restored soon after cultivation. If crops are growing over the path you have every right to walk or ride through them, following the line of the right of way as closely as possible. If you find a path blocked or impassable you should report it to the appropriate **highway authority**. Highway authorities are respon-sible for maintaining public rights of way. Along the Ridgeway the highway authorities are **Wiltshire County Council**, **Swindon Borough Council**, **Oxfordshire County Council**, **West Berkshire Council**, **Buckinghamshire County Council** and **Hertfordshire County Council** (see box p56). The coun-cils are also the surveying authorities with responsibility for maintaining the official definitive maps of the public rights of way.

Right to roam

The Countryside & Rights of Way Act 2000 (CRoW), or 'Right to Roam' as dubbed by walkers, gives the public access to areas of countryside, deemed to be uncultivated open country, in England and Wales – this essentially means moor-land, heathland, downland and upland areas. Some land is covered by restrictions (ie high-impact activities such as driving a vehicle, cycling, horse-riding are not permitted) and some land is excluded (such as gardens, parks and cultivated land). Full details are given on the Natural England website (see box p56).

With more freedom in the countryside comes a need for more responsibil-ity from the walker. Remember that wild open country is still the workplace of farmers and home to all sorts of wildlife. Have respect for both and avoid dis-turbing domestic and wild animals.

The Countryside Code

The countryside is a fragile place which every visitor should respect. It seems like common sense but sadly some people still seem to have no understanding of how to treat the countryside they walk in. Everyone visiting the countryside has a responsibility to minimise the impact of their visit so other people can enjoy the same peaceful landscapes. It does not take much effort; it really is common sense. Below is an expanded version of the Countryside Code, launched under the logo, 'Respect, Protect and Enjoy':

● **Be safe – plan ahead and follow any signs** Walking on the Ridgeway is pretty much hazard-free but you're responsible for your own safety so follow the simple guidelines outlined on pp51-3.

● **Leave all gates as you found them** Normally a farmer leaves gates closed to keep livestock in but may sometimes leave them open to allow livestock access to food or water. Leave them as you find them and if there is a sign, fol-low the instructions.

● **Leave livestock, crops and machinery alone** Help farmers by not interfer-ing with their means of livelihood.

● **Take your litter home** 'Pack it in, pack it out'. See p47.

● **Keep your dog under close control** Across farmland, dogs should be kept on a lead. During lambing time (see box opposite) they should not be taken with you at all.

● **Enjoy the countryside and respect its life and work** Access to the country-side depends on being sensitive to the needs and wishes of those who live and work there. Being courteous and friendly to those you meet will ensure a healthy future for all based on partnership and co-operation.

MINIMUM IMPACT & OUTDOOR SAFETY

❏ **Lambing**
A great deal of the Ridgeway passes through private farmland some of which is pasture for sheep. Lambing takes place from mid-March to mid-May and dogs should not be taken along the path at this time. Even a dog secured on a lead is liable to disturb a pregnant ewe. If you should see a lamb or ewe that appears to be in distress contact the nearest farmer.

● **Guard against all risk of fire** Accidental fire is a great fear of farmers and foresters. Never make a camp fire and take matches and cigarette butts away with you to dispose of safely.
● **Keep to paths across farmland** Stick to the official Ridgeway path across arable/pasture land. Minimise erosion by not cutting corners or widening the path.
● **Use gates and stiles to cross fences, hedges and walls** The Ridgeway path is well supplied with stiles where it crosses field boundaries. On some of the side trips you may find the paths less accommodating. If you have to climb over a gate because you can't open it always do so at the hinged end.
● **Help keep all water clean** Leaving litter and going to the toilet near a water source can pollute people's water supplies. See p48 for more advice.
● **Take special care on country roads** Drivers often go dangerously fast on narrow winding lanes. To be safe, walk facing the oncoming traffic and carry a torch or wear highly visible clothing when it's getting dark.
● **Protect wildlife, plants and trees** Care for and respect all wildlife you come across. Don't pick plants, break trees or scare wild animals.
● **Make no unnecessary noise** Enjoy the peace and solitude of the outdoors by staying in small groups and acting unobtrusively.

Outdoor safety

AVOIDANCE OF HAZARDS

With good planning and preparation most hazards can be avoided. This information is just as important for those out on a day walk as for those walking the entire Ridgeway.

Ensure you have **suitable clothes** (see pp33-4) to keep you warm and dry whatever the conditions, and a spare change of inner clothes. A compass, whistle, torch and first-aid kit should be carried and are discussed further on p34. The **emergency signal** is six blasts on the whistle or six flashes with a torch.

Remember to take your **mobile phone**; you can get a decent signal on nearly all of the Ridgeway and not only will you be able to contact someone in an emergency, but the signal from your phone can be traced to pinpoint your location.

Take plenty of **food** with you for the day and at least one litre of **water** although more would be better, especially on the long western stretches. It is a good idea to fill up your bottle whenever you pass a water tap as they aren't very common. You will eat far more walking than you do normally so make sure you have enough for the day, as well as some high-energy snacks (chocolate, dried fruit, biscuits) in the bottom of your pack for an emergency.

Stay alert and **know exactly where you are** throughout the day. The easiest way to do this is to regularly check your position on the map. If visibility suddenly decreases with mist and cloud, or there is an accident, you will be able to make a sensible decision about what action to take based on your location.

If you choose to walk alone you must appreciate and be prepared for the increased risk. It's a good idea to leave word with someone about where you are going and remember to contact them when you have arrived safely.

WEATHER FORECASTS

The western section of the Ridgeway is particularly exposed. The difference in conditions between the villages below the Ridgeway and the path itself can be quite dramatic. You often only notice just how cold and windy it is when you stop for a few minutes.

Try to get the local weather forecast from the internet, newspaper, TV, radio or one of the telephone forecasts before you set off. Plan the day accordingly.

Telephone and internet forecasts

These are frequently updated and generally reliable. **Weather call** (☎ 09068 500406; 🖳 www.weathercall.co.uk) is useful, but calls are charged at the expensive premium rate (60p per minute from a UK landline).

You can get a localised five-day forecast from 🖳 www.bbc.co.uk/weather if you enter a postcode. Useful postcodes for the Ridgeway are: SN8 (Marlborough); OX12 (Wantage); OX10 (Wallingford); OX39 (Chinnor); HP27 (Princes Risborough) and HP23 (Tring).

HEALTH

Blisters

It is important to break in new boots before embarking on a long walk. Make sure the boots are comfortable and try to avoid getting them wet on the inside. Air your feet at lunchtime, keep them clean and change your socks regularly. If you feel any hot spots stop immediately and apply a few strips of zinc oxide tape and leave them on until the area is pain free or the tape starts to come off.

If you have left it too late and a blister has developed you should surround it with 'moleskin' or any other blister kit to protect it from abrasion. Popping it can lead to infection. If the skin is broken keep the area clean with antiseptic and cover with a non-adhesive dressing material held in place with tape.

Hypothermia

Also known as exposure, this occurs when the body can't generate enough heat to maintain its normal temperature, usually as a result of being wet, cold, unprotected from the wind, tired and hungry. It is usually more of a problem in upland areas. However, even on the Ridgeway in bad weather the body can be exposed to strong winds and driving rain making the risk a real one. The western stretches of the path are particularly exposed and there are few villages making it difficult to get help should it be needed.

Hypothermia is easily avoided by wearing suitable clothing, carrying and eating enough food and drink, being aware of the weather conditions and checking the morale of your companions. Early signs to watch for are feeling cold and tired with involuntary shivering. If

> ❏ **Dealing with an accident**
> ● Use basic first aid to treat the injury to the best of your ability.
> ● Work out exactly where you are. If possible leave someone with the casualty while others go to get help. If there are only two people, you have a dilemma.
> ● If you decide to get help leave all spare clothing and food with the casualty.
> ● Telephone ☎ 999 and ask for the ambulance service.

this occurs, find some shelter as soon as possible and warm the person up with a hot drink and some chocolate or other high-energy food. If possible give them another warm layer of clothing and allow them to rest until feeling better.

If the patient's condition deteriorates, strange behaviour, slurring of speech and poor co-ordination will become apparent and they can quickly progress into unconsciousness, followed by coma and death. You should get the patient out of wind and rain quickly, improvising a shelter if necessary. Rapid restoration of bodily warmth is essential and is best achieved by bare-skin contact: someone should get into the same sleeping bag as the patient, both having stripped to their underwear, putting any spare clothing under or over them to build up heat. Send urgently for help.

Hyperthermia

Hyperthermia is the general name given to a variety of heat-related ailments. Not something you would normally associate with England, heatstroke and heat exhaustion are serious problems nonetheless. Symptoms of **heat exhaustion** include thirst, fatigue, giddiness, a rapid pulse, raised body temperature, low urine output and, if not treated, delirium and finally a coma. The best cure is to drink plenty of water.

Heatstroke is another matter altogether, and even more serious. A high body temperature and an absence of sweating are early indications, followed by symptoms similar to hypothermia (see opposite) such as a lack of coordination, convulsions and coma. Death will follow if treatment is not instantly given. Sponge the victim down, wrap them in wet towels, fan them, and get help immediately.

Sunburn

It can easily happen even on overcast days and especially if you have a fair complexion. The only surefire way to avoid it is to stay wrapped up, but that's not really an option. What you must do, therefore, is to smother yourself in sunscreen (with a minimum factor of 15) and apply it regularly throughout the day. Don't forget your lips, nose, ears, the back of your neck if wearing a T-shirt, and even under your chin to protect against rays reflected up off the ground.

MINIMUM IMPACT & OUTDOOR SAFETY

3

THE ENVIRONMENT & NATURE

At first glance, the Ridgeway path doesn't seem to be very distinctive. It doesn't have wide beaches or impressive mountains like many other long-distance trails in the UK. But when you look closer you see a wide variety of terrains and habitats from one end of the path to the other: grasslands, chalk downs, beech woodlands and a section along the banks of the River Thames. These varied environments are home to an equally diverse collection of animals, birds and plants. This book is not designed to be a comprehensive guide to all the wildlife you may encounter, but serves as an introduction to the flora and fauna the walker is likely to find along the Ridgeway.

Making that special effort to look out for wildlife and appreciating what you are seeing will enhance your enjoyment of the walk. To take it a step further is to understand a little more about the species you may encounter, appreciating how they interact with each other and learning a little about the conservation issues that are so pertinent today.

Conservation

NATURAL ENGLAND

The official responsibilities of Natural England are to 'enhance biodiversity and our landscapes and wildlife in rural, urban, coastal and marine areas; promote access, recreation and public well-being, and contribute to the way natural resources are managed, so they can be enjoyed now and for future generations'. Essentially this organisation gives advice and information, designates **Sites of Special Scientific Interest** (SSSIs), **National Parks**, **Areas of Outstanding Natural Beauty** (AONBs), manages **National Nature Reserves** (NNRs) and enforces existing regulations. Natural England also manages England's National Trails: they provide most of the funding and resources for path maintenance and promote the conservation of wildlife, geology and wild places in England.

Although no part of the Ridgeway is inside a National Park, the route does lie within two pieces of land designated **Areas of Outstanding Natural Beauty** (AONB) which are administered by the relevant local authorities. The western part of the path is in the 1730 sq km **North Wessex Downs AONB** that was created in 1972. It lies within the County Council boundaries of Wiltshire, Hampshire and Oxfordshire.

The eastern part of the trail is included in the 833 sq km **Chilterns AONB** that was created in 1965 and lies within the County Council boundaries of Bedfordshire, Buckinghamshire, Hertfordshire and Oxfordshire.

There are over 220 **NNR**s in England and the course of the Ridgeway includes Fyfield Down NNR (see p92), just a couple of miles from the beginning of the route and Aston Rowant NNR (see Map 35, p154) near Watlington. These two areas are also **SSSI**s along with over 4100 others in England. Other SSSIs along the Ridgeway include White Horse Hill SSSI and Chinnor Chalk Pit SSSI. **Special Areas of Conservation** (SACs) are designated by the European Union's Habitats Directive and provide an extra tier of protection to the areas that they cover. Along the Ridgeway, Aston Rowant NNR and SSSI is also a SAC along with the Chilterns' beechwoods and Hackpen Hill (see p92). More information on NNRs, SSSIs and SACs can be found on the Natural England website (see box p56).

There is no doubt that these designations play a vital role in safeguarding the land they cover for future generations. However, the very fact that we rely on these labels for protecting limited areas begs the question: what are we doing to the vast majority of land that remains relatively unprotected? Surely we should be aiming to protect the natural environment outside protected areas just as much as within them.

Natural England oversees a National Trails Management Group that has administered both the Ridgeway and the Thames Path national trails since 1997. This Management Group includes a team of National Trails staff who are responsible for the day-to-day management and running of the Ridgeway. They employ wardens and conservation officers – many of them volunteers – to maintain the trail and they also organise guided events and publish information about the Ridgeway for the public.

General maintenance of the trail includes such things as surface repairs, signpost and waymark installation and replacement, converting stiles to gates and installing water taps and troughs. They are also responsible for the protection of endemic species and habitats, as well as geological features, along the Ridgeway. If necessary this may involve access restrictions, especially for motorised vehicles. However, promoting public access and the appreciation of the Ridgeway's natural heritage is also of importance, as is educating locals and visitors about the significance of the environment.

❏ **National Trails**
The Ridgeway is one of 15 National Trails in England and Wales. These are Britain's flagship long-distance paths which grew out of the post-war desire to protect the country's special places, a movement which also gave birth to National Parks and AONBs (see opposite). The first National Trail was the Pennine Way in 1965. Since then over 2500 miles (4000km) of walking routes have been designated.

THE ENVIRONMENT & NATURE

❑ **Statutory bodies**
● **Department for Environment, Food and Rural Affairs** (🖳 www.defra.gov.uk) Government department responsible for sustainable development in the countryside.
● **Natural England** (see pp54-5; 🖳 www.naturalengland.gov.uk)
● **County/Borough Councils: Wiltshire** (🖳 www.wiltshire.gov.uk); **Oxfordshire** (🖳 www.oxfordshire.gov.uk); **Buckinghamshire** (🖳 www.buckscc.gov.uk); **Hertfordshire** (🖳 www.hertsdirect.org); **Swindon** (🖳 www.swindon.gov.uk); **West Berkshire Council** (🖳 www.westberks.gov.uk).
● **English Heritage** (🖳 www.english-heritage.org.uk) Organisation whose central aim is to make sure that the historic environment of England is properly maintained. It is officially known as the Historic Buildings and Monuments Commission for England. Most of the sites around Avebury (see pp71-81) are English Heritage properties though a number are actually managed by the National Trust (see below).
● **Forestry Commission** (🖳 www.forestry.gov.uk) Government department for establishing and managing forests, including Hale Wood (see p170), for a variety of uses.

CAMPAIGNING AND CONSERVATION ORGANISATIONS

The **Friends of the Ridgeway** (🖳 www.ridgewayfriends.org.uk) group focuses specifically on the trail and is particularly vocal on the subject of motorised vehicles using and damaging the tracks. They also have a volunteer scheme for people who wish to get actively involved in preserving the Ridgeway.

The **National Trust** (🖳 www.nationaltrust.org.uk) is a charity with over three million members which aims to protect, through ownership, threatened coastline, countryside, historic houses, castles, gardens and archaeological remains. The Trust manages land and sites along the Ridgeway including the sites in the Avebury area (see pp71-81), the Uffington White Horse area (p109) and the nearby Wayland's Smithy neolithic long barrow (p106). However, all these sites are actually owned by English Heritage (see box above).

The **Wildlife Trusts** (🖳 www.wildlifetrusts.org) is the umbrella organisation for the 47 wildlife trusts in the UK. Regional branches relevant to the Ridgeway are: **Wiltshire Wildlife Trust** (🖳 www.wiltshirewildlife.org); **Berks, Bucks & Oxon Wildlife Trust** (🖳 www.bbowt.org.uk); **Hertfordshire & Middlesex Wildlife Trust** (🖳 www.hertswildlifetrust.org.uk). Reserves include a 70-acre site on Chinnor Hill, just east of Chinnor, a mixture of open grassland and woodland comprising oak, ash and beech. Another reserve, Dancersend & Crong Meadow, is between Wendover and Hastoe.

The **Woodland Trust** (🖳 www.woodlandtrust.org.uk) aims to conserve, restore and re-establish native woodlands throughout the UK: it cares for over a thousand woods around the UK. The Ridgeway passes through one of their woods, Tring Park (p171), towards the end of the trail.

Butterfly Conservation (🖳 www.butterfly-conservation.org) was formed in 1968. They now have 31 branches throughout the British Isles and operate over 30 nature reserves and also sites where butterflies are likely to be found. The branches relevant to the Ridgeway are Wiltshire (🖳 www.wiltshire-butterflies.org.uk) and the Upper Thames (🖳 http://upperthames-butterflies.org.uk).

The **Royal Society for the Protection of Birds (RSPB**; 🖳 www.rspb.org. uk) is the largest voluntary conservation body in Europe focusing on providing a healthy environment for birds, with 200 reserves in the UK.

Although the RSPB doesn't have any reserves directly on the course of the Ridgeway they are running projects on some areas of it. In particular they are involved in a scheme to encourage stone curlew to breed in the Wessex area. In 2009 they recorded 123 breeding pairs and aim to have 350 by 2015.

Flora and fauna

MAMMALS

You could walk the length of the Ridgeway and come to the conclusion that there isn't much wildlife on the route. Obviously walking in a group and making unnecessary noise will dramatically reduce your chances of seeing anything, but if you take some time to look carefully and become aware of your surroundings you are likely to see much more than just the back end of a rabbit diving into the undergrowth. You can be fairly certain that the wildlife you are looking for will have seen you well before you see it and will often be making its escape by the time you do. You'll have to be either very patient or very quick if you want to get photographs.

As a brief 'checklist', depending on the time of year, you can expect to see the following animals along the Ridgeway: deer, foxes, rabbits, hares, stoats, weasels, grey squirrels and perhaps even a badger.

The biggest wild animal you will see along the Ridgeway is the deer. There are two different species in this region: the **fallow deer** (*Dama dama*) and the **roe deer** (*Capreolus capreolus*). They have basically the same lifestyle, usually living in woodland but sometimes on open land with plenty of hedges and copses for cover. Both species are most likely to be seen in the early morning and early evening when they are feeding. The easiest way to tell them apart, if you are close enough, is their size. The adult roe deer grows to about 60cm high at the shoulder while the fallow deer can be up to 90cm at the shoulder. Male fallow deer have large, flat antlers unlike the roe deer whose antlers are spiky. The rutting season for fallow deer is July and August; this is when the males fight each other both for females and territory. You are most likely to see deer in the open during these months. At other times of year you might be able to spot one or two of them together against a hedge on the edge of a field or at the perimeter of a clearing in the woods.

The much-maligned **fox** (*Vulpes vulpes*) inhabits woods and farmland. Despite relentless persecution it is a born survivor, even having adapted to life in cities where they are quite tolerant of human presence. They aren't exclusively nocturnal and in areas where they feel less threatened they are quite likely to be active during the day. Although they can be seen year-round, sight-

THE ENVIRONMENT & NATURE

ings of foxes are usually brief and at a distance, perhaps as one crosses a field.

Among other denizens of woods and farmland are a number of common but shy mammals. One of the most difficult to see is the **badger** (*Meles meles*), a sociable animal with a distinctive black-and-white-striped muzzle. Badgers live in family groups of around ten in large underground setts, coming out to root for worms on the pastureland after sunset, though they will eat practically anything. Some setts can be in use for well over a hundred years if left undisturbed by humans. They do sometimes emerge during daylight hours and the best time for spotting them is between May and September. Unfortunately, the most common sight of badgers is as a bloody mess on the road; they are one of the most frequent animal road casualties.

The animal you are most likely to see on the Ridgeway is the **rabbit** (*Oryctolagus cuniculus*). In fact, at numerous places, especially on the trail near the aptly named Warren Farm just before Streatley, you'll find it hard to miss them. You can see them at all times of year when they come out during the day and at night to find food such as grass and farm crops. Despite the fact that they won't hang around after they have detected your presence, you can still get a good look at them.

Like rabbits, **hares** (*Lepus capensis*) also feed on grass and farm crops and although they live above ground and like open countryside they are far harder to spot. They generally keep well hidden during the day, except for the months of March and April when you might see them dashing around fields or getting involved in 'boxing matches' with other hares. This isn't, as you might presume, an exclusively male preserve as mixed boxing has also been witnessed. If you are hoping to get a photo of a hare be aware that they can run at speeds up to 40mph/65kph!

The carnivorous **stoat** (*Mustela erminea*) and its smaller cousin the **weasel** (*Mustela nivalis*) are common along the Ridgeway and can be seen year-round but just as with the hares you'll have to be quick if you want to see more than the tail-end of one. They can be difficult to tell apart, especially if you only get a glimpse, but the weasel is noticeably smaller than the stoat. Weasels eat mice, shrews and birds' eggs but owing to their size stoats can tackle larger prey such as adult rabbits and farm birds. This has led to their persecution by farmers who lose poultry to them. Weasels and stoats are by nature very inquisitive so just because they dart for cover as you approach doesn't mean they might not poke their head out for another look just after you have passed.

The **grey squirrel** (*Sciurus carolinensis*) was introduced to Britain from North America in the late 19th century and its outstanding success in colonising the country is very much to the detriment of other native species including songbirds and, most famously, the red squirrel. Grey squirrels inhabit woodlands, parks and gardens and are a common sight from January to June during their breeding season. You might also see them during the autumn on the woodland floor, burying nuts to keep themselves supplied throughout the winter.

At dusk during the summer months **bats** can be seen hunting for moths and flying insects along hedgerows, over rivers and around street lamps. As the weather gets colder they will hibernate though can sometimes still be seen on warmer evenings. Bats have had a bad press thanks to Dracula and countless other horror stories but anyone who has seen one up close knows them to be harmless and delightful little creatures. As for their blood-sucking fame, the matchbox-sized species in Britain would not even be able to break your skin with their teeth let alone suck your blood. Their reputation is improving all the time thanks to the work of the many bat conservation groups around the country and all fourteen species found in Britain are protected by law. The most numerous species is the **common pipistrelle bat** (*Pipistrellus pipistrellus*).

Some other small but fairly common species which can be found in the grassland and hedgerows on the Ridgeway include the **hedgehog** (*Erinaceus europaeus*) and a variety of **voles**, **mice** and **shrews**.

BIRDS

The two halves of the Ridgeway provide distinctly different environments for birds. On the whole the western half, up to Streatley, is exposed with few trees while the eastern half is mostly wooded. Both sections provide ample opportunity for bird spotting with the western section providing the most variety. Early mornings and early evenings are generally the best times for spotting birds.

The western half

One of the most common birds on the open downs is the **skylark** (*Alauda arvensis*). Its dull brown plumage with a darker stripe doesn't make it the most distinctive of birds but when in flight you can recognise it by the white edges of the outer tail feathers. It nests on the ground in a hollow and makes little attempt to conceal its eggs.

SKYLARK
L: 185MM/7.25"

The **corn bunting** (*Emberiza calandra*) can often be heard singing its sharp jangly song along the path. It doesn't look dissimilar to the skylark though it has no white edging on its tail feathers and its beak is shorter and more rounded. You are also likely

to see some **yellowhammers** (*Emberiza citrinella*) among the hedgerows and bushes along the path. Although the young birds only have a yellow head, as they grow older the entire body takes on a yellow base colour. Their song is a single repetitive note with a higher note to finish.

Another common sight on this section is the **meadow pipit** (*Anthus pratensis*). Its light brown plumage, blending into buff on its underside, is marked with darker brown bars all over. You can often see it hopping quickly along the ground where it nests but it conceals its home well with thick brambles.

YELLOWHAMMER
L: 160MM/6.25"

THE ENVIRONMENT & NATURE

LAPWING/PEEWIT
L: 320mm/12.5"

The **lapwing** (*Vanellus vanellus*) with its long legs, short bill and distinctive long headcrest feeds on arable farmland. Sadly, this attractive bird is declining in numbers. The name comes from its lilting flight, frequently changing direction with its large rounded wings. It's also identified by a white belly, black and white head, black throat patch and distinctive dark green wings.

There are also several larger birds that you might see on the Ridgeway. The **buzzard** (*Buteo buteo*) is the most common and can often be seen hovering in the sky, looking for prey such as mice, rabbits and snakes. It has a deep brown plumage with a rounded black and brown banded tail. The **kestrel** (*Falco tinnunculus*) can also be seen hovering above the ground, hunting for prey. Both the male and female are of a reddish brown colour, though the male has a blueish head. Their wings are broad and flat and widely spread when hovering.

You might also be lucky enough to see an owl, even in the daytime. The **barn owl** (*Tyto alba*) is normally nocturnal, but when it has young, or if it is desperate for food, it will hunt during the day. The back of the owl is a sandy brown colour with grey spots while the front is white with brown spots. The white face is heart-shaped, set with deep, dark eyes. The legs are covered with dense, short white feathers. If you can see one of these birds perched where you can get a good look at it you really have been fortunate.

Pheasants (*Phasianus colchicus*) are common around hedgerows and bushes; they can often be spotted in open fields when feeding. The male can be seen strutting around, showing off his long brown and black striped tail and colourful neck and head. The females are buff and brown all over with a shorter tail than the males. You can usually get a good look at these birds as they aren't particularly shy which might go some way to explaining why they are also the most popular game bird in England.

Other game birds you may see in the fields along the western part of the Ridgeway include the partridge and the quail. The **partridge** (*Perdix perdix*) is often seen in pairs during the spring and summer. Although there are many colour variations in its plumage, it is often light grey with brown bars and the head is usually brown. This bird feeds mainly on insects and seeds. The **quail** (*Coturnix coturnix*) feeds on similar fare, though it is much smaller than the partridge, at half the size. It is only found in England during the late spring and summer and resembles a partridge but its colouring is reddish-tan with dashes of cream and black. It's not easily spotted as it often hides in grass when disturbed.

If you are very lucky, you might see a **stone curlew**, but realistically, the chances are very low. This long-legged summer visitor nests on the ground and its colouring of light brown with dark brown and cream streaks camouflages it well in such an environment. Their large yellow eyes are ideal for spotting any far-off danger from which they are more inclined to hide rather than take flight.

The eastern half

Common birds seen in the woodlands of the eastern section of the Ridgeway include the **nuthatch** (*Sitta europaea*) which can often be seen clinging to tree trunks looking for insects. It's a distinctive small bird with a blue back, white throat and chestnut-coloured underside. The nuthatch nest will often be in a hole in a tree trunk. If the hole is too big, the nuthatch will partially block it with mud, thus making it quite easy to spot.

Various species of tit also live in the woodlands with the **great tit** (*Parus major*) being the largest and one of the most common. It has a black and white head, green back, blue and white wings and a yellow underside. Other tits seen in the woodlands include the **long-tailed tit** (*Aegithalos caudatus*) which is black and white with a long black tail with white edging and the **coal tit** (*Parus ater*), another black and white specimen found in more open areas of woodland.

The numbers of **red kites** in the Chilterns is increasing owing to reintroduction programmes run by Natural England and the RSPB and there is a good chance that you will see one or more. Their large size – adults have a wingspan of around 1.8m – make them easy to spot and their long forked red tail makes them easy to identify. They have reddish brown bodies with darker wings which also have large patches of white, visible when they are in flight.

You should be able to see woodpeckers during your walk and will certainly hear them hammering away at tree trunks. The most common is the **great-spotted woodpecker** (*Dendrocopos major*) which has mainly black and white plumage enhanced by red patches on the back of its head and on its lower underside. Where the woods are on the edge of open country, you can find **green woodpeckers** (*Picus viridis*). The lifestyle of this bird is similar to that of the great-spotted woodpecker. Its striking green body, white underside and red head with black dashes make this a very attractive bird. The woodpecker bores into trees, not only to find insects and their larvae but also to hollow them out to make a nest. **Blackbirds** (*Turdus merula*) appear all along the Ridgeway and are unmistakable as the males are jet-black with orange beaks. The females are the same size but have brown bodies, graduating to black at the tail, and brown beaks.

If you, by chance, spot a **jay** (*Garrulus glandarius*) before it spots you and flies off, you are doing well. They are members of the crow family but are notoriously shy. Their plumage is a brownish-red overall with the top of the head white with black dashes. The tail is black with dark blue flashes.

BUTTERFLIES

The chalk downlands along the Ridgeway provide a habitat in which many species of butterfly can flourish. The most common species seen during the summer is the **meadow brown** (*Maniola jurtina*), overall a dusty brown colour, but with orange patches on its forewings, inside which are black eye-spots. This is

THE ENVIRONMENT & NATURE

one of the most common butterflies in Europe, as well as on the Ridgeway. Also likely to be flitting around at this time is the **small heath** (*Coenonympha pamphilus*), recognisable by its dull-orange wings edged with grey; it has black eye-spots on the underside of its forewings. You'll probably see some **large white** (*Pieris brassicae*) and **small white** (*Pieris rapae*) butterflies too. These are both essentially white with dark-grey wing tips. On the large white, both male and female have two black eye-spots on the underside of the forewings, but only the female has them on the upper side. On the small white, both sexes have two black eye-spots on the underside of their forewings, but on the upperside, the female has two small spots and the male only a single spot.

There are several different kinds of blue butterfly that you may see on the chalklands. The most likely is the **common blue** (*Polyommatus icarus*). The male is violet-blue with a fine black edging to its wings; the female is actually brown though has a row of red spots along her wings which are edged with black. Less common is the **chalkhill blue** (*Lysandra coridon*); the male is altogether duller than the common blue but has more extensive black and white edging around the wings. The female is dark brown and has the same wing edging.

There are usually some **small copper** (*Lycaena phlaeas*) butterflies around that are distinctive despite their size. The forewings are bright orange with heavy black spots and black fringing whereas the hindwings are predominantly black with a thick band of bright orange edging at the bottom.

Two common day-flying moths are the **five-spot burnet** (*Zygaena trifolii*) and **six-spot burnet** (*Zygaena filipendulae*). Each has very dark wings, patterned with five or six orange/red spots.

TREES

You'll see few trees along the western half of the Ridgeway. Most of those you do see have been planted by man over the centuries to serve a specific purpose, eg coppices, windbreaks and plantations. Though many of these are no longer maintained you can still see evidence of them if you look. The eastern half of the Ridgeway is often wooded, usually with beech.

Coppices are areas of woodland, usually oak, hazel or elm, managed by man through the periodic cutting of the trees right back to the ground; multiple fast-growing shoots then appear from the cut trees and are harvested.

Many coppices were fenced to keep animals out and often the fence sat on a raised earth ridge that you can still see around many disused coppiced areas. Coppices were an important supply of wood until the mid-1800s after which demand declined. However, most coppices were still maintained and today some are being fully used once more to supply wood for charcoal, greenwood furniture and craft items.

Windbreaks, such as hedges, serve multiple purposes. They give livestock a place to shelter from the wind and also provide shade. They also prevent soil erosion and provide a habitat for varied wildlife such as birds, insects, rabbits and pheasants. With the correct maintenance a hedge can last indefinitely and they are an extremely effective way of containing animals. Despite fences providing none of these benefits, they have often been a more popular choice with farmers who want to maximise their field size or change the layout of their fields. To a small extent, hedges are starting to make a comeback as their full benefits are realised and you'll see some recently planted hedges along parts of the Ridgeway.

Plantations were most common between 1600 and 1900; popular species included oak, beech, elm and ash. It was intended that when the trees were mature they would be used for ship-building, furniture-making and other tasks. Many plantations did provide wood for these purposes, like the beech plantations on the eastern section of the Ridgeway, but others, especially the oak plantations, which took years to mature, were never used owing to the availability of cheap coal and imported timber being sourced from around the British Empire. These unused plantations form some of what we now consider traditional woodland.

During World War I there was a timber shortage that led to large conifer plantations being started. However, these weren't ready for cutting during World War II and this meant that large tracts of private woodland had to be felled. After World War I the increased need for food led to the felling of plantations and removal of hedges to increase the size of available farmland.

Today the creation of new plantations has virtually stopped. Many of the conifer plantations, started between the wars, have matured and been felled though there are still many which are managed for their timber. In a country where so many of the ancient forests have long since disappeared, plantations are now as near as some of us can get to the real thing.

FLOWERS

You'll be walking amongst many different species of wild flowers on the Ridgeway, though unless you keep an eye out it can be easy to miss some of them. Despite the trail being constantly exposed to wind and direct sunlight there will still be a wide selection of common flowers at any time between March and November though the biggest selection appears during the summer months. You'll also have the chance to see some of the more uncommon flowers native to chalk grassland. The best time for spotting these is during the summer months in the areas around Barbury Castle, Uffington Castle, the Pitstone Hills and Ivinghoe Beacon.

There will be plenty of **scentless mayweed** (*Tripleurospermum inodorum*), **common mouse-ear** (*Cerastium glomeratum*) and **common vetch** (*Vicia sativa*) at any time between April and November along most stretches of the Ridgeway. Another common flower is the **red campion** (*Silene dioica*), but this is found mainly in wooded areas and hedgerows. Despite its name, you'll recognise it by the profusion of shocking pink flowers it produces. A common flower with an even more misleading name is the **black medick** (*Medicago lupulina*) that grows mainly on grassland and has yellow flowers. **Herb robert** (*Geranium robertianum*) also flowers throughout the spring, summer and early autumn. It has attractive pink and white flowers and is found in shady, often rocky areas.

THE ENVIRONMENT & NATURE

In the spring, flowers such as **greater stitchwort** (*stellaria holostea*) and **dovesfoot cranesbill** (*Geranium molle*) are common in the hedgerows while the distinctive **cowslip** (*Primula veris*) with its clusters of yellow, funnel-shaped flowers is widespread in more open areas. The **common dog** and **heath dog violets** (*Viola riviniana, V. canina*) can be found in shady, open woodlands during the spring while another violet-coloured flower, the **common field speedwell** (*Veronica persica*), prefers cultivated land.

During the late spring and summer months, the variety of flowers along the Ridgeway is at its best. An aptly named example is the **traveller's joy** or **old man's beard** (*Clematis vitalba*) that climbs over hedgerows and displays dense clumps of white, feathery flowers with a strong scent. Another climber you are likely to see is the large-leafed, white-flowered **white bryony** (*Bryonia dioica*). Summer is also when you can see the striking flowers of the **common mallow** (*Malva sylvestris*) that can grow to 150cm high. The yellow, star-shaped flowers of the medicinal **St John's wort** (*Hypericum perforatum*) can be spotted in wooded areas and is so named as it flowers around St John's Day, 24th June.

Upright hedge parsley (*Torilis japonica*) is common along the hedgerows and on the edges of woodland whereas the similar-looking **wild parsnip** (*Pastinaca sativa*) grows mainly on grassland. **Wild carrot** (*Daucus carota*) can sometimes be seen in open grassy areas, distinguished by its large dome-shaped clusters of white flowers. Large **oxeye daisies** (*Leucanthemum vulgare*) are difficult to miss and you may also see **silverweed** (*Potentilla anserina*) along the trail showing grey/silver sharply toothed leaves and yellow flowers.

Flowers that grow only on chalk grassland areas of the Ridgeway include **devil's-bit scabious** (*Scabiosa pratensis*) that can flower as late as October, **squinancywort** (*Asperula cynanchica*) that has slender stems bearing pale-pink and white flowers and **viper's bugloss** (*Echium vulgare*) with its tall thick stem and purple funnel-shaped flowers. This type of chalky ground also plays host to various orchids including the **common spotted** (*Dactylorhiza fuchsii*) that has pale leaves spotted with crimson and the **fragrant** (*Gymnadenia conopsea)* and **pyramidal** (*Anacamptis pyramidalis*), both with reddish petals but with the pyramidal variety being darker.

(Colour section (following pages)
- **C1-C3** Some common flora.
- **C4 Top**: Snowy view of the ancient standing stones along West Kennet Avenue (see p75) towards Avebury. **Bottom**: Crop circles (see p76) near Overton Hill.
- **C5** In good weather paragliders launch themselves off White Horse Hill (see p107).
- **C6-7 Top**: Looking out along grassy Smeathe's Ridge (p94), shortly after Barbury Castle. **Bottom left**: West Kennet Long Barrow (see p78) dates back to 3600BC. **Bottom right**: Chinnor station (p156), the start of the seven-mile Chinnor & Princes Risborough Railway.
- **C8 Top**: Walking down Liddington Hill (see p100). **Bottom**: An unusual double-railway via-duct (p136) with diagonally-laid brickwork crosses the Thames near South & North Stoke.
- **C9** There's no shortage of hostelries to delay your progress along the Ridgeway. The Swan at Streatley (see p130) has an inviting terrace right beside the River Thames.
- **C10-11** Wayland's Smithy (see p106) is a Neolithic long barrow. Legend says that the shoes for the Uffington White Horse were made here. ● **C12** Some common butterflies.

Viper's Bugloss
Echium vulgare

Rosebay Willowherb
Epilobium angustifolium

Foxglove
Digitalis purpurea

Bluebell
Endymion non-scriptus

Red Campion
Silene dioica

Herb-Robert
Geranium robertianum

Early Purple Orchid
Orchis mascula

Spotted Orchid
Dactylorhiza fuchsii

Pyramidal Orchid
Anacamptis pyramidalis

Gorse
Ulex europaeus

Common Ragwort
Senecio jacobaea

St John's Wort
Hypericum perforatum

Tormentil
Potentilla erecta

Birdsfoot-trefoil
Lotus corniculatus

Scarlet Pimpernel
Anagallis arvensis

Yarrow
Achillea millefolium

Hogweed
Heracleum sphondylium

Ramsoms (Wild Garlic)
Allium ursinum

Common Vetch
Vicia sativa

Old Man's Beard
Clematis vitalba

Germander Speedwell
Veronica chamaedrys

Silverweed
Potentilla anserina

Self-heal
Prunella vulgaris

Violet
Viola riviniana

Meadow Buttercup
Ranunculis acris

Primrose
Primula vulgaris

Cowslip
Primula veris

Dog Rose
Rosa canina

Common Hawthorn
Crataegus monogyna

Ox-eye Daisy
Leucanthemum vulgare

C6

C10

Peacock
Inachis io

Small Tortoiseshell
Aglais urticae

Common Blue
Polyommatus icarus

Small Garden/Cabbage White
Pieris rapae

Chalkhill Blue
Lysandra coridon

Painted Lady
Cynthia cadui

Large
Garden/
Cabbage White
Pieris brassicae

Small
Copper
*Lycaena
phlaeas*

Small
Heath
*Coenonympha
pamphilus*

Red Admiral *Vanessa atalanta*

White Admiral
Limenitis camilla

Meadow
Brown
*Maniola
jurtina*

Using this guide

This route guide has been divided according to logical start and stop points. However, these are not intended to be strict daily stages since people walk at different speeds and have different interests. The maps can be used to plan how far to walk each day. The route summaries below describe the trail between significant places and are written as if walking the path from west to east. To enable you to plan your own itinerary practical information is presented clearly on the trail maps. This includes walking times for both directions, all places to stay, camp and eat, as well as shops where you can buy supplies. Further service details are given in the text under the entry for each place.

For an overview of this information see Itineraries, pp25-31.

TRAIL MAPS

Scale and walking times

The trail maps are to a scale of 1:20,000 (1cm = 200m; $3^1/_8$ inches = one mile). Walking times are given along the side of each map and the arrow shows the direction to which the time refers. Black triangles indicate the points between which the times have been taken. **See box on walking times below.**

The time-bars are a tool and are not there to judge your walking ability. There are so many variables that affect walking speed, from the weather conditions to how many beers you drank the previous evening. After the first hour or two of walking you will be able to see how your speed relates to the timings on the maps.

Up or down?

Other than when on a track or bridleway the trail is shown as a dotted line. An arrow across the trail indicates the slope; two arrows show that it is steep. Note that the arrow points towards the higher part of

---

❏ **Important note – walking times**
Unless otherwise specified, **all times in this book refer only to the time spent walking**. You will need to add 20-30% to allow for rests, photography, checking the map, drinking water etc. When planning the day's hike count on 5-7 hours' actual walking.

the trail. If, for example, you are walking from A (at 80m) to B (at 200m) and the trail between the two is short and steep it would be shown thus: A— — — >> — — — — B. Reversed arrow heads indicate downward gradient.

Accommodation

Apart from in large towns where some selection of places has been necessary, almost everywhere to stay that is within easy reach of the trail is marked. Details of each place are given in the accompanying text. The number and type of rooms is given after each entry: S = single room, T = twin room, D = double room, F = family room sleeping at least three people; family rooms can also often be let as a double or twin.

The text also mentions whether rooms are en suite, or have private/shared facilities, and if a bath is available (□) in at least one room and also whether dogs (🐾) are welcome. Most places will not take more than one dog in a room and also accept dogs subject to prior arrangement. Some make an additional charge while others may require a deposit which is returnable if the dog doesn't make a mess. See p14 and p23 for details on rates.

Other features

Other features are marked on the map only when they are pertinent to navigation. To avoid clutter, not all features are marked all the time.

Marlborough

Marlborough is the nearest town to the start of the Ridgeway. It has all the shops and services you might need before setting off and boasts a large array of pubs, cafés and restaurants for you to enjoy. Convenient bus links to the start of the Ridgeway, and its proximity to Avebury, also make this a useful place to base yourself before you start.

Although there is evidence of human activity in the area dating back to around 3700BC, the first mention of the town is in the Domesday Book of 1087. A royal charter was granted by King John in 1204 that allowed the town to hold markets on Wednesdays and Saturdays, a practice that remains to this day. In 1653 a devastating fire destroyed around 250 houses in Marlborough and it was decreed that from then on no house in the town could have a thatched roof. The long-term prosperity of the town was assured by its position on the old coach road between London and Bristol; the town still has an air of affluence, perhaps owing in part to the presence of the exclusive Marlborough College, founded in 1843.

SERVICES

The town's shops and services are concentrated along the High St and include a **post office** (Mon-Fri 9am-5.30pm, Sat 9am-12.30pm) in the **One Stop** convenience store (daily 6am-10pm) and various **banks**, all with **ATMs**.

   In the **library** (☎ 01672 512663; Mon 2-7pm, Wed & Fri 9.30am-5pm, Thur 9.30am-7pm, Sat 9.30am-1pm, closed Tue and Sun), at the southern end of the High St, offers free **internet access** but it is limited to an hour per session and non-members must have some ID.

   At the other end of the High St, **White Horse Bookshop** (☎ 01672 512071; Mon-Sat 9am-5.30pm) has a good selection of books about the local area. There is also a **chemist** (Boots; Mon-Sat 9am-5.30pm, Sun 10am-4pm) and a **supermarket** (Waitrose; Mon-Thur 8.30am-8pm, Fri 8.30am-9pm, Sat 8am-7pm, Sun 10am-4pm) on the High St. If you're here on the second Saturday or last Sunday of the month, visit the **farmers' market** (see box p15).

   For outdoor equipment and supplies try **Landmark** (☎ 01672 515000, 🖥 www.landmarkstores.com; Mon-Sat 9.30am-5.30pm, to 6pm on Sat in the summer, Sun 10am-5.30pm) on the High St. They have a good range of outdoor clothing and accessories in case you have forgotten something.

   If you need repairs to your bike head to **Bertie Maffoons Bicycles** (☎ 01672 519119; Mon-Fri 10am-6pm, Sat 9am-5pm) in Hughenden Yard. Alternatively, go to **Acceler8** (☎ 01672 513414; Mon-Sat 9am-5.30pm, Sun 11am-2pm) which sells motoring accessories but also some for cycling and walking.

   Taxi firms include Arrow (☎ 01672 515567, 🖥 bookings@arrowph.com) and Marlborough Taxis (☎ 01672 512786) though the bus services are good so you shouldn't need them. There are regular **bus** services to: Avebury and Calne (Connect2Wiltshire's Line 4); Swindon (Wilts & Dorset's No X5, Thamesdown's No 48 and Stagecoach's No 70); and Ogbourne St George (Stagecoach's No 70). See public transport map and table, pp42-5, for more details.

   Several National Express **coach** services (see box p40) also call here.

WHERE TO STAY

On the High St the rather grand-looking *Castle & Ball Hotel* (☎ 01672 515201, 🖥 www.castleandball.com; 25D/4T/4D, T or F, all en suite, ☐; 🐾) dates back to the 15th century; B&B costs from £85 for either single or double occupancy, and from £110 for four in a family room. Just as atmospheric is *The Ivy House Hotel* (☎ 01672 515333, 🖥 www.ivyhousemarlborough.co.uk; 16D/3D or 1/5T/3D, T or F, all en suite, ☐; 🐾 £25). B&B in this well-kept Georgian house starts from £95 two sharing, £75 for single occupancy. Just along from here is *The Merlin* (☎ 01672 512151, 🖥 www.merlin-bed-and-breakfast-marlborough. co.uk; 3S/5D/1D, T or F, all en suite, ☐). This B&B is in the large, cream-coloured Georgian building and shares an entrance with the Pizza Express restaurant (see p70). Singles/doubles start from £50/60, the family room costs from £80; breakfast costs an extra £5pp.

   Several pubs in town also offer accommodation. *The Bear* (☎ 01672 512134; 2D en suite, 4D share shower room) charges from £30pp. Breakfast is not included, nor is it available, but an evening meal is which makes this good value. Around the corner from The Bear is *The Lamb Inn* (☎ 01672 512668, 🖥 www.thelambinnmarlborough.com; 4D/1T/1D, T or F, all en suite) that has light, airy rooms for £75-105, or £50-85 single occupancy. The family room costs £120 for four sharing. Just past The Lamb Inn is *The Crown Hotel* (☎ 01672 511344; 💻 www.thecrownmarlborough.co.uk; 4D/1D, T or F, all private facilities) where they charge £30pp (£37.50 with breakfast). The family room has two double beds.

At the other end of the High St is *The Sun Inn* (☎ 01672 515011, 💻 www.thesunmarlborough.co.uk; 5D, all en suite) offering rather stylish rooms for £60; no discount for single occupancy. A continental breakfast is included in the rate; a full English is an additional £5pp.

WHERE TO EAT AND DRINK

A good choice during the day is *Armadillo Café* (☎ 01672 516933; Mon-Fri 8am-5pm, Sat 9am-5pm) on the High St. They serve hot breakfast baguettes with a sausage and bacon filling, home-made pies, sandwiches, seven types of Scotch egg, salads, cakes, ice cream and good coffee. *The Food Gallery* (☎ 01672 514069, 💻 www.thefoodgallery.co.uk; Mon-Sat 8.30am-5pm, Sun 10am-3pm) is also on the High St. They take great pride in the quality of their coffee and produce some excellent eat-in or takeaway sandwiches (£2.50-3.60).

Located down Hilliers Yard *Bytes Café* (☎ 01672 511377; Mon-Sat 9am-4.30pm, Sun 11am-4pm) serves toasted paninis, home-made soup and pasties, amongst other items. There is also wi-fi **internet access** here; access is free but is only available for a limited period of time.

In Hughenden Yard you'll find *Azuza* (☎ 01672 513380, 💻 www.azuza.co.uk; food Mon-Sat 9am-5pm, Sun 10am-5pm), a café/bar which serves an all-day breakfast, paninis, wraps and baguettes. Azuza is licensed all day but after 5pm it changes into a Sports bar showing major sports events on their large screens; the night club (Fri 11pm-2.30am, Sat to 3am) is upstairs.

Also good for breakfast is *Polly Tea Rooms* (☎ 01672 512146; Mon-Fri 8.30am-5pm, Sat 8am-6pm, Sun 9am-6pm) which has been here since 1932. Apart from cooked breakfasts (£4.95-8.95) they also have plenty of home-made lunches, such as sausages with yorkshire pudding (£8.50). However, they are probably best known for their cream teas (£5.50; available all day).

Most of the pubs on the High St serve food both at lunchtime and in the evening and are licensed to serve drinks all day. You could head to *The Wellington Arms* (☎ 01672 512954; food Mon noon-2.30pm & 6-9pm, Tue-Sat 11am-2.30pm & 6-9pm, Sun noon-2.30pm & 6-8.30pm) where there are specials (eg curry, or pasta, or fish and chips) most nights of the week, or the 15th-century *Sun Inn* (see above; food Mon-Sat noon-3pm & 6-9pm, Sun noon-2.30pm) where *moules frites* is £9.95.

The *Royal Oak* (☎ 01672 512064; food daily 11am-10pm) has Greene King ales to go with a ploughman's lunch (£7.25). *Castle & Ball Hotel* (see p67; food Mon-Fri 7am-10pm, Sat & Sun 8am-10pm) serves breakfasts and pastries in the morning. From lunchtime onwards they have choices such as a tandoori vegetable burger (£7.69) or slow-cooked duck leg (£11.39). Continuing on the pub crawl you might like to visit ***The Bear*** (see p67; food daily Mon-Sat noon-9pm, Sun noon-3pm) for Arkell's beers and pub grub such as cod and chips (£6.95) or steak and ale pie (£7.25), or the ***Green Dragon*** (☎ 01672 512366; food Mon 10am-2pm, Tue-Sat 10am-2pm & 6-9pm, Sun noon-3pm) for a late breakfast (from £5.50) and, later on, to try some locally brewed 6X from the Wadworth brewery.

   The Crown Hotel (see opposite; food daily noon-2pm & 6.30-9pm) specialises in fish but does have some meat dishes (main courses cost around £13-15) and the menu changes regularly. Not to be left out, ***The Lamb Inn*** (see p67; food Mon-Thur noon-2.30pm & 6.30-9pm, Fri-Sun noon-2.30pm) also serves food. A Thai beef salad costs £9 and fillet of sea trout is £9.50.

   For a non-alcoholic lunch you could head to ***Krumbz*** (☎ 01672 516333; Mon-Fri 7.30am-3pm) which charges £2.70-4.50 for its breakfast baguettes. They have an interesting selection of sandwich fillings (such as roast veg and goat's cheese, or poached salmon and lime mayonnaise) and make their own cakes. On the High St, ***Greggs*** (Mon-Sat 7.30am-5pm) also sells a variety of sandwiches.

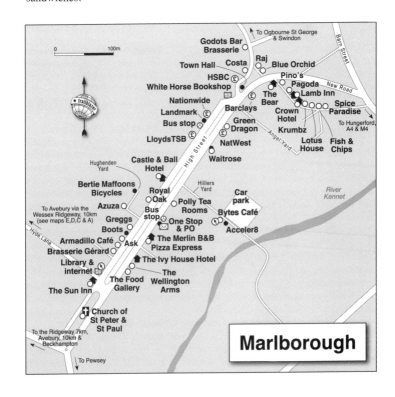

Marlborough

There is a *coffee shop* (Mon-Fri 10am-5pm, Sat 9am-5pm, Sun 10am-3pm) in the redundant church of St Peter and St Paul at the end of the High St. It shares the former church with a craft shop and art exhibition. It's well worth a visit to sample a generous wedge of home-made cake with a nice cup of tea. They also serve simple but tasty lunches costing from £4 to £7.50. *Costa* (Mon-Sat 7.30am-6pm, Sun 9am-5pm) serves pretty much exactly the coffees, teas and light lunches you would expect from a coffeeshop chain. There is also a small *café* (Mon-Thur 8.30am-7pm, Fri 8.30am-8pm, Sat 8am-6pm, Sun 10am-3pm) at the front of the Waitrose supermarket (see p67).

Of course, there is an Indian restaurant here, too: it's called *Raj* (☎ 01672 515661; Mon-Sat noon-2pm, Sun noon-3pm, Sun-Thur 5.30-11.30pm, Fri & Sat 5.30pm-midnight) and is always busy. They have the usual extensive menu with most main dishes costing £4.95-10.95. On Sunday there is a buffet. If you just want a takeaway you could head to *Spice Paradise* (☎ 01672 519959; Sun-Mon & Wed-Thur noon-2pm & 5-11pm, Fri & Sat noon-2pm & 5-11.30pm). *Blue Orchid* (☎ 01672 513353, 🖥 www.blueorchidthai.co.uk; Mon-Sat noon-2pm & 5.30-11pm) serves authentic Thai food. They have an extensive menu that includes traditional curry dishes (£8.50-11.50) but also specials; try the delicious *goong pad khing pak* (tiger prawns fried with ginger and vegetables) if it is on the menu.

A minute or so away is *Pagoda* (☎ 01672 512886, 🖥 www.pagodapeking. co.uk; Mon-Sat 5.30-11pm); it's a pretty standard Peking Chinese restaurant with a lengthy menu and reasonable prices (£6.20 for *kung po* chilli chicken) which also does takeaway. Alternatively, *Lotus House* (☎ 01672 512715; daily 5.30-11.30pm) cooks Chinese food for takeaway only. Just next door is *Fish & Chips* (Mon-Sat noon-2pm & 5-11.30pm).

There is also a scattering of eateries serving Italian food. *Pizza Express* (☎ 01672 519229; Sun-Mon 11.30am-10pm, Tue to 10.30pm, Wed-Sat to 11pm), at The Merlin (see p67), has a sunny courtyard and the usual selection of pizza and pasta. On the other side of the High St, *Ask* (☎ 01672 515797; daily noon-11pm) has a more interesting selection and the menu changes regularly. It's always busy and has an easy-going atmosphere. Slightly more expensive but the best Italian in town is *Pino's* (☎ 01672 512969, 🖥 www.pinosristorante.co.uk; Mon-Sat noon-2.30pm, daily 6-10pm) where *tonno grigliatio* (marinated tuna steak) is £14.95 and *agnello con crosta di erbe* (rack of lamb with herb crust) is £16.95. Pizzas are £8.45-11.95.

The French-style chain *Brasserie Gérard* (☎ 01672 511181, 🖥 www.bras seriegerard.co.uk; Mon-Sat 9am-11pm, Sun to 10.30pm) serves light meals: *poulet* baguette (£8.95) or steak baguette (£9.95) as well as classic French dishes such as *coq au vin* (£11.95) and *boeuf bourguignon* (£13.95) in a relaxed atmosphere.

For something a little more stylish there is *Godots Bar Brasserie* (☎ 01672 514776, 🖥 www.godotsrestaurant.co.uk; Tue-Sat noon-2.30pm & 7-10pm, last orders 9.30pm), a short walk from the High St. Reservations are necessary. Expect to pay £13-17 for a main course such as half a duck roasted with

Madeira jus, or sauté of chicken breast with fennel and tarragon. They have a delightful courtyard garden.

Avebury and around

AVEBURY [See map p75]

This small village, spread around one of the most important Neolithic sites (see box pp72-3) in Europe, attracts thousands of visitors every year, but for all that, it's still essentially a quiet and unassuming place. Most tourists are here for just a couple of hours on a whistle-stop coach tour and those day trippers who arrive by car are usually gone by mid-afternoon, too. It's remarkable how you can walk just a few minutes away from the throngs of visitors around the stone circle and be on your own in the countryside. Another remarkable thing about this place, that's impossible to miss, is how the busy A4361 road from Beckhampton to Swindon zig-zags straight through the stone circle itself. It really couldn't be any less subtle.

It is well-worth spending as much time as you can in and around Avebury. There is so much to see and the walking is easy – an ideal warm-up for the Ridgeway proper. Not only is there the stone circle, but the Great Barn and museums, West Kennet Avenue, Silbury Hill, West Kennet Long Barrow, the Sanctuary and Windmill Hill. And if you're really lucky you might even see a crop circle (see box p76)! A useful website for information about the sights is 🖳 www.avebury-web.co.uk.

The **Alexander Keiller Museum** (☎ 01672 539250, 🖳 www.nationaltrust. org.uk; daily Easter-Oct 10am-6pm, Nov-Easter 10am-4pm) is spread over two locations: the **Barn Gallery**, in the magnificent late 17th-century **Great Barn** and the **Stables Gallery**, a few minutes' walk away. This museum was started in 1935 to gather together archaeological finds from Avebury and the surrounding area dating back 6000 years. A visit is recommended as it really helps to put the surviving monuments in and around the village in context. Entry is £4.90/2.45 for adults/children, £3.90/1.95 for cyclists or people arriving by public transport (on production of a bus ticket). Entry is free for members of all National Trust (NT) organisations and English Heritage (EH). One ticket admits you to both galleries.

Close to the Stables Gallery is **Avebury Manor and Gardens** (contact details as above). There was originally a Benedictine Priory on this site dating back to the 13th century, but the current buildings date from the 16th century with renovations made by a Colonel Jenner in the early 20th century. The immaculate gardens, with their box hedges and medieval walls, are open to the public (Easter-Oct daily 11am-5pm; £3.50/1.75 adults/children; free for NT members but not for EH members). At the time of writing the Manor was not open to visitors but it is expected to be open in 2012. *(continued on p74)*

❏ Avebury Stone Circle

A visit to the Neolithic stone circle complex at Avebury is undoubtedly one of the highlights of the Ridgeway. This is one of the largest stone circles in the world though it's often overshadowed by the more famous Stonehenge, about 24 miles away. Although most tourists are here for just a couple of hours, it would be easy to spend a day or two investigating Avebury and the surrounding monuments.

The immense task of constructing this site spanned about 500 years, starting around 2500BC. The irregularly shaped stones come from the Marlborough Downs, a few miles from where they were set up in the henge, and were transported here with great effort though it's still unclear why. There are several clear solar alignments within the formation but an overall theory about the purpose and usage of the stone circle remains elusive. If you are in need of an answer, you'll find plenty of ideas out there, with many entering the realms of fantasy, but none of which can comprehensively explain this huge site.

Starting from the outside and working in there is a roughly circular earth bank about 400 metres in diameter immediately dropping down into a deep ditch. Lining the other side of this ditch is the main stone circle. It is highly significant that the earth bank is on the outside of the ditch as this means that the site cannot have been defensive in nature, unlike all the later hill forts which have the ditch outside the bank and therefore are defensive. The alignment of outer bank and inner ditch is what defines a 'henge', though there is one exception to this of course – Stonehenge itself!

The main stone circle once consisted of nearly 100 stones, but today just 30 are standing. There are two main reasons for the disappearance of the stones: some were pulled over and buried in pits during the 14th century and others were broken up and used as building materials for houses in the village in the late 17th and 18th centuries. Most of the stones standing today were unearthed during excavations and re-erected. Within the outer circle are two smaller circles, both about 100 metres in diameter. Like the outer circle, many of the stones that once formed these circles are now missing and have been replaced by concrete markers.

Two of the best-known stones in the outer circle are the 'Swindon Stone' and the 'Barber Surgeon Stone'. The '**Swindon Stone**', roughly square in shape, is one of the largest and marks the northern entrance to the circle. It weighs in at an estimated 60 tonnes and is one of the only stones never to have fallen.

The '**Barber Surgeon Stone**', towards the south of the outer circle, is so named because a skeleton was found under it during excavations in the 1930s. The story goes that, during the 14th century when many of the stones were pulled over and buried one unfortunate man happened to be in the wrong place and was squashed. When Alexander Keiller excavated this stone the man's skeleton was found underneath it, along with a pouch containing scissors and some coins. Research indicated this unfortunate individual was probably an itinerant craftsman who performed many roles including that of a barber and a surgeon.

What you can see today is the result of immense excavation work and restoration projects, mainly led by Alexander Keiller during the 1920s and 1930s; up till then, the site had suffered centuries of deliberate damage and neglect. Keiller relied heavily on

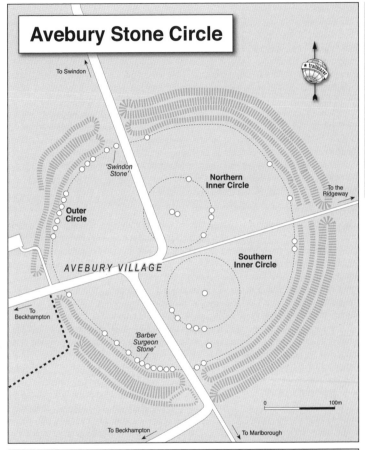

Avebury Stone Circle

To Swindon

'Swindon Stone'

Northern Inner Circle

To the Ridgeway

Outer Circle

AVEBURY VILLAGE

Southern Inner Circle

To Beckhampton

'Barber Surgeon Stone'

0   100m

To Beckhampton

To Marlborough

ROUTE GUIDE AND MAPS

the previous work of two antiquarians, John Aubrey and William Stukeley, to interpret the remains of the stone circle. Aubrey was the first person to study Avebury in detail and record what he found. His main findings were written up in 1690 and proved an invaluable resource for William Stukeley who in the 18th century drew maps of the entire complex of stones and also wrote extensively about his findings. As the period following Aubrey's and Stukeley's work was one of the most destructive in Avebury's history, had it not been for their surviving records much of Keiller's work, and indeed even modern archaeology in the Avebury area, would have proved an impossible task.

There is no entrance fee to the circle, mainly because it would be impractical to enforce such a scheme; hence it is open for visitors all day, every day.

Services

The **post office** in the small car park on the High St operates limited hours (Mon 9am-noon, Wed-Fri 2-5pm) and the **village shop** (Mon-Fri 9am-5pm, Sat 9.30am-3.30pm, Sun 10.30am-4.30pm) stocks a selection of groceries and a range of sandwiches. Sadly the tourist information centre has now closed. However, the **National Trust Shop** (NT; ☎ 01672 539384; daily Apr-Oct 10am-5.30pm, Nov-Mar 10.30am-4pm) close to the Great Barn has some tourist information leaflets. They also have a good range of postcards and souvenirs.

If you need cash you should head to The Red Lion pub (see opposite) where there is an **ATM** (£1.85 charge per withdrawal). **The Henge Shop** (☎ 01672 539229; daily 9.30am-5pm) is a large souvenir shop that sells some interesting Avebury paraphernalia as well as shelf upon shelf of generic tourist tat.

There are frequent **bus** services to Marlborough (Connect2Wiltshire's Line 4) and to Swindon (Stagecoach's No 49); see pp42-5 for further details. For a **taxi**, call one of the firms in Marlborough, see p67.

Where to stay

B&B options in Avebury village are expensive and even if you can afford to stay here you should book well ahead to secure a room.

There is, however, one slightly cheaper option just outside the village at *No 6 Beckhampton Road* (☎ 01672 539588; 1D/1T, shared bathroom, ▣). It's run by the friendly Mrs Dixon who charges £60, or £40 if you are on your own. A packed lunch is available for £3 if requested in advance. You could walk here from the village as it's only about half a mile (1km) along the A4361 towards Beckhampton though there isn't a pavement all the way. The B&B is in the line of cottages on the main road at the top of the hill. A quieter and safer but less straightforward route would be to follow the High St to its western end then take the series of paths to Trusloe village and cut through to the B&B. Alternatively, you could get a bus (Stagecoach's No 49, see pp42-5) here: the first bus stop out of Avebury village is more or less opposite the B&B.

Manor Farm (☎ 01672 539294, 🖥 www.manorfarmavebury.com; 1D/1S or T, ▣) is a large red-brick farmhouse offering B&B for two sharing from £85 (single occupancy from £75). The rooms share a bathroom but only one room is let out at a time, unless a group book, so effectively the bathroom is private. Note: this is a different Manor Farm from the one on Green St (see map p77).

The Lodge (☎ 01672 539023, 🖥 www.aveburylodge.co.uk; 1D en suite/1D private bathroom; ▣), just up the High St, charges £150-175 (single occupancy £120). The food is vegetarian and, where possible, organic.

Where to eat and drink

Most people head to *The Circle Restaurant* (☎ 01672 539514; daily Apr-Oct 10am-5.30pm, Nov-Mar 10.30am-4pm, lunch served noon-2pm) which is in a good location next to the Great Barn. They only serve vegetarian, vegan and gluten-free food. Hot dishes are from £6.95, home-made flan and salad is £6.95 and a cheese ploughman's is £6.50. They also have various sandwiches and rolls from £3.25 and, of course, cakes, tea and coffee.

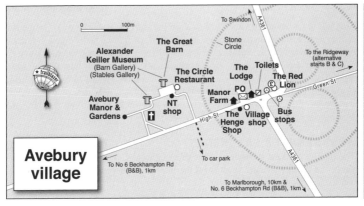

Avebury village

To Swindon — A4361
Stone Circle
The Great Barn
Alexander Keiller Museum (Barn Gallery) (Stables Gallery)
The Circle Restaurant
The Lodge
Toilets
To the Ridgeway (alternative starts B & C)
The Red Lion
Green St
Avebury Manor & Gardens
NT shop
Manor Farm
PO
The Village shop
Bus stops
High St
The Henge Shop
To No 6 Beckhampton Rd (B&B), 1km
To car park
To Marlborough, 10km & No. 6 Beckhampton Rd (B&B), 1km
0 — 100m

The Red Lion (☎ 01672 539266, 🖥 www.red-lion-pub-avebury.co.uk; food daily noon-10pm, winter Mon-Sat noon-8pm) is right in the centre of the stone circle and is also the only pub in the village. The building dates back to the early 17th century but it was only in the early 18th century that it became a pub. Since then the original building has been enlarged. Naturally, the place has its own ghost – a murdered lady – who might or might not put in an appearance depending on how long you've spent at the bar. The pub is always busy and lunchtimes can be particularly crowded with long waiting times for food. There is a large restaurant area at the back of the pub serving a wide variety of dishes: lunches, such as ham, egg and chips or a ploughman's, cost from £7.19 to £7.49. Main courses in the evening include crab mezzaluna pasta (£7.29) and gammon steak, chips and peas (£7.49). Note that the pub's car park is pay and display but if you spend more than £5 in the pub they will refund the cost of your ticket.

❏ **West Kennet Avenue** **[see map p77]**
West Kennet Avenue dates from about 2400BC and runs south from the henge at Avebury to The Sanctuary, a distance of about 1½ miles (2.5km). The course of the avenue was originally marked by two parallel rows of around one hundred sarsen stones, though today only the first 750 metres of the avenue is lined with them.
These stones were excavated and re-erected by Maud Cunnington in 1912 and by Alexander Keiller in the 1930s. As with the henge at Avebury, concrete markers replace stones that have disappeared or been destroyed. Despite various sources of evidence – the 18th-century records of William Stukeley and excavations in both the 20th century and in 2002 – the exact course of the avenue is still a subject of debate.
There is a second avenue of stones at Avebury, leading away from the henge to the west. This was first noticed by William Stukeley in the 18th century, but no longer shows above ground and was only rediscovered following excavations in 1999. It is called Beckhampton Avenue because it heads out towards the long stones at Beckhampton.

WEST OVERTON   [see map opposite]

This village is about one mile/1.6km from the start of the Ridgeway. On the A4 at the main turning for the village is *The Bell* (☎ 01672 861099, 🖳 www.the bellwestoverton.co.uk; Sun-Fri bar noon-3pm & 6-11pm, food noon-2.30pm & 6-9pm, Sat bar noon-11pm, food available all day), which has a very good reputation for its food. Main courses (£11-24) include a range of fresh fish from Cornwall. They also serve around four locally brewed real ales.

Buses (Connect2Wiltshire's Line 4) stop here en route between Avebury and Marlborough; see pp42-5 for further details.

WEST KENNET & EAST KENNET   [see map opposite]

The hamlet of **West Kennet** consists of a pet hotel and a few houses spread out along the main A4 road. Apart from the bus stops, there is nothing of practical use to the traveller. **East Kennet**, a very picturesque village, provides the closest accommodation to the Ridgeway, though very little else.

The Old Forge (☎ 01672 861686, 🖳 www.theoldforge-avebury.co.uk; 1T/1D/1D, T or F, all en suite, 1D private bathroom; ☐; 🐾£5) really is a lovely B&B. They charge £65-80 (£55-70 for single occupancy; up to £120 for

---

❏ **Crop circles**
If you are in the Wiltshire area, particularly around Avebury, during the summer months you have a good chance of seeing a crop circle. It's usually free to go into the field to have a look inside the formation but as you'll be just one of many doing this they get damaged very quickly. It's not often easy to get good photographs of crop circles because although they are generally on hillsides, the gradient isn't steep enough to present a clear view of the pattern.

However, nearly every formation that appears in Wiltshire will have an aerial photograph taken of it and these are easily found on the internet. Websites such as 🖳 www.cropcircleconnector.com often have photos of crop circles within a day of them first being reported.

The appearance of crop circles in Wiltshire certainly dates back as far as the early 1980s and some farmers say they noticed them earlier than that. In the 1990s, when the more elaborate designs started to appear, the media became interested. However, within a few years much of the media interest faded, though the circles continue to appear, getting more elaborate every year. In 2010 there were over 60 reported crop circles in the UK and the tally for 2011 was already up to 50 by the end of July.

Theories abound as to how the circles are created. There is no doubt that some are man-made and people have comprehensively demonstrated how to make complex designs in just a few hours. But that still leaves some designs which appear simply too intricate to be created in a few hours in the middle of the night. You can take your pick of the theories out there, some more 'out there' than others. Are they created by a 'plasma vortex', UFOs, the presence of ley lines, or something completely different that no one has even thought of yet?

If it all gets a bit confusing, you might like to unwind with a pint of Crop Circle, a beer produced by Hop Back Brewery (see pp16-17) in Downton, near Salisbury, and available in some local pubs. Alternatively, head to the Barge Inn at Honeystreet – the 'HQ of the crop circle fraternity' – for a pint of Croppie.

four sharing). This place is often busy so book as far in advance as possible. Small well-behaved dogs are welcome. If requested in advance they can provide a packed lunch (about £6). For an evening meal The Bell (see opposite) at West Overton is about ten minutes' walk down the road.

From East Kennet the start of the path is only about half a mile/750m away. Should you need a shop, it's a straightforward half-hour stroll along West Kennet Avenue to Avebury.

Connect2Wiltshire's Line 4 **buses** stop both here and at West Kennet. However, if you want to board the bus at East Kennet you must phone in advance; see pp42-5 for further details.

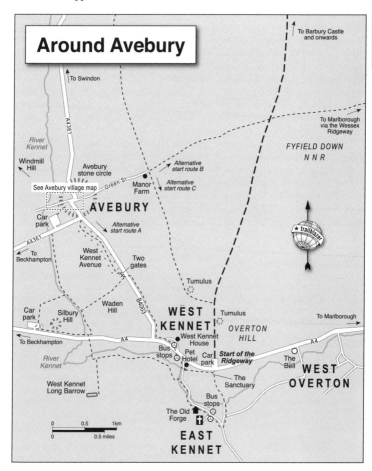

Around Avebury

To Barbury Castle and onwards

To Swindon

To Marlborough via the Wessex Ridgeway

FYFIELD DOWN NNR

River Kennet

Windmill Hill

Avebury stone circle

Alternative start route B

Alternative start route C

See Avebury village map   Green St

Manor Farm

AVEBURY

Car park

Alternative start route A

To Beckhampton

West Kennet Avenue

Two gates

Tumulus

★ trailblazer

Car park

Silbury Hill

Waden Hill

WEST KENNET

Tumulus

To Marlborough

OVERTON HILL

To Beckhampton

A4

West Kennet House

River Kennet

Bus stops

Pet Hotel

Car park

Start of the Ridgeway

The Bell

WEST OVERTON

West Kennet Long Barrow

The Sanctuary

Bus stops

0   0.5   1km
0   0.5 miles

The Old Forge

EAST KENNET

A WALK AROUND AVEBURY   [MAP A p80; MAP B p81]

If you have some spare time before starting the Ridgeway, you might like to explore the area around Avebury. Detailed below is a walk designed to take in the main attractions outside the village. As this walk is circular and starts from the centre of Avebury, you can do it in either direction. It will take between 2½ and 4 hours. The general theme of this walk is Avebury–West Kennet Avenue–Silbury Hill–West Kennet Long Barrow–East Kennet village–The Sanctuary–Ridgeway–Green St–Avebury. It's about 6 miles/10km and the walking is generally easy going with just a couple of mildly tiring uphill stints.

Starting from **The Red Lion** follow the main road south through the stone circle then enter the field and follow **West Kennet Avenue** (see box p75). When you reach the gates at the end of the field follow the fence line up **Waden Hill** from the top of which you get very good views of Silbury Hill. At the bottom of the hill you should turn right and follow the stream to the junction where you need to take the left turn and go over the bridge – straight ahead leads back to Avebury, if you are already tired. After turning left you will skirt around **Silbury Hill** (see box opposite), eventually arriving at a car park. Here you can get a closer view of the Hill from a special viewing area. You are not allowed to walk any nearer than this though the road does in fact pass much closer.

From the car park, follow the busy and fast A4 road towards and then past Silbury Hill. You must then look for a turning on the other side of the road which leads up to **West Kennet Long Barrow** (see box below). The climb up is a bit tiring but will get you in good shape for the Ridgeway.

After visiting the Long Barrow and admiring the views you should retrace your steps to the path junction where you need to take a right turn, heading for **East Kennet** village. This is an idyllic place. Take a few minutes to look at the

---

❏ **West Kennet Long Barrow**
Even if you don't plan to do the whole walk described above you should make the effort to walk up to West Kennet Long Barrow, located on a ridge about a mile from Silbury Hill. At 100 metres long it's one of the largest Neolithic burial mounds in the country and dates back to 3600BC, nearly a thousand years before Wayland's Smithy (see box p106). It's thought that this long barrow was used for around a thousand years before it was filled in with earth and sealed with the huge sarsen stones that currently stand across the entrance. During several excavations, the last in 1955-6, the remains of 45 people of all ages were discovered in the various chambers.

The main advantage this site has over Wayland's Smithy is that you can actually enter this long barrow and walk into all five of the burial chambers, but don't expect the underground passage to take you along the entire length of the long barrow – it only extends about ten metres into the mound. There is no entrance fee for the long barrow and it is open all the time. Take a torch though.

❏ Silbury Hill

Despite the enormity of this hill it's often neglected in favour of the stone circle up the road. But do make the effort to come here as it's only at this closer proximity that you can start to understand the almost super-human effort that must have been required to build this structure.

The history of the hill dates back to around 2600BC when construction started. The first phase created a stepped structure. The steps were then filled in with chalk and after that earth was shaped over the steps to create a smooth face. You can still see one of these steps near the top of the hill but it's only clear when viewed from the eastern side. The top of the mound was left flat, but not level, and is 39m high and 30m wide. The base is perfectly round with a diameter of 167m. Just to really impress you, the hill contains around a quarter of a million cubic metres of chalk.

Why was it built? No one really knows, but there have been some earnest efforts to find out. The first of these was in 1776 when a shaft was dug from the summit down to the base. Nothing was found apart from construction materials. In 1849 another approach was tried, this time digging a tunnel from the base to the centre. Again, nothing was found. Yet another investigation took place in the late 1960s but the new tunnel into the base, again, revealed no evidence to point to Silbury Hill's raison d'être.

The hill was previously open to the public but slippages of the top soil were detected and any more human trampling would have only accelerated this deterioration. In 2000 a large hole also opened up on the summit, owing to a collapse of the shaft dug in 1776. It was infilled with polystyrene blocks and then covered with chalk. Investigations by English Heritage around the base of Silbury Hill in 2007 discovered evidence of a Roman settlement and later in the same year a major task was undertaken to stabilise the hill. Tunnels which had previously been dug into the hillside were filled with hundreds of tonnes of chalk to prevent any more collapses. As this work was sealing up the tunnels for good, English Heritage also took the opportunity to undertake one final archaeological survey in a bid to finally understand why the hill was built. Although they ultimately didn't come any closer to finding an answer to the question, the stabilisation work on the hill was carried out successfully.

Naturally, various theories regarding Silbury Hill's purpose have been developed to fill the vacuum, among them that it was a solar observatory or was symbolic of a Mother Goddess, but none really explains why such a gargantuan effort was made to build something so seemingly purposeless.

church and wander past the attractive village houses before you get to the fork in the road. At this point you should follow the other lane, almost doubling back on yourself. This lane turns into a path and you cross the River Kennet once more, heading up to **The Sanctuary** (see box p82) by the side of the A4.

When you feel you have soaked up the atmosphere of this place you should cross the road to the official start of the Ridgeway and make your way up the hill to the junction with **Green St**. Turn left onto this track and follow it down to the Red Lion at Avebury. It's a handy place to finish for obvious reasons.

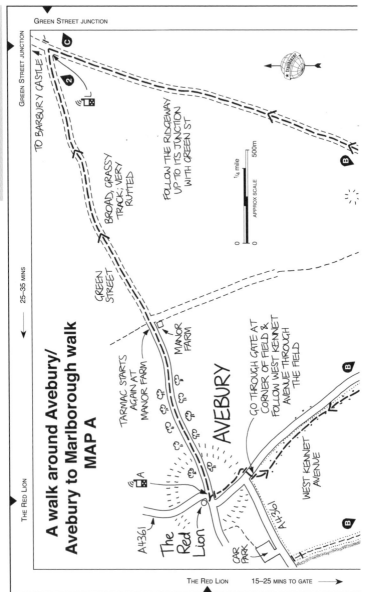

A walk around Avebury/
Avebury to Marlborough walk
MAP A

GREEN STREET JUNCTION

TO BARBURY CASTLE

BROAD, GRASSY TRACK; VERY RUTTED

FOLLOW THE RIDGEWAY UP TO ITS JUNCTION WITH GREEN ST

¼ mile

APPROX SCALE

500m

GREEN STREET

25-35 MINS

THE RED LION

MANOR FARM

TARMAC STARTS AGAIN AT MANOR FARM

AVEBURY

GO THROUGH GATE AT CORNER OF FIELD & FOLLOW WEST KENNET AVENUE THROUGH THE FIELD

WEST KENNET AVENUE

A4361

The Red Lion

A4361

CAR PARK

THE RED LION   15-25 MINS TO GATE

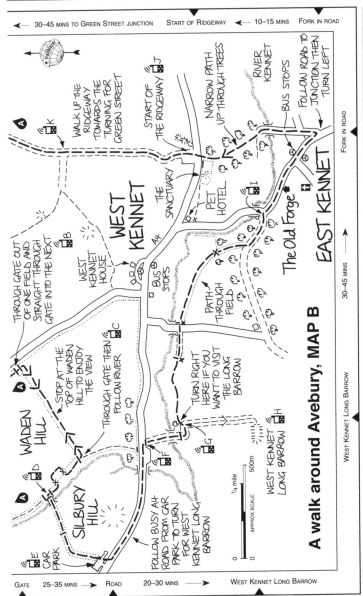

← 30–45 MINS TO GREEN STREET JUNCTION   START OF RIDGEWAY ← 10–15 MINS   FORK IN ROAD

WALK UP THE RIDGEWAY TOWARDS THE TURNING FOR GREEN STREET

START OF THE RIDGEWAY

NARROW PATH UP THROUGH TREES

RIVER KENNET

BUS STOPS

FOLLOW ROAD TO JUNCTION THEN TURN LEFT

K

J

A

WEST KENNET

THE SANCTUARY

PET HOTEL

I

The Old Forge

FORK IN ROAD

EAST KENNET

THROUGH GATE OUT OF ONE FIELD AND STRAIGHT THROUGH GATE INTO THE NEXT

WEST KENNET HOUSE

B

A4

BUS STOPS

PATH THROUGH FIELD

30–45 MINS

STOP AT THE TOP OF WADEN HILL TO ENJOY THE VIEW

C

THROUGH GATE THEN FOLLOW RIVER

TURN RIGHT HERE IF YOU WANT TO VISIT THE LONG BARROW

A

WADEN HILL

F

G

WEST KENNET LONG BARROW

H

WEST KENNET LONG BARROW ▶

A

D

SILBURY HILL

¼ mile   500m

APPROX SCALE

A walk around Avebury, MAP B

FOLLOW BUSY A4 ROAD FROM CAR PARK TO TURN FOR WEST KENNET LONG BARROW

E

CAR PARK

0   0

GATE   25–35 MINS →   ROAD   20–30 MINS →   WEST KENNET LONG BARROW

ROUTE GUIDE AND MAPS

❏ **The Sanctuary**
Opposite the official start of the Ridgeway is The Sanctuary. It's not one of the more memorable relics in the Avebury area but is worth a visit nonetheless. It consists of various concentric circles marked out with small concrete posts in the ground.

This was the site of a circular wooden building, possibly a temple, dating back as far as 2500BC. The smaller circle marks out the boundary of the original building while the larger ones suggest that the structure was considerably and repeatedly expanded over the course of the next thousand years. Eventually, the wooden buildings were replaced by two stone circles, noted by John Aubrey in 1648, and these were connected to Avebury by a stone avenue (West Kennet Avenue), parts of which you can still follow. The views from here over to Silbury Hill and West Kennet Long Barrow are particularly good.

AVEBURY TO MARLBOROUGH WALK
[MAP A p80, MAP C p83, MAP D p84, MAP E p85]

If you're spending time around the beginning of the Ridgeway, the chances are you'll need to get from Avebury to Marlborough, or vice versa, at some point. You could always take one of the regular buses but walking the route is far more interesting.

The route in fact follows the course of the Wessex Ridgeway (see pp183-4) and is an easy 6 miles/10km across the Marlborough Downs with the only mildly strenuous section being at the Avebury end of the route. Although most of this route is very exposed to the elements, the conditions underfoot are generally excellent, consisting mainly of hard gravel tracks. From The Red Lion at Avebury to Marlborough High St it'll take 2-3 hours in either direction.

From The Red Lion leave the village via **Green St**. The road soon fades into a track that broadens into a series of roughly parallel deep ruts as it climbs up to meet the Ridgeway. At this junction you walk straight across the Ridgeway and through the gate into **Fyfield Down NNR** (Map C). To most people it's just another attractive area for a stroll, but for geologists it's one of the most important sites in Britain. The sides and bottom of the valley in the reserve are littered with sarsen stones – the very same type of stones that were used to build Avebury and many of the more recent buildings in the vicinity. Some of these sarsens are also home to rare mosses and lichens. There is something of a fantasy-world feel to this place, as if you might pass a wandering hobbit or see an elf resting on a sarsen.

You'll pass an underground **reservoir** to the left of the path which looks rather anomalous in this landscape and as the well-made gravel track meanders along with various paths and other tracks joining it, you'll notice plenty of evidence of the racehorse business (see box p96). Gallops parallel the track for long stretches; if you're lucky you could see some thoroughbreds being exercised. When walking on the edge of the grassy gallops instead of on the gravel track you'll notice just how soft and springy the ground is; this is one of the main reasons that this area is so favourable for training racehorses. You'll also

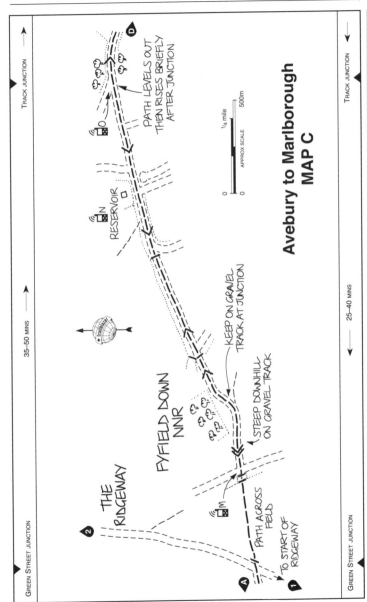

Avebury to Marlborough
MAP C

TRACK JUNCTION

GREEN STREET JUNCTION

35–50 MINS

25–40 MINS

THE RIDGEWAY

FYFIELD DOWN NNR

RESERVOIR

PATH ACROSS FIELD

TO START OF RIDGEWAY

STEEP DOWNHILL ON GRAVEL TRACK

KEEP ON GRAVEL TRACK AT JUNCTION

PATH LEVELS OUT THEN RISES BRIEFLY AFTER JUNCTION

¼ mile
APPROX SCALE
500m

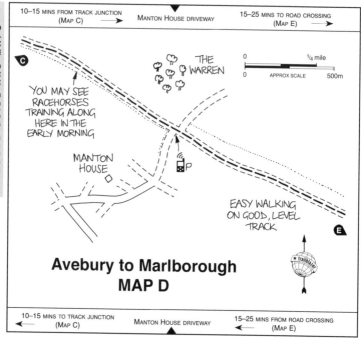

10–15 MINS FROM TRACK JUNCTION (MAP C) ⟶   MANTON HOUSE DRIVEWAY   15–25 MINS TO ROAD CROSSING (MAP E) ⟶

THE WARREN

0   ¼ mile

0   APPROX SCALE   500m

YOU MAY SEE RACEHORSES TRAINING ALONG HERE IN THE EARLY MORNING

MANTON HOUSE

P

EASY WALKING ON GOOD, LEVEL TRACK

Avebury to Marlborough MAP D

★ trailblazer

10–15 MINS TO TRACK JUNCTION (MAP C) ⟵   MANTON HOUSE DRIVEWAY   15–25 MINS FROM ROAD CROSSING (MAP E) ⟵

pass the driveway for Manton House where there is a well-established stable and stud that has been operating since the 19th century.

At the end of the long, neat, straight track you come to a minor road that you must cross and you eventually end up walking on the edge of a golf course for a spell before crossing the road to two **cemeteries**. You should pass the new one but enter the old one via the rusty iron double gates. Someone has thoughtfully provided a roughly hewn wooden seat to rest on in the middle of this peaceful place. Identical iron gates bound the other side of the cemetery and once through these you simply have to turn left and follow the road, down into Marlborough town centre, passing by some immaculate cricket, rugby and hockey pitches.

The road joins the southern end of the High St with the library on your left (see map p69) and **The Sun Inn** on your right. There is a bench outside the library should you need it but it's perhaps a better idea to head to one of the many pubs lining the High St for a well-earned drink.

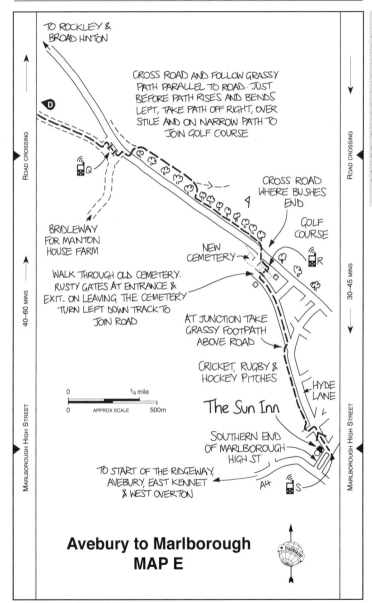

TO ROCKLEY &
BROAD HINTON

CROSS ROAD AND FOLLOW GRASSY
PATH PARALLEL TO ROAD. JUST
BEFORE PATH RISES AND BENDS
LEFT, TAKE PATH OFF RIGHT, OVER
STILE AND ON NARROW PATH TO
JOIN GOLF COURSE

D

ROAD CROSSING

ROAD CROSSING

Q

CROSS ROAD
WHERE BUSHES
END

GOLF
COURSE

BRIDLEWAY
FOR MANTON
HOUSE FARM

NEW
CEMETERY

R

40-60 MINS

30-45 MINS

WALK THROUGH OLD CEMETERY.
RUSTY GATES AT ENTRANCE &
EXIT. ON LEAVING THE CEMETERY
TURN LEFT DOWN TRACK TO
JOIN ROAD

AT JUNCTION TAKE
GRASSY FOOTPATH
ABOVE ROAD

CRICKET, RUGBY &
HOCKEY PITCHES

HYDE
LANE

The Sun Inn

0   ¼ mile

0   APPROX SCALE   500m

MARLBOROUGH HIGH STREET

MARLBOROUGH HIGH STREET

SOUTHERN END
OF MARLBOROUGH
HIGH ST

TO START OF THE RIDGEWAY,
AVEBURY, EAST KENNET
& WEST OVERTON

A4

S

Avebury to Marlborough
MAP E

trailblazer

The Ridgeway route guide

ALTERNATIVE STARTS TO THE RIDGEWAY   [See map p77]

If you are staying in Avebury before you start the Ridgeway, there are three options for starting the walk from the village. It is generally agreed that starting by walking out from Avebury makes for a far more exciting beginning than simply being dropped off at the official start by the side of the A4 road.

Alternative start – Route A

This is the longest alternative start. It involves walking out of the village along West Kennet Avenue which runs parallel to the B4003. It's easy walking on the soft grass along here with the large sarsen stones flanking you on either side. After a hundred metres or so the B4003 road cuts into the stone avenue before gently curving away from it a hundred metres later.

The avenue finishes all too soon and you must leave the field through a gate and continue on the grass verge by the side of the road. Although this is a narrow road, some people drive too fast along here so take care.

Follow this road until you reach the T-junction and turn left onto the A4. Don't cross the road until you have passed the rather grand West Kennet House as it is easier and safer to continue walking on the southern side of the road. You'll reach a right-hand turning for East Kennet and the pet hotel – there are always plenty of dogs here barking at each other – on the corner and should take this turning off the A4. Just after the pet hotel and shop there is a stile on your left leading into a field. Climb over this and walk up the field, parallel to the

---

❏ **Signposts on The Ridgeway**
The Ridgeway is one of the most comprehensively signposted long-distance trails in the country. At nearly every junction on the path there will be a dedicated and distinctive black 'Ridgeway' signpost (see photo p10), not only to keep you going in the right direction, but also to inform you of other options.

At a glance these waymarkers look to be made in the traditional manner from wood that has been treated with creosote, but in fact the material used is Plaswood. This is an environmentally friendly plastic material made from 30% consumer waste and 70% from other waste sources. It is strong, durable and impervious to water so it will not rot or splinter as wood does. This also means that it is maintenance free.

You will see many traditional wooden signs along the Ridgeway in various states of decay but the Plaswood signs will remain looking the same as the day they were set into the ground for years to come. Some have been there for more than ten years already.

Plaswood is now used for many other products, often as a substitute for wood in outdoor areas. Items such as benches, planters, walkways and street furniture are all being constructed from the material.

❏ **Change to the start of the Ridgeway?**

Anyone who has walked the Ridgeway will agree that the official start is really rather lacking in atmosphere. This is surprising when one considers how packed with character the surrounding area is. With this in mind, there have been calls to change the starting point, though at the time of writing the situation hasn't changed much from when the first edition of this book was published. It is still very much on the wish list but these things tend to take a long time to be agreed and organised, not to mention the costs involved. However, a more fitting starting point could be a serious possibility in the future.

Avebury is the obvious place for the relocation of the starting point. The path would then lead out of the village along Green St and join the Ridgeway just 1.8 miles (3km) into its current route. It's probable that many people choose to walk this route anyway and as you really don't lose anything by not walking the first couple of miles of the trail it is a sensible choice. If you'd like to do this, follow alternative start routes B or C.

A4, to reach the top corner where you should climb over another stile and find yourself in the Sanctuary. From here you simply have to cross the A4 to arrive at the official start of the Ridgeway.

Alternative start – Routes B & C

Both these routes leave Avebury via Green St. The only part of Green St that could be vaguely described as a conventional 'street' peters out very quickly before becoming a sealed track.

Even on the busiest days in Avebury, you don't have to take many steps down Green St before leaving the crowds behind. You'll pass several houses on your right as Green St clears the village and then come to Manor Farm. This is the last building on the 'street' and is where the tarmac finishes. It can be muddy around here owing to the farm vehicles.

You will see Green St stretching into the distance up the hillside; it's at this point that you need to make the first decision of your walk. Either follow Green St up the hill (B), or take the signposted track that turns off right, immediately after Manor Farm (C).

If you choose to follow Green St straight up the hill (B) you'll find that the track broadens out and becomes grassy, making for easy walking despite the increasing gradient. Look behind on your way up here to see the view getting better all the time.

Green St joins the Ridgeway at the top of the climb and from here you have a choice of turning left or right. Turning left will take you onto the Ridgeway, heading towards Barbury Castle, whereas turning right will take you onto the Ridgeway and down to the official start. It's up to you, though there seems little point turning right, walking down to the beginning of the Ridgeway, then doing an about-turn and walking back up again. However, you might feel a bit of a cheat if you miss out this 1¾ miles/3km of the path, especially as it's the first part.

A compromise solution is to take the right turn after Manor Farm (C) as described earlier. Soon after joining this track it becomes grassy but deeply rutted and can be really muddy after rain. The path is level for the first half-mile

> ❏ **Tumuli**
> Especially on the first half of the Ridgeway, and in particular on the first 15 miles of it,
> you will see many tumuli – burial mounds dating from around 4000 to 4500 years ago
> which now just look like raised grassy humps. In fact there are three right next to the
> start of the Ridgeway (see Map 1, opposite) and you'll see a couple more just ten
> minutes up the path. Sometimes they are planted over with trees, so if you see an iso-
> lated bunch of trees in the middle of a field, this could suggest a tumulus underneath.
>   They are generally marked on Ordnance Survey maps, though not all marked
> tumuli are necessarily burial mounds. They could be just, as yet, unidentified lumps
> on the landscape.

after which it bends left and begins to climb the side of Overton Hill.

As you reach a **tumulus** (see box above) with a coppice on top, the path
bends left more sharply than before and you'll see ahead where you will join
the Ridgeway. When you do so you'll have the same choice as walkers on
Alternative start route B.

Although Alternative start route C isn't as attractive as route B it finishes a lot
closer to the start of the Ridgeway, giving less backtracking, should you prefer.

OVERTON HILL TO FOXHILL   [MAPS 1-10]
Overview
This first **16½-mile/26.3km (6¾-8½hrs)** stage of the Ridgeway includes many
interesting sights but most of them are before Ogbourne St George. By com-
parison, thereafter, it can seem a bit of a slog in parts, especially the last section
from Liddington Hill to Foxhill.

The full length of this stage will leave you tired after your first day but
you'll have to push on to Bishopstone to find accommodation. Alternatively
you could stay at Ogbourne St George which is only 9 miles/14.5km from the
start of the Ridgeway. It would make an easy first day's walking and would also
allow time to investigate Fyfield Down National Nature Reserve and take a long
break at Barbury Castle.

Route
There are several alternative starts to the Ridgeway (see pp86-7) that are all
more interesting than the official one. It just depends how serious you are about
following every step of the real path.

The official, but rather uninspiring, starting point is at the side of the
Beckhampton to Marlborough road (the A4) and if you've taken Alternative
start route A you will arrive here. However, you soon gain enough height on the
broad track on Overton Hill to lose the sight and noise of the busy road. It's at
this point that Alternative start route C joins the Ridgeway from the left.

In clear weather there are excellent views west to the obelisk monument on
Cherhill Hill, 5 miles/8km away. It was built on an Iron Age hillfort in 1845/6
in memory of Sir William Petty, the 17th-century economist. **Windmill Hill**
(see box p92), 2½ miles/4km to the west, is another easily spotted landmark.

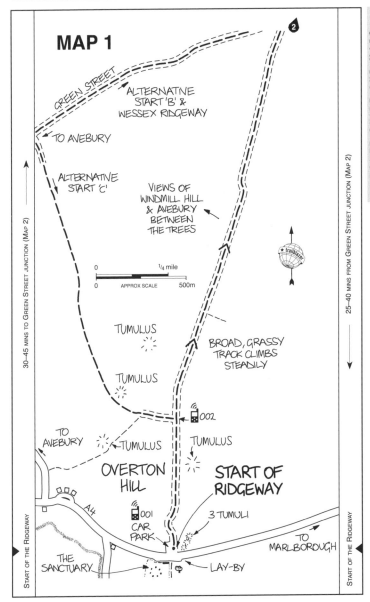

MAP 1

GREEN STREET

ALTERNATIVE
START 'B' &
WESSEX RIDGEWAY

TO AVEBURY

ALTERNATIVE
START 'C'

VIEWS OF
WINDMILL HILL
& AVEBURY
BETWEEN
THE TREES

0   ¼ mile

0   500m
APPROX SCALE

★ trailblazer

TUMULUS

TUMULUS

BROAD, GRASSY
TRACK CLIMBS
STEADILY

002

TO
AVEBURY

TUMULUS

TUMULUS

OVERTON
HILL

START OF
RIDGEWAY

001
CAR
PARK

3 TUMULI

TO
MARLBOROUGH

A4

THE
SANCTUARY

LAY-BY

30–45 MINS TO GREEN STREET JUNCTION (MAP 2)

25–40 MINS FROM GREEN STREET JUNCTION (MAP 2)

START OF THE RIDGEWAY

START OF THE RIDGEWAY

2

ROUTE GUIDE AND MAPS

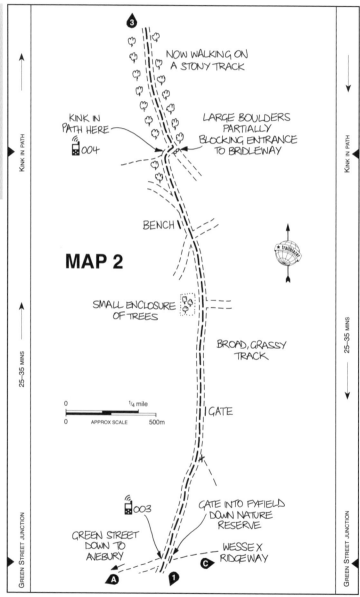

KINK IN PATH

KINK IN PATH

25-35 MINS

25-35 MINS

GREEN STREET JUNCTION

GREEN STREET JUNCTION

NOW WALKING ON
A STONY TRACK

KINK IN
PATH HERE
📱004

LARGE BOULDERS
PARTIALLY
BLOCKING ENTRANCE
TO BRIDLEWAY

BENCH

MAP 2

SMALL ENCLOSURE
OF TREES

BROAD, GRASSY
TRACK

0   1/4 mile

0   APPROX SCALE   500m

GATE

📱003

GATE INTO FYFIELD
DOWN NATURE
RESERVE

GREEN STREET
DOWN TO
AVEBURY

WESSEX
RIDGEWAY

Ⓐ   ❶   Ⓒ

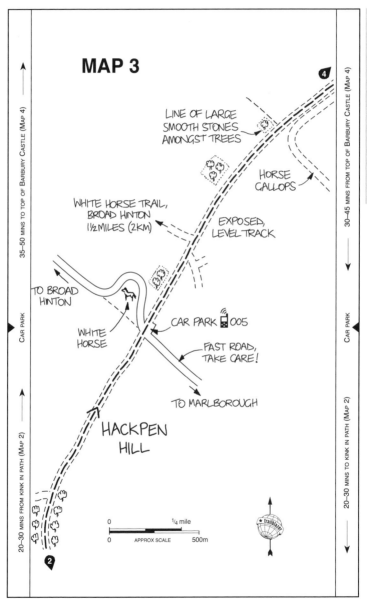

MAP 3

LINE OF LARGE SMOOTH STONES AMONGST TREES

HORSE GALLOPS

WHITE HORSE TRAIL, BROAD HINTON 1½ MILES (2KM)

EXPOSED, LEVEL TRACK

TO BROAD HINTON

WHITE HORSE

CAR PARK 📱 005

FAST ROAD, TAKE CARE!

TO MARLBOROUGH

HACKPEN HILL

35–50 MINS TO TOP OF BARBURY CASTLE (MAP 4)

CAR PARK

20–30 MINS FROM KINK IN PATH (MAP 2)

30–45 MINS FROM TOP OF BARBURY CASTLE (MAP 4)

CAR PARK

20–30 MINS TO KINK IN PATH (MAP 2)

4

2

0   ¼ mile
APPROX SCALE
0   500m

★ trailblazer

❑ **Windmill Hill**

This 20-acre site forms the largest of the 66 known Neolithic causewayed enclosures in Britain, with evidence of activity here dating from about 3700BC. A causewayed enclosure is a piece of land, usually oval in shape, bounded by one or more seg-mented banks or ditches. Windmill Hill has three such series of banks and ditches, with the outermost series being by far the most substantial. These sites represent the earliest examples of artificially enclosing an open area in Britain.

The findings of excavations by Rev H G O Kendall and Alexander Keiller, that took place here in the 1920s, not only established Neolithic causewayed enclosures as a distinct class, but also granted Windmill Hill its status as the most important one in Britain. The site even lent its name to 'Windmill Hill Ware', a distinctive type of pot-tery found at this and other similar sites in Britain.

From the 1920s onwards, the theory was that Neolithic people had lived in 'pit dwellings' – in the ditches of the enclosure – owing to the large quantity of animal bones and pottery found there. Keiller's findings from the 1920s were not properly written up at the time and it wasn't until 1965 that a summary of the excavations was published. This led to renewed excavations on the site and by the late 1960s the the-ory of 'pit dwellings' had totally lost favour. Although we now know that this was not a site of permanent settlement it is still unclear exactly what its purpose was. We can presume that ceremonies and feasts took place here, but the size of the enclosure would suggest a more substantial use. Several round burial mounds on Windmill Hill have also been excavated but these have been dated to the Bronze Age.

Despite the significance of Windmill Hill to archaeologists, a casual visit can prove disappointing. Apart from the views of the surrounding countryside there really isn't much to see on the hill itself as large sections of the banks and ditches have been ploughed into farmland. It's certainly far less visually dramatic than an Iron Age hill fort like Barbury Castle, only 5 miles (8km) along the Ridgeway from Avebury.

If you want to visit Windmill Hill you should walk to the western end of Avebury High St and follow the signposts from there; it's about 2 miles (3km) from the village.

After the track levels out, you'll arrive at the Green St junction (Map 2).

If you have taken Alternative start route B from Avebury you will join the Ridgeway from the left, while to the right is a gate leading into **Fyfield Down NNR**. Up here it's exposed to the elements with few trees or bushes to shelter you and the walking is mainly level on a broad, grassy track with numerous byways and bridleways joining from both sides.

When you get to the junction (Map 3) where the Broad Hinton to Marlborough road crosses the Ridgeway you'll have the opportunity to see the **Hackpen White Horse** (see box p108) cut into the chalk of the hillside. You can't see it from the track as you are above it so you'll need to make a slight diversion. It is not an ancient White Horse – this one was cut into Hackpen Hill in 1838 – so don't feel the steep detour is obligatory, especially as you will be seeing the original white horse at White Horse Hill, further along the Ridgeway. This section of the Ridgeway path is also part of the White Horse Trail (see box p108).

At the foot of **Barbury Castle** (Map 4) the 'Ridgeway Route For Vehicles' continues straight ahead across the road but walkers, cyclists and horses can follow the steep grassy slopes up onto the top of Barbury Castle itself. Apart

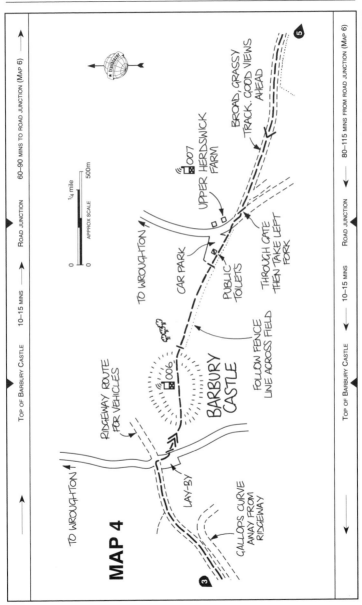

MAP 4

TO WROUGHTON

TO WROUGHTON

RIDGEWAY ROUTE FOR VEHICLES

LAY-BY

GALLOPS CURVE AWAY FROM RIDGEWAY

1006

BARBURY CASTLE

FOLLOW FENCE LINE ACROSS FIELD

CAR PARK

PUBLIC TOILETS

THROUGH GATE THEN TAKE LEFT FORK

UPPER HERDSWICK FARM

1007

BROAD, GRASSY TRACK. GOOD VIEWS AHEAD

APPROX SCALE

0   ¼ mile
0   500m

trailblazer

from this one there are two more Iron Age forts on the Ridgeway (Liddington Castle, p97, and Uffington Castle, p108), but this is the only one that the path cuts directly through. The 11-acre fort is ringed by double ramparts and deep ditches with entrances at both ends through which the Ridgeway passes. Some Iron Age finds from the castle are on display at Devizes Museum. Its defensive position is indisputable and this guaranteed its importance long after the Iron Age finished. In fact the name 'Barbury' is thought to come from the Old English name, 'Bera', after the Saxon chief who controlled the castle around AD550. Even as late as World War II it was being used as a potentially defensive position by allied troops.

The views from up here on a clear day are fantastic and it's a popular place at weekends with walkers, cyclists and horseriders. On some weekends it's also home to the White Horse Kite Fliers. You might wonder how all the people managed to get up here but when you get to the other side of the castle you'll understand. There you'll find a large car park, picnic tables, public toilets and the road north to Wroughton, 3¹/₂ miles/5.5km away.

When the weather is good the walking on **Smeathe's Ridge** (Map 5) makes for some of the most enjoyable parts of this stage; the soft grass under foot means walking is easy. Although the official path doesn't go into **Ogbourne St George** you can follow the signposted footpath (see Map 6), about half a mile/1km, into this attractive village if you want to stop here.

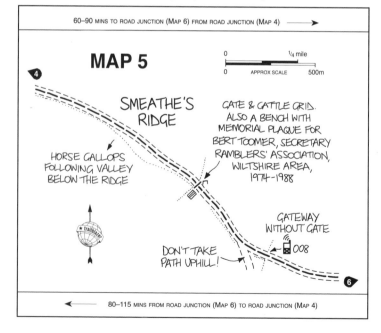

60–90 MINS TO ROAD JUNCTION (MAP 6) FROM ROAD JUNCTION (MAP 4) ⟶

MAP 5

0   ¹/₄ mile

0   APPROX SCALE   500m

SMEATHE'S RIDGE

GATE & CATTLE GRID. ALSO A BENCH WITH MEMORIAL PLAQUE FOR BERT TOOMER, SECRETARY RAMBLERS' ASSOCIATION, WILTSHIRE AREA, 1974–1988

HORSE GALLOPS FOLLOWING VALLEY BELOW THE RIDGE

★ trailblazer

GATEWAY WITHOUT GATE

008

DON'T TAKE PATH UPHILL!

80–115 MINS FROM ROAD JUNCTION (MAP 6) TO ROAD JUNCTION (MAP 4) ⟵

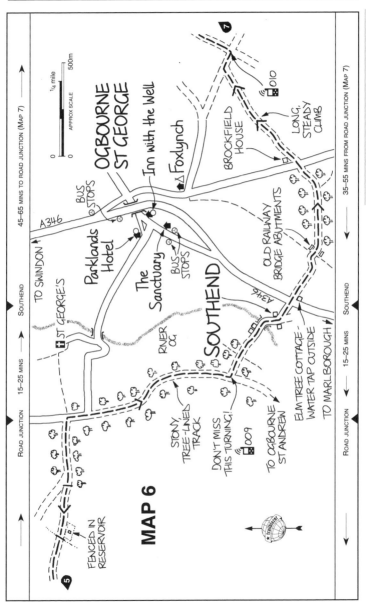

❏ **Racehorses**
From virtually the start of the Ridgeway up until past East Ilsley you are likely to see racehorses. They won't be on the path itself, but will be training along the gallops that often run parallel to the path, sometimes with brushwood hurdles set up on them. As you may have noticed, the ground here is soft and springy and very open which makes it ideal for racehorse training. The early morning is the best time to see the small groups of horses being put through their paces with their trainers. When the Ridgeway is right next to the gallops you can feel the power of the horses as they thunder by.

When you are at Barbury Castle you can look down onto the Marlborough Downs and see Barbury Castle racecourse, but it's the Lambourn Downs area, further east, that is really famous as a centre for racehorse training. There are around 50 racing yards around Lambourn which train up to 2000 horses at any one time.

If you visit East Ilsley (see pp125-6) and the Crown & Horns pub there, you'll notice that the walls in the bar are covered with horse-racing memorabilia, connected to the landlord's involvement in the business.

OGBOURNE ST GEORGE
[MAP 6, p95]
The name of this village refers to the river Og (Map 6) and the name of its church, St George's. A mile (1.5km) or so south of here is the village of Ogbourne St Andrew, named in the same way. Ogbourne St George is a pretty-enough village but unless you are planning to stay the night, there really isn't much point making the detour. There aren't any shops but there is a range of accommodation options and two good places offering food and drink.

Stagecoach's No 70 **bus**, which operates between Swindon and Marlborough, stops in the village, and Wilts & Dorset's No X5 (Pewsey to Swindon) stops on the A346 just outside the village; see pp42-5 for further details.

If you need a **taxi**, call one of the firms in Marlborough, see p67.

Where to stay, eat and drink
The Inn with the Well (☎ 01672 841445, 🖳 www.theinnwiththewell.co.uk; 2D/3T or D/1D, T or F, all en suite, ❏; 🐾; food served summer Wed-Sun noon-2.30pm & daily 6.30-8.30pm, winter Wed-Sun noon-2.30pm & Mon-Sat 6.30-8.30pm) is a deservedly popular place with both locals and people travelling from the surrounding area. They serve a range of real ales including Wadworth 6X alongside some delicious food. Their varied menu has dishes

such as St George's chicken with walnuts (£10.95) and duck breast with gooseberry sauce (£13.95). Packed lunches (£4.95) are available on request. B&B costs from £65 (£60 if you are on your own and from £85 for the family room).

A couple of minutes away is *The Sanctuary* (☎ 01672 841473, 🖳 www.the-sanctuary.biz; 1D/1T, both en suite, 1D, T or F, private facilities; ❏; 🐾), a well-run, friendly B&B that's used to walkers. They serve large, tasty breakfasts to set you up for the day. B&B for two sharing costs from £70 (the family room is from £87.50; single occupancy £52.50). They welcome dogs (donation to the dog charity they support would be appreciated) but be aware that they also have chickens running free in their garden. Packed lunches (from £3.50) are available if requested in advance.

Surprisingly for such a small village there is a hotel: *Parklands Hotel* (☎ 01672 841555, 🖳 www.parklandshoteluk.co.uk; 8D/4D or T, all en suite) has modern rooms starting at £95 (single occupancy from £85). The restaurant here, *Bentley's Chophouse* (Mon-Thur 6.30-8.30pm, Fri-Sat noon-2pm & 6.30-8.30pm, Sun 6-7.30pm) changes its menu regularly but dishes may include sausages, mash and red onion gravy (£11) or steaks (£11.50-15.75). Booking in advance is essential for both lunch and dinner though they can always serve sandwiches/snacks.

They are used to walkers and don't have a strict dress code.

Campers should head for *Foxlynch* (☎ 01672 841307; open all year). It costs £5pp to camp here including use of a toilet and shower. Breakfast (£5) is available if requested in advance, as are packed lunches (£3.50). They also offer **B&B** in a bunk-room with a sofa bed and a bunk bed so up

to four can sleep here; it is centrally heated and also has an en suite shower room. The rate including breakfast is £20pp though it must be booked in advance. Although Foxlynch is not quite in the village, it's only about five minutes' walk away and, better than that, it's only 500m from the Ridgeway: for the most direct route, see Map 6.

The official path skirts around the south of the village on shady farm tracks. You get occasional glimpses of Ogbourne St George through the trees on your left and you soon arrive in the hamlet of **Southend** (Map 6). This must rate as one of the most picturesque collections of cottages anywhere and is so perfect it's almost twee. Apart from the few buildings at Barbury Castle, this is the most heavily built-up area you have passed through since setting off.

After the hamlet you start a steady climb up a stony track closed in by trees and bushes and come to pass between the hefty stone abutments of an old railway bridge which was once the route of the Midland and South Western Junction Railway. This section opened in the 1880s but has long since disappeared. It linked Swindon and Chiseldon, to the north, with Marlborough, to the south. It's now been developed into the Chiseldon & Marlborough Railway Path and is popular but muddy.

Much later on when you arrive at the crossroads with the **reservoir** (Map 7) on the left corner that looks like a fortified concrete bunker, there is the opportunity to visit the former village of **Snap**. A small farming community existed on this site for hundreds of years until the late 19th century when farming became less economically viable owing to cheap imports and spare land was bought up by wealthy local landowners for use as sheep-grazing. Most of the population left the village to find work elsewhere and by the early 20th century the village was empty. To get there turn right and follow the track straight on for about half a mile/1km. Since being abandoned, the village has all but disappeared into the landscape, so unless you have plenty of time...

The 'Snap crossroads' is worth noting because just a short way down the track to the left is the **radio mast** that you'll probably have seen by now. If you haven't it will certainly be a prominent landmark every time you do look back, all the way to Liddington Castle. When you eventually reach **Liddington Castle** (Map 9) you'll get views of the M4 over to the north-east and if you turn around you'll see the aforementioned radio mast, now on the horizon behind you.

The Ridgeway does not actually go through Liddington Castle so if you'd like to visit follow the signpost that directs you along the fence line rather than going directly to the castle; it's about 500m. The trig point on top of the castle displays a height of 277m and the hill is a popular launch site for paragliders.

After descending Liddington Hill and joining the fast B4192 you'll have the possibility of walking to Liddington; though it is only worth going if you want a drink or meal, or to get a bus. To get there simply continue down the B4192 for about half a mile/1km, crossing the M4 en route.

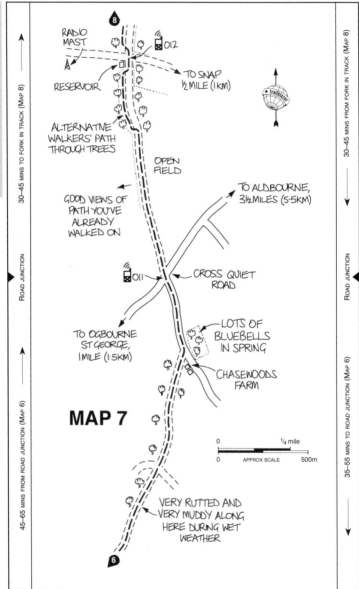

8

RADIO MAST

☐ 012

TO SNAP ½ MILE (1KM)

RESERVOIR

ALTERNATIVE WALKERS' PATH THROUGH TREES

OPEN FIELD

GOOD VIEWS OF PATH YOU'VE ALREADY WALKED ON

TO ALDBOURNE, 3½ MILES (5·5KM)

☐ 011

CROSS QUIET ROAD

TO OGBOURNE ST GEORGE, 1 MILE (1·5KM)

LOTS OF BLUEBELLS IN SPRING

CHASEWOODS FARM

MAP 7

0   ¼ mile
0   APPROX SCALE   500m

VERY RUTTED AND VERY MUDDY ALONG HERE DURING WET WEATHER

6

30-45 MINS TO FORK IN TRACK (MAP 8) ↑

◀ ROAD JUNCTION

45-65 MINS FROM ROAD JUNCTION (MAP 6) ↑

30-45 MINS FROM FORK IN TRACK (MAP 8) ↓

ROAD JUNCTION

35-55 MINS TO ROAD JUNCTION (MAP 6) ↓

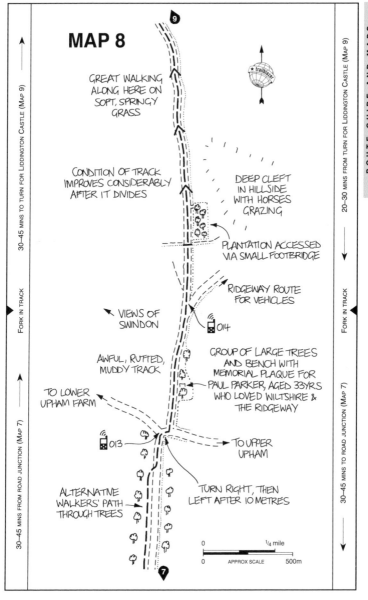

ROUTE GUIDE AND MAPS

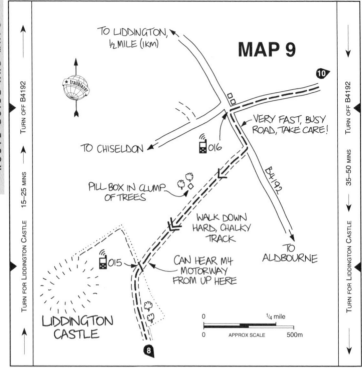

LIDDINGTON

The Village Inn (☎ 01793 790314, 🖥 www
.villageinn-liddington.co.uk; 1D/1T, shared
bathroom, ⬜; bar Mon-Sat 11.30am-
2.30pm & 6.30-11pm, Sun noon-2.30pm &
7-10.30pm; food Mon-Sat noon-2pm &
6.30-9pm; Sun noon-2pm & 7-8.30pm)
provides a friendly focus for the village and
is usually busy. This creeper-clad inn, originally called The Bell, was built in the late
19th century. They serve Arkell's ales and
their excellent food keeps the place full,
particularly at weekends. B&B costs £50
(£40 for single occupancy); packed lunches
are available if requested in advance.

There are three **bus** stops.
Thamesdown's No 46A service stops by
The Village Inn on its way between
Swindon and Hungerford and their No 48

(Swindon to Marlborough) calls at Spinney
Close. RH Buses' X47 service to Foxhill
stops at the turning off the B4192 into the
village; see pp42-5 for further details.

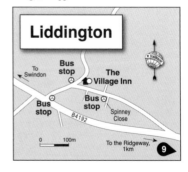

After enduring a stretch of road walking you must cross the bridge over the M4. You'll be surprised just how noisy and smelly it is; although the fumes disappear quickly when you reach the other side, the noise will stay with you all the way to Foxhill at the end of this stage. There is still about 700m of walking to go after the bridge but it's all on a neat grassy verge.

The crossroads at Foxhill are dominated by *The Burj* (☎ 01793 791888, ⌨ www.theburj.co.uk; daily 11.30am-2.30pm & 5.30-11.30pm), an Indian restaurant. This place used to be Shepherds Rest pub – the sign is still standing outside – a most welcoming stop during a Ridgeway walk. Since the closure of this pub, there are now none directly on the western half of the Ridgeway. Anyway, The Burj does cook some very tasty food from an extensive menu and has plenty of interesting vegetarian options, too. Main courses cost £9-18 but they also have set menus (£10-20). Thamesdown's Nos 46 & 48 **buses** call here as does RH Buses' X47 service; see pp42-5 for further details.

FOXHILL TO COURT HILL (& WANTAGE) [MAPS 10-16]

Overview
This second stage of the Ridgeway totals **11½ miles/18.5km (3¾-5½hrs)**; on the whole the walking is easy along very broad grassy tracks. Although there are a few ascents, they're not too draining. There are some great views plus several interesting archaeological sites and natural phenomena worth investigating. This is also the most remote section of the Ridgeway and is completely exposed to the elements with little shelter available. If it rains there is little you can do but continue walking and get very wet.

Route
About 200m past the Foxhill crossroads you leave the road that goes to the villages of Hinton Parva and Bishopstone and take the track on the right. If you are heading to Bishopstone it is best to wait and take the first turning on Map 11. A large **transmitter mast** will be in the field on your right protected by a gate with a dozen padlocks on it. The path levels out after a short climb and you can see the trig point on **Charlbury Hill** ahead and to the left of the path.

The ever-spreading town of Swindon is clearly visible to the west and you can also see villages down in the valley, parallel to the Ridgeway. These include Hinton Parva, Bishopstone, Idstone and Ashbury. Paths run down off the Ridgeway to these villages and many people from the surrounding area bring their dogs up here for exercise.

The first turning off (on Map 11) left to Bishopstone is a bridleway down a very steep-sided cleft, followed just a few hundred metres later by a narrow surfaced road headed to the same place from the crossroads at **Ridgeway Farm**. From this latter turning it's about half a mile/1km to the village.

BISHOPSTONE [see map p102]
Although this is a fairly large village, facilities for the walker are a little thin on the ground. There is no shop or post office, but there are a couple of great places to stay and the pub serves delicious food. It's an attractive place for a wander, especially by

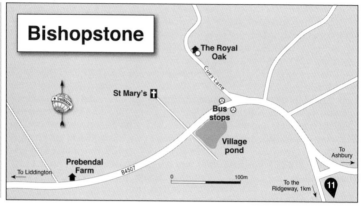

the village pond and on the shady shortcut paths around the village. However, like some of the other settlements on this stretch of the walk, it's only worth coming all the way down off the Ridgeway if you plan to stay or eat here.

Thamesdown's No 47 **bus** passes through on its way from Swindon to Ashbury and Lambourn. You can also take RH Buses X47 service to Foxhill or Ashbury; see pp42-5 for further details.

Where to stay and eat
The Royal Oak (☎ 01793 790481, 🖳 www. royaloakbishopstone.co.uk; 1D/1D, T or F, both en suite; 🏠; bar Mon-Fri noon-3pm & 6-11pm, Sat noon-midnight, Sun noon-10pm; food Mon-Sat noon-2.30pm & 6-9.30pm, Sun 12.30-3pm & 6.30-8pm), in a grand building set on a quiet lane, has

been here for about two hundred years and is well worth stopping off at. They serve Arkell's ales, amongst others, and have an excellent restaurant (booking is recommended) serving a regularly changing selection of organic food. Much of the meat comes from their own farm. As regards their accommodation they charge £35 for one person, £60 for two and £85 for three. Breakfast is extra (£8.50-10pp); packed lunches are also £10pp. Both should be requested in advance.

Prebendal Farm (☎ 01793 790485, 🖳 www.prebendal.com; 3D/1T, ☐; 🏠), a stately Victorian house set in truly beautiful gardens on a working farm, offers B&B from £45pp. Two of the doubles share a bathroom and the other rooms are en suite; wi-fi is available. Packed lunches (£5) are available if requested in advance.

After the junction at Ridgeway Farm the track becomes lined with trees on both sides and the walking is easy along here owing to the track being surfaced with stone chippings and the banning of motor vehicles.

At the next farm there is a track left, down Idstone Hill, to the hamlet of Idstone. From this junction to Bishopstone, via Idstone, it's a little over 1¼ miles/2km. There is also a **water tap** by the barn a few metres down the Idstone Hill turning. The next tap is 5½ miles/9km further on, but at the time of writing the tap had been removed and the pipe capped.

You're likely to hear the noise of the upcoming B4000 road crossing a good few minutes before you reach it. It comes up Ashbury Hill from Shrivenham and Ashbury, in the north, to cross the Ridgeway and continue south to the

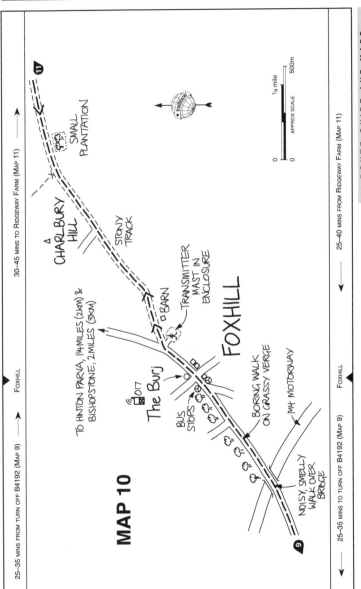

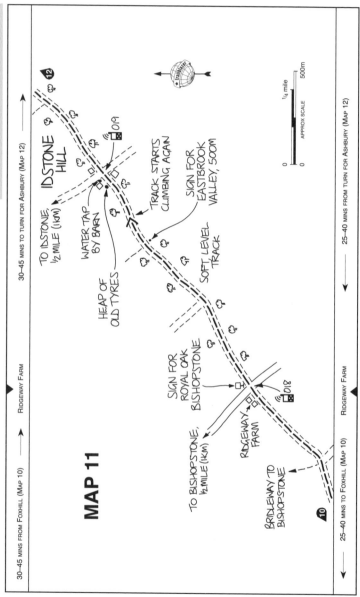

MAP 11

30–45 MINS FROM FOXHILL (MAP 10) ⟶

RIDGEWAY FARM

30–45 MINS TO TURN FOR ASHBURY (MAP 12) ⟶

25–40 MINS FROM FOXHILL (MAP 10) ⟶

RIDGEWAY FARM

25–40 MINS FROM TURN FOR ASHBURY (MAP 12) ⟶

TO IDSTONE, ½ MILE (1KM)

IDSTONE HILL

019

WATER TAP BY BARN

HEAP OF OLD TYRES

TRACK STARTS CLIMBING AGAIN

SIGN FOR EASTBROOK VALLEY, 500M

SOFT LEVEL TRACK

SIGN FOR ROYAL OAK, BISHOPSTONE

RIDGEWAY FARM

TO BISHOPSTONE, ½ MILE (1KM)

BRIDLEWAY TO BISHOPSTONE

018

APPROX SCALE

0   ¼ mile

0   500m

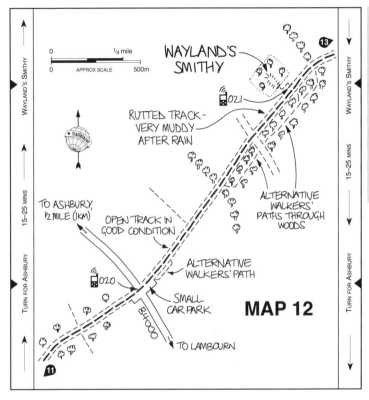

WAYLAND'S SMITHY

⌕ 021

RUTTED TRACK - VERY MUDDY AFTER RAIN

TO ASHBURY, ½ MILE (1KM)

OPEN TRACK IN GOOD CONDITION

⌕ 020

ALTERNATIVE WALKERS' PATHS THROUGH WOODS

ALTERNATIVE WALKERS' PATH

SMALL CAR PARK

MAP 12

B4000

TO LAMBOURN

WAYLAND'S SMITHY

15-25 MINS

TURN FOR ASHBURY

WAYLAND'S SMITHY

15-25 MINS

TURN FOR ASHBURY

Lambourns. From this crossing (Map 12) it is about half a mile/1km down to the village of Ashbury.

ASHBURY

This is another delightful village in the string of settlements running parallel to the Ridgeway. Unfortunately, like the other villages along here, there is no shop, but there is still a **post office**, though it has limited opening hours.

Thamesdown's Nos 47 **bus** service stops here as does RH Buses' X47; see pp42-5 for further details.

The *Rose & Crown Hotel* (☎ 01793 710222, 🖳 www.roseandcrownashbury. co.uk; 1S/3D/3T, all en suite, ☐; 🐾; bar daily noon-3pm, Mon-Thur 6-11pm, Fri &

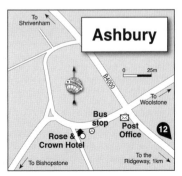

Ashbury

To Shrivenham

B4000

To Woolstone

Bus stop

Post Office

Rose & Crown Hotel

To Bishopstone

To the Ridgeway, 1km

Sat 6pm-midnight, Sun 7-10.30pm; food Mon-Sat noon-2pm & 6-9pm, Sun noon-2.30pm), a large Arkell's establishment, occupies a commanding position in the centre of the village. Bar snacks are available and the menu includes a wide range of main courses; their Sunday roast (£8.95-12.95) is good value. The single room is £55 a night; it is £70 for two sharing a room. This is a popular place for Ridgeway walkers to stay and they are always made to feel welcome.

> ❑ **Wayland's Smithy**
>
> This is a Neolithic long barrow. It was built in stages but was started around 2800BC as a burial place for members of the important ruling families in this area. The barrow itself is set in a small fenced wood and the entrance passageway that leads to the burial chamber is flanked by four huge sarsen stones. It's not possible to go into the underground chambers but nevertheless it's still an impressive construction when viewed just from the outside.
>
> The name of this long barrow dates from a couple of thousand years after it was built and comes from 'Wayland', the Saxon god of smiths. Apparently he made the shoes for the Uffington White Horse and will even shoe your horse for you if you leave it here, overnight, with some payment – cash only.

Around 15 minutes further along the closed-in track you will come to a short path on your left for Wayland's Smithy and by this time tall stands of trees will also be lining the track to your right. There is something a little eerie about this place, especially on a misty morning. **Wayland's Smithy** (see box above) isn't, and never really was, a smithy (a blacksmith's/forge).

The village of Woolstone can be reached by taking a left turn down the hill at the next crossroads (Map 13). It's about 1¼ miles/2km to the village.

WOOLSTONE

This is a very small, picturesque village at the foot of the steep Uffington Hill. There are many attractive buildings and the only place offering food and accommodation is one of the most enchanting buildings of all, *The White Horse* (☎ 01367 820726, 💻 www.whitehorsewoolstone.co.uk; 4D/1T/1D, T or F, all en suite, 🖵; 🐾; food daily noon-2.30pm & 6-9pm). It is an attractive 16th-century coaching inn situated in the 'centre' of the village. The pub serves Arkell's ales and, worth noting, it's open every day 11am-11pm. They serve food in the bar and the restaurant; delicious doorstep sandwiches cost from £5.95 and in the evening main courses such as steak and chips (£17.95), or warm lemon chicken & pine nut salad (£11.95) are on the menu; there are also specials every day. The comfortable en suite accommodation is in the

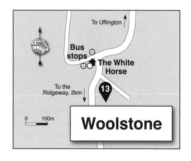

more modern building next to the pub and costs £75 for two sharing, or £60 for single occupancy; the family room, which is really a suite, can accommodate up to six people and costs £130-150.

RH Buses X47 **bus** service stops here; see pp42-5 for further details.

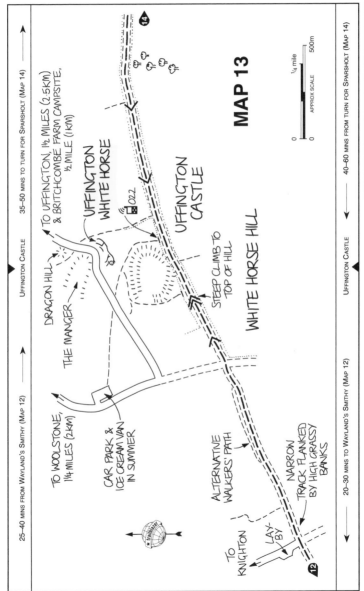

The climb up White Horse Hill to Uffington Castle (Map 13) is on a good track but it certainly gets steep towards the top; this is the toughest climb of this section but it doesn't last for long so count yourself lucky.

The National Trust area around this hill contains not only the aforementioned Uffington Castle and Uffington White Horse but also The Manger, a stunning coombe, lined with terraces, best viewed from the White Horse itself, and the perfectly formed, flat-topped Dragon Hill, just north of the White Horse, where St George battled with and slew the dragon.

Uffington Castle is the third of the big Iron Age hill forts you will have passed – the previous two being Barbury Castle (see p92) and Liddington Castle (see p97). The setting is certainly no less dramatic than Barbury's, though it's seven metres lower and only two-thirds its size. The double banks

---

❑ **White horses**
The **Uffington White Horse** (see Map 13) is the one that inspired them all. Scientists now think, after much debate, that it was first cut into the hillside around 800BC. It's over 100 metres long and superbly suggests the form of a horse rather than simply defining its outline. It's a mystery how the creators of the horse could cut it so well, given that the whole horse is only properly viewable from around a mile (1.5km) away in the valley.

Without a shadow of a doubt, Uffington White Horse is the best of the lot, but there are various other white horses scattered around the countryside near here. None of them is nearly as ancient and they don't even get close to the fluid beauty of the Uffington horse. By the time you reach this horse you'll have already passed another example at Hackpen Hill (Map 3) that was cut into the hillside in 1838.

The oldest and one of the most visible of all the modern horses is the **Westbury White Horse**. This was cut in 1778 but at some point in the 1950s it was concreted over. The concrete was then painted white. Owing to some unsightly deterioration and discolouration in the concrete, the horse was given another coating of concrete and paint in 1995. The logic was that concrete is easier to maintain. Using that logic maybe we should concrete over the Ridgeway, too? **Cherhill White Horse** is on a hill of the same name that is south of the A4 near Cherhill village, 3¾ miles/6km west of Avebury. This horse is one of the older ones in the area having been cut into the hillside in 1780. It was fully restored in 2002 and is easily visible from the A4.

There are other **white horses**: between Milk Hill and Walkers Hill, close to the village of Alton Barnes, about 3¾ miles/6km due south of Avebury is a good specimen, cut in 1812 and cleaned up in 2002. There is a further example of a well cared for horse near Broad Town on a north-west-facing slope. This horse is about 5km north-west of the Hackpen Hill horse though it's unclear when it was cut – probably in the 1860s. On Pewsey Hill, just south of the village of Pewsey, about 4¼ miles/7km south of Marlborough, is a well-groomed 1937 white horse.

The youngest white horse in the area is on Roundway Hill in Devizes, about 7½ miles/12km south-west of Avebury. It was created for the millennium and is uncommon in that it faces to the right. There was a much older white horse close to here but it has long since disappeared.

There is now a recognised **White Horse Trail** that follows a roughly circular route and visits all the white horses in Wiltshire. The trail is around 90 miles/145km long and illustrated guides can be bought from tourist information centres in the area.

For further information visit 🖳 www.wiltshirewhitehorses.org.uk.

and ditches are still steep and well defined and the views from up here are magnificent.

Uffington White Horse lies on the side of the hill to the north of the fort and although it really is spectacular this is certainly not the best place from which to view it. In fact it's very difficult to get a good view of the horse from the ground. Short of hiring a helicopter, the better views are from down in the valley: a steep descent and a very disappointing walk back up. If you don't think you can manage it, don't worry – even from down there the views are frustratingly incomplete. Perhaps remember to drive along the B4507 (the road running parallel to the Ridgeway along here) another time for views of the horse.

The **White Horse Hill area** really is one of the highlights of the Ridgeway trail so do take some time out to relax here and enjoy it. You've also got a fairly long stretch of plodding ahead, so you'll need the energy.

If you have decided to finish your day's walking at this point, you can walk down to the **campsite** at *Britchcombe Farm* (☎ 01367 820667; 70 pitches, 3 tipis and 1 yurt); the location is hard to beat. Pitches are £7pp per night including use of the shower/toilet facilities. You are also allowed to have an open fire as long as it is on a site where there has previously been a fire and also is not near the tents – bags of firewood are sold by the campsite owner. The tipis and yurt cost from £60 per night (plus the pitch fee above; from £90 for two nights) and sleep up to four people. They share toilet/shower facilities with the campsite and you need to bring your own bedding. There is also a tearoom called *The Teapot* (Mar-Dec, weekends and Bank Holidays 3-6pm) that serves cream teas.

This is also the place to leave the trail and head down to the village of Uffington, if you so desire.

UFFINGTON

It's a bit of a trek to get to Uffington from the Ridgeway, and certainly a strenuous start to the day if walking back up to the trail, but there are a couple of very good places to stay here, along with a decent pub, a shop with a post office, and even a museum.

Tom Brown's School Museum (🖳 www.museum.uffington.net; Easter-end Oct, weekends and Bank Holidays only, 2-5pm, free admission) is logically located in the classroom featured in the 1857 novel *Tom Brown's School Days* by Thomas Hughes. Exhibits centre on local history and archaeology.

The **Post Office and Stores** (☎ 01367 820221; Mon, Tue, Thur & Fri 7.15am-5.30pm, Wed 7.15am-2pm, Sat 7.30am-4pm, Sun 8.30am-noon; post office Mon, Tue, Thur & Fri 9am-5.30pm, Wed 9am-1pm, Sat 9am-12.30pm) is well stocked with groceries and general supplies.

However, they are expecting to move to a new site during 2012 and the opening hours may change at that time. When they

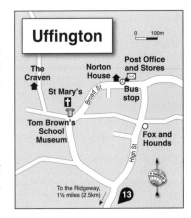

do move there will be directions from the current site to the new one.

In the centre of the village is the cream-coloured *Norton House* (☎ 01367 820230, 🖥 www.smoothhound.co.uk/ho tels/nortonfaringdon; 1S shared bathroom, 1D/1D, T or F, both with private bathroom; ▢; 🐾) which offers B&B in a large 18th-century family home. The double is £60, the single is £35-40 and the family room costs £90-100. Packed lunches are available and the owners can pick you up from, or drop you off at, the Ridgeway which could be a godsend if you're finding the going a bit tough.

The Craven (☎ 01367 820449, 🖥 www .thecraven.co.uk; 2S share facilities/2D/1F, all en suite; ▢) in a quiet location on the outskirts of the village offers distinctively styled rooms – one of them even has a four-poster bed! B&B starts from £60 for a single, £85-105 for two sharing. Packed lunches and delicious evening meals (set menu; £25 for three courses with coffee) are available if booked in advance.

The other option for eating in the village is at the *Fox & Hounds* (☎ 01367 820680, 🖥 www.uffingtonpub.co.uk; bar Mon-Sat 11am-11pm, Sun noon-10.30pm; food Mon-Fri noon-2pm & 6-9pm, Sat noon-2.45pm & 6-9pm, Sun noon-2.45pm). It's not often that you find a village pub with such accommodating opening hours and as such there is little excuse to pass it by. Being a freehouse, there is a good selection of real ales; there may be some that you might not have tried before. The menu is fully of hearty pub grub which should satisfy the hungry walker. Sandwiches (£5), ploughman's (£8) or local pork sausages with mashed potato and onion gravy (£8.50), for example. There's also a board with home-made puddings and vegetarian options too.

RH Buses' X47 **bus** (Swindon to Wantage) and their 67 (Faringdon to Wantage) stop in the village; see pp42-5 for further details.

At the next crossroads (Map 14) a sealed road cuts across the Ridgeway. Turn right here for Seven Barrows, a group of, well, yes, seven barrows. Turn left for **Kingston Lisle** where you'll find *The Blowing Stone* (☎ 01367 820288, 🖥 www. theblowingstone.co.uk; daily 11am-11.30pm; food Mon-Sat noon-2pm & 6.30-9pm, Sun 12.30-2.30pm). This freehouse has a good selection of real ales and a friendly atmosphere. They also have a sterling reputation for their food; the bar menu includes generous portions of kedgeree with a poached egg (£12.95), or Wiltshire ham with double egg and chips (£10.50). An interesting selection of mains is on offer (£12.95-17.95); the prices aren't the cheapest, but the quality makes it very well worth it.

RH Buses' No 67 and X47 **buses** stop in Kingston Lisle; see pp42-5 for further details.

After you descend Kingston Hill you will reach a crossroads that you should head straight across. It's also at this crossroads that you need to turn right to reach the B&B and camping at Down Barn Farm, about half a mile/1km away. The turning is marked as a byway though there is no sign for Down Barn Farm. The farm itself is not visible from here as it's round a corner and in a dip.

DOWN BARN FARM   [MAP 14]

For a unique experience you might like to stay at *Down Barn Farm* (☎ 01367 820272, mob ☎ 0779 983 3115, 🖥 pendomeffect@ aol.com; 1D/2T, ▢; 🐾£5). This place really is out on its own, set on a grassland farm that rears organic pigs and cattle. You might occasionally hear the cows mooing or the cock crowing but that's about it at

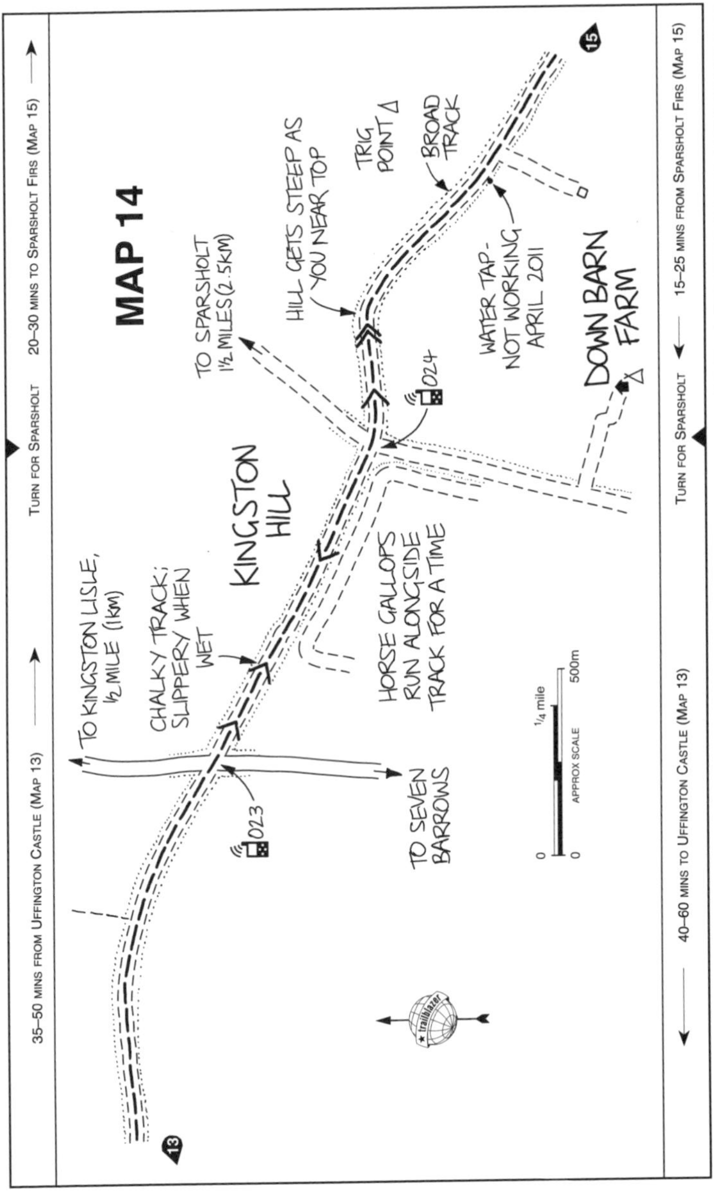

MAP 14

TURN FOR SPARSHOLT — 20–30 MINS TO SPARSHOLT FIRS (MAP 15) —

35–50 MINS FROM UFFINGTON CASTLE (MAP 13) — TURN FOR SPARSHOLT

15–25 MINS FROM SPARSHOLT FIRS (MAP 15)

40–60 MINS TO UFFINGTON CASTLE (MAP 13)

TO KINGSTON LISLE, ½ MILE (1km)

CHALKY TRACK; SLIPPERY WHEN WET

KINGSTON HILL

TO SPARSHOLT 1½ MILES (2.5KM)

HILL GETS STEEP AS YOU NEAR TOP

TRIG POINT △

BROAD TRACK

WATER TAP – NOT WORKING, APRIL 2011

DOWN BARN FARM △

HORSE GALLOPS RUN ALONGSIDE TRACK FOR A TIME

TO SEVEN BARROWS

024

023

15

13

¼ mile

500m

APPROX SCALE

0

0

❏ Morris dancing

If you hang around the pubs along the Ridgeway for long enough during the summer, you are likely to see some Morris dancing. Essentially the Morris teams (or sides) are performing traditional country dances and will often be accompanied by musicians. Each group of Morris men has its own particular outfit: embroidered smocks, waist-coats, decorated hats, neckerchiefs and clusters of bells abound. Depending on the dance they might also be waving handkerchiefs or hitting sticks together, sometimes with great force.

It is thought that these dances, often named after the villages where they were originally performed (such as Adderbury, Bampton, Ducklington or Stanton Harcourt), have also been influenced by traditional European dances. It's fairly safe to say that they were performed as long as 500 years ago, though many traditions died out in the 18th and 19th centuries.

The beginning of the 20th century saw a concerted effort to record the dances and music before they disappeared forever and the last 30 years in particular have seen an increased interest in performing the traditions.

Morris groups based in the Ridgeway area include White Horse Morris Men (🖥 www.whitehorsemorris.tk), Liddington Hall and Icknield Way Morris Men (🖥 www.icknieldwaymorrismen.org.uk), the latter being one of the more prolific.

Many of the village pubs along the first half of the Ridgeway are popular venues for Morris dancers including the Rose & Crown at Ashbury, The Bell at Aldworth, the Royal Oak at Bishopstone, and The Greyhound at Letcombe Regis to name a few.

---

this haven of peace and quiet. One twin is en suite and the other rooms share a bathroom if both are let. **B&B** costs £65-85, or £45 if you're on your own.

Outdoors there are several pitches for **campers** (£5pp) that are available all year, but it is exposed up here. Campers can use the toilet and a sink; a shower costs £3.

Booking is essential, even if you are camping. The owner can prepare evening meals (£15-20pp for three courses), packed lunches (£4.50) and breakfast for campers (£8), which is just as well as the next nearest place offering food is a good couple of miles (3km) away.

Alternatively, if you want to head to the Star Inn at Sparsholt, you could turn left here for the 1¹/₂-mile/2.5km walk to the village. Follow the track to the main road, turn right onto the road and follow it for 500m before turning left into the quiet village of Sparsholt. You can also reach Sparsholt via the turning off Map 15, but this route requires more road walking.

SPARSHOLT [off MAP 14]

The *Star Inn* (☎ 01235 751539; 2D/4T/2D, T or F, all en suite, ▯; 🐾 ; food Mon 6.30-9.30pm, Tue-Sun noon-2.30pm & 6.30-9.30pm; bar Mon-Fri 12.30-2.30pm & 6-11pm, Sat noon-4.30pm & 6pm-midnight, Sun noon-4.30pm & 6.30-11pm) is an inviting 17th-century country inn with accommodation in a converted barn. They have plenty of filling dishes on their menu to satisfy the hungry walker and if you are

staying here overnight a continental breakfast is included in the rate but if you want a full English it is an additional £5pp. The well-kept accommodation starts at £55 for a twin, £60 for a double, £55 for single occupancy and £70 for a family room.

There is no shop or post office in the village, but RH Buses' No 67 and X47 stop here; see pp42-5 for further details.

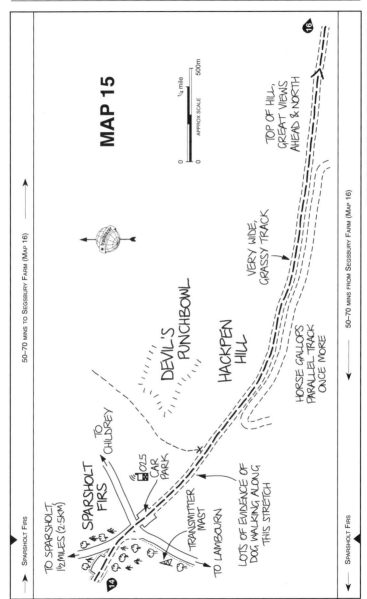

On your way up Hackpen Hill the valley drops away very steeply to the north giving excellent views of the **Devil's Punchbowl** (Map 15). You can get closer to the punchbowl by taking the path that branches left from the track where there is a stile structure marking the path junction. Although this should be a path, it seems to run straight through a planted field with no visible trail.

You'll soon cross the road junction (Map 16) that has a left turn down to Letcombe Bassett and further on there is a track on the left that joins up with the road; using either of these turnings Letcombe Bassett is about half a mile (1km) away. You could also use these to walk to Wantage but it'd probably be better to wait for the next road junction for that. Shortly ahead there is a path on the left – yet another opportunity to head down to Letcombe Bassett. If you have no pressing matters to attend to in the village, it's probably not worth a detour. However, RH Buses Nos 67 and X47 (see pp42-5) do stop there.

It was just a little further on from here that, several years ago, I passed a nun on the track. She had walked from St Mary's Convent in Wantage, around three miles (5km) away. You might have some unlikely encounters on the Ridgeway – owls or deer, for instance, but I think that meeting a nun up here must now be added to the list.

On reaching **Segsbury Farm** (on your right), there is a 100-metre track (to the left) up to **Segsbury Camp**: this is also called Letcombe Castle. It's more than double the size of Barbury Castle but far less popular; you'll usually have the place to yourself. Like Barbury Castle (see p92), this was an Iron Age hill fort and evidence of roundhouses were found during excavations in the 1990s.

It's also this track that you should take if you want to visit Letcombe Regis. This isn't the only way to the village – you could follow the road past the Court Hill Centre – but it's the most convenient. You'll also have the bonus of passing through Segsbury Camp on your way. From the junction with the Ridgeway, it's about 1 1/4 miles/2km to the centre of the village.

LETCOMBE REGIS

This village, another in the chain of 'spring line' settlements below the Downs, dates back well over a thousand years although the 'Regis' part of the name was only added during the reign of Richard II (1377-99). However, the regal connections date from well before then as it was the property of King Stephen in the 12th century and there was a royal hunting lodge here in the 13th and 14th centuries.

The oldest remaining building in the village is the church, St Andrew's, parts of which date back to the 12th century though some of the houses don't look as if they are a great deal younger.

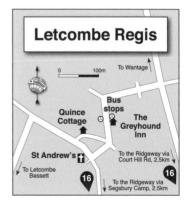

Letcombe Regis

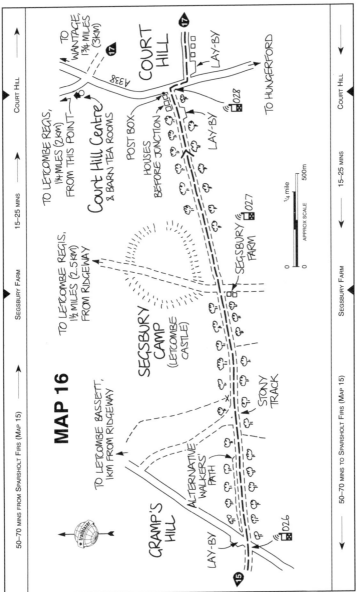

MAP 16

50–70 MINS FROM SPARSHOLT FIRS (MAP 15)

SEGSBURY FARM

15–25 MINS

COURT HILL

GRAMP'S HILL

LAY-BY

TO LETCOMBE BASSETT, 1KM FROM RIDGEWAY

ALTERNATIVE WALKERS' PATH

STONY TRACK

026

SEGSBURY CAMP (LETCOMBE CASTLE)

TO LETCOMBE REGIS, 1½ MILES (2.5KM) FROM RIDGEWAY

SEGSBURY FARM 027

TO LETCOMBE REGIS, 1¼ MILES (2KM) FROM THIS POINT

Court Hill Centre & Barn Tea Rooms

POST BOX

HOUSES BEFORE JUNCTION

LAY-BY

028

TO HUNGERFORD

TO WANTAGE, 1¾ MILES (3KM) 17

A338

COURT HILL 17

LAY-BY

¼ mile

500m

APPROX SCALE

0   0

Letcombe Regis and its neighbour, Letcombe Bassett, are known for the watercress beds that covered the land between them though 'Regis' is also home to four racing stables, which generate considerably more income.

There aren't any shops or services but nevertheless it would make a convenient and enjoyable overnight stop. RH Buses No 67 **bus** stops here (Wantage to Faringdon) as does the X47 (Wantage and Swindon); see pp42-5 for further details.

Where to stay, eat and drink

The Greyhound Inn (☎ 01235 771093; bar daily noon-11.30pm, food Tue-Sat noon-3pm & 6-9pm, Sun roast noon-4pm) is a Georgian-style, traditional country inn serving standard pub fare.

Nearby is *Quince Cottage* (☎ 01235 763652, 🖥 www.bodenfamily.info; 1S/1T or F, private facilities, 🚻; 🐾 £not fixed), a charming 18th-century thatched cottage that charges from £75/£90 for two/three people sharing; the single room is £35-40. Packed lunches (about £5) are available if requested in advance. This is a great place to stay and you are assured a friendly welcome. An excellent cooked breakfast is also served. Book well ahead as this place is deservedly popular with walkers!

Soon after here, at the foot of **Court Hill**, the Ridgeway crosses the main A338 road coming from Wantage in the north and Hungerford in the south. Turn left for Wantage (see below), a town with plenty of shops, banks and other services just over two miles/3km away, and also for Court Hill Centre, about 500 metres along the road.

Court Hill Centre (☎ 01235 760253, 🖥 www.courthill.org.uk; 60 beds) is virtually on the Ridgeway and has accommodation in a **bunkhouse**: there are family and dormitory rooms at £17.50pp (£13 for under 18s). A limited number of **camping pitches** (£8.50 per night, £6 for under 18s) is also available. Breakfast, from £5, and an evening meal, from £8.50, are available as are packed lunches but all must be ordered in advance. There is a small food shop, open during hostel hours, and a self-catering kitchen. The hostel also has wi-fi access. Campers have access to the toilet during the night and use of the other facilities during opening hours. Advance booking for both the bunkhouse and the campsite is recommended.

If you're just passing by and not staying the night, you could always stop off at *Barn Tea Rooms* (daily 10.30am-5pm) where you'll find teas, coffees and cold drinks along with cakes, light lunches and ice-creams.

WANTAGE

Despite the lengthy walk from the Ridgeway, Wantage is a good place to stop and recharge your batteries. The town is famous as the birthplace of King Alfred the Great (849-99), the only Anglo-Saxon ruler who was not defeated by the Vikings. You can see his statue in the centre of Market Place. Wantage has a compact centre with most of the shops, restaurants and pubs within a few minutes' walk of Market Place.

Vale and Downland Museum & Visitor Centre (☎ 01235 771447; 🖥 www.wantage-museum.com; Mon-Sat 10am-4pm, free admission but donations appreciated) is well worth a visit if you have some free time. There is lots of free information here about local attractions, a gift shop, café (see Where to eat and drink), permanent historical exhibition and art gallery. The exhibition concentrates on the history of the town and features plenty of artefacts from King Alfred's time to the present.

Part of the museum is housed in an 18th-century barn that was moved from a

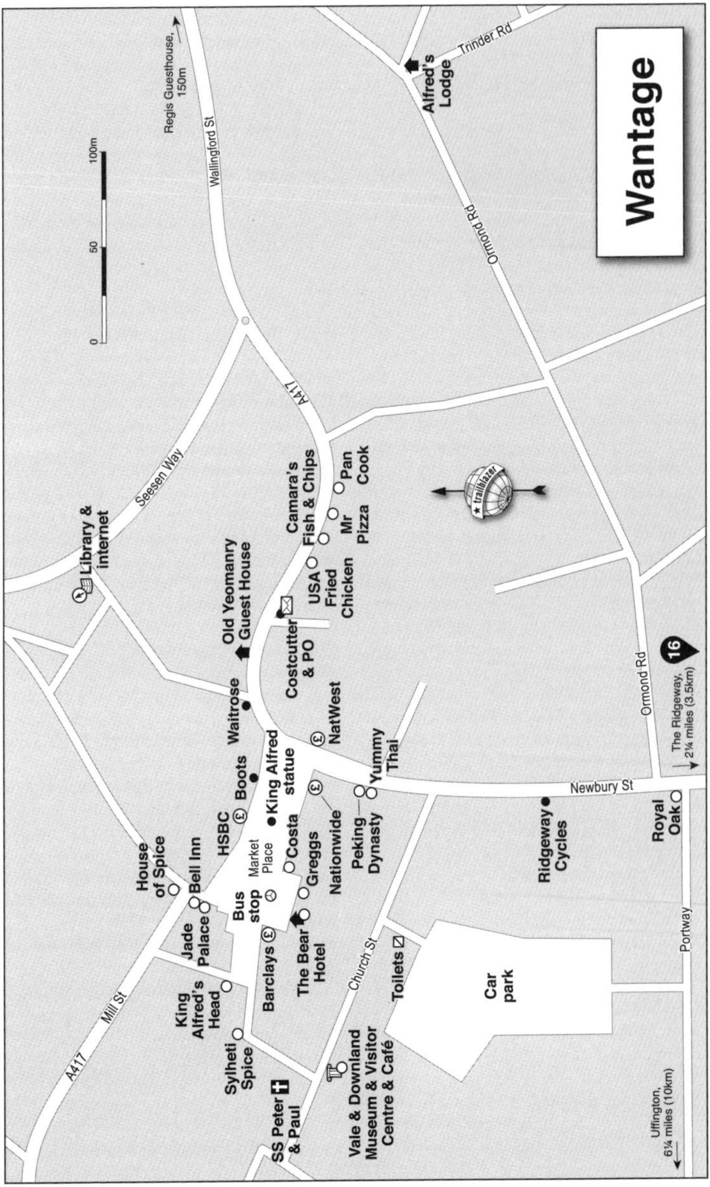

Wantage

Regis Guesthouse, 150m

Wallingford St

Trinder Rd

Alfred's Lodge

Ormond Rd

100m

50

0

Seesen Way

Library & internet

Old Yeomanry Guest House

Camara's Fish & Chips

Mr Pan Pizza Cook

Trailmaster

A417

USA Fried Chicken

Costcutter & PO

16

NatWest

The Ridgeway, 2¼ miles (3.5km)

Waitrose

Boots

King Alfred statue

Yummy Thai

Ormond Rd

HSBC

Market Place

Costa

Newbury St

House of Spice

Bell Inn

Greggs

Nationwide

Peking Dynasty

Royal Oak

Ridgeway Cycles

Jade Palace

Bus stop

Barclays

The Bear Hotel

Portway

King Alfred's Head

Church St

Sylheti Spice

SS Peter & Paul

Vale & Downland Museum & Visitor Centre & Café

Toilets

Car park

A417

Mill St

Uffington, 6¼ miles (10km)

nearby village and rebuilt here. The visitor centre part is able to do accommodation booking; they charge £2.50 but this is then deducted from the bill at wherever you stay.

Services

There are plenty of **banks** (such as HSBC, Barclays, NatWest and Nationwide), all with **ATMs**, around Market Place. You'll also find a Boots **pharmacy** (Mon-Sat 8.45am-5.30pm) on Market Place and a large Waitrose **supermarket** (Mon-Thur 8.30am-8pm, Fri 8.30am-9pm, Sat 8.30am-7pm, Sun 10am-4pm) just a few steps away. There's also a **farmers' market** (see box p15).

The **library** (☎ 01235 762291; Mon 9am-8pm, Tue & Wed 9am-5.30pm, Thur 9am-1pm, Fri 9am-8pm, Sat 9am-4.30pm), a few minutes' walk north of Market Place, offers **internet access** for free (up to 1hr/day). The **post office** (Mon-Fri 9am-5.30pm, Sat 9am-12.30pm) is in the Costcutter shop.

If you need **bike repairs** you should head to Ridgeway Cycles (☎ 01235 764445; 🖳 www.ridgewaycycles.com; Mon-Sat 9am-5.30pm) on Newbury St. There are free **public toilets** at the entrance to the pay and display car park.

Buses stop on Market Place and include services to Oxford (Stagecoach's Nos 31 & X30); Letcombe Regis, Sparsholt, Kingston Lisle, Uffington and Swindon (RH Buses Nos 67 & X47) and Didcot (Thames Travel Nos 32A, 36 & X36); Didcot Parkway and Abingdon (Thames Travel No 32); see pp42-5 for further details.

Where to stay

If you are walking from the Ridgeway to Wantage, the chances are you'll be intending to stay overnight here, too. *Regis Guesthouse* (☎ 01235 762860; 🖳 www. regisguesthouse.com; 3D/2T or D, private facilities, Jacuzzi available) is a well-appointed place just a few minutes' walk from the town centre. All the rooms have wi-fi. B&B costs £70-80 (single occupancy is £45-55). The owners can pick you up

from/drop you off at Court Hill Centre by prior arrangement and can also provide packed lunches. An evening meal is available if booked in advance.

At the junction of Ormond Rd and Trinder Rd is *Alfred's Lodge* (☎ 01235 762409; 🖳 www.bwithme.co.uk, 23 Ormond Rd; 1D/2T/2D, T or F, all en suite; 🐾). It's close to the town centre and offers wi-fi. B&B is £65 for two sharing plus about £10 for an additional person in a family room; single occupancy costs from £45.

Just a stone's throw from Market Place is *Old Yeomanry Guest House* (☎ 01235 772778; 🖳 www.yeomanryhouse.co.uk; 2S/2D/1T, all en suite). The location of this 17th-century town house is hard to beat and the modern rooms are good value costing £55 for two sharing and £30 for a single.

Right on Market Place is *The Bear Hotel* (☎ 01235 766366; 🖳 www.thebear wantage.co.uk; 9S/16D/8T/2D, T or F, 🖵). This grand building was completely renovated in 2010. B&B costs £49 for single occupancy, £59/69 for two/three sharing. There is free wi-fi in every room.

Where to eat and drink

There are plenty of places in Wantage offering food and drink. *King Alfred's Head* (☎ 01235 765531; 🖳 www.kingalfredshead. com; bar daily 11am-11pm, food daily noon-3pm, Tue-Sat 6.30-9pm) is one of the best. Their lunchtime snack menu includes sandwiches such as pork and leek sausage with onion and apple sauce for £4.95. Prices on the bistro-style dinner menu range from £7.95 to £16.95; dishes vary but may include rib-eye steak, lemon sole and wild mushroom risotto. They also serve a good and regularly changing selection of real ales and have free wi-fi.

The Bear Hotel (see Where to stay; Mon-Fri 7-9am, Sat 8-10am, Mon-Sat noon-2.30pm & 6-9pm, Sun noon-2.30pm) is also a good place for food. They serve a full English breakfast (£7) which might be just the thing to prepare you for a day of walking. In the evening, main courses cost from £7.95 to £13.50 and include honey-glazed pork belly with crackling, confit potatoes and bacon for £12.95. They are a bit light on vegetarian options though. The bar serves Arkell's beers.

Lunchtime options include Vale and Downland Museum and Visitor Centre (see p116) where you can enjoy home-made soup for £3.60 or a range of salads with jacket potatoes for £6.10 in the light and airy **café** area (9.30am-3.45pm).

The *Bell Inn* (☎ 01235 763718; food served Mon-Sat noon-3pm & 6-9pm, Sun noon-3pm) also has plenty of choice for lunch including ciabattas, jacket spuds and ploughman's, all from £4.95. They also have an evening menu with 'pub classics' and a few vegetarian options (£8.95-13.95).

Tasty Thai food can be found at *Yummy Thai* (☎ 01235 768222; 🖥 www.yummythai.com; Thur-Sun noon-3pm, daily 6-11pm) who also provide a takeaway service. The menu is guaranteed to make your mouth water and the prices are very reasonable – main dishes are from £6.25. The *masaman* chicken curry for £7.50 is recommended.

Next door is *Peking Dynasty* (☎ 01235 771338; 🖥 www.pekingdynasty.co.uk; Mon-Sat 6-11pm, Sun noon-2pm & 6-10.30pm), a Chinese restaurant and take-away. You won't find any surprises on the menu but it is extensive enough. Main dishes typically cost £5.50-7.

There are two 'Indian' restaurants in town vying for your custom – *House of Spice* (☎ 01235 760707; 🖥 www.houseof spice.uk.com; Sun noon-2pm, Sun-Thur 6-11.30pm, Fri & Sat 6pm-midnight), which is part of a chain (see also p151 and p163) and *Sylheti Spice* (☎ 01235 764164/762651; Sun-Thur 6-11.30pm, Fri & Sat 6pm-midnight). They are just what you would expect and there really isn't much to choose between them though you can take your own alcohol to Sylheti.

Fast food and takeaway outlets abound and include: *Greggs* (Mon-Sat 8am-5.30pm), *Camara's Fish & Chips* (daily 11am-10.30pm), *Mr Pizza* (daily 5-11pm) and *USA Fried Chicken* (daily noon-11pm). *Pan Cook* (☎ 01235 766287; daily 5-11.30pm) and *Jade Palace* (☎ 01235 762832; Wed-Mon 5-11pm) are standard Chinese takeaways.

If you are after an excellent selection of real ales in a friendly atmosphere, you couldn't do better than head to the *Royal Oak* (☎ 01235 763129; 🖥 www.royaloak wantage.co.uk; bar Mon-Fri 5.30-11pm, Sat noon-2.30pm & 7-11pm, Sun noon-2pm & 7-10.30pm). With up to a dozen local ales on at any one time, not to mention a similar number of ciders, you'll be spoiled for choice – well worth a post-walk visit! Food is not served but they are happy for walkers to bring their own.

There is a *Costa* (Mon-Sat 8am-6pm, Sun 9am-4pm) coffee shop on Market Place if you fancy a hot drink and a snack.

COURT HILL TO GORING   [MAPS 16-25]
Overview
This is an easy **14-mile/22.5km** (4¼-6hrs) section. From Court Hill up to the crossing of the A34 road, the path is level, broad, grassy and exposed, similar to what you've become used to from the previous stages. After the A34 there is more tree cover and the path starts to undulate, though it hardly ever gets steep. The Ridgeway then gradually descends into the small town of Streatley, on the west bank of the river Thames, before crossing into Goring on the opposite bank. At the time of writing, the water tap on Map 21 had been removed and the pipe capped; therefore there is no source of drinking water on the trail between Court Hill and Streatley.

Route

Where the Ridgeway arrives at the A338 (Map 16) to Wantage you need to make a right turn and follow it for all of a minute before turning left, back onto the track. The track is sealed for a while now and you'll pass several houses on your right before reaching Whitehouse Farm (Map 17) on the left; the tarmac fades to soft grass or mud, depending on the weather conditions. When you arrive at the T-junction, you'll have another chance to visit Court Hill Centre by turning left.

When you arrive at the B4494 you can turn right and walk for 750m to reach *Lockinge Kiln Farm B&B* (☎ 01235 763308, 🖳 www.lockingekiln.co .uk; 1D or F en suite/1T private shower room; Mar-Dec). As the name suggests, this B&B is on a working farm with accommodation in the 200-year-old farmhouse. The rate is £64-68 for two sharing (single occupancy is £35-45). The owners can provide packed lunches (£3.50) if given advance notice and can also give you a lift into Wantage in the evening for dinner. This place is ideally located for Ridgeway walkers and the opportunity to stay on a working farm adds to the attraction.

After you have crossed the B4494 and rejoined the broad grassy track, you will come to a large **monument**, on your right. It consists of a marble column set on a large square base with steps on all sides. At the top of the column is a cross. It is in memory of Baron Wantage (1832-1901) who, amongst other things, expanded the nearby Lockinge estate.

A further mile (1.5km) down the track, but this time on the left, you will see a **reservoir** (Map 18). It's a low, square red-brick structure, surrounded by trees and fenced in. The walking along here is on the same broad grassy track you have been on for some time and it will be with you for a while yet.

Around 20 minutes after passing the reservoir you will come to a sealed road (Map 19) crossing the Ridgeway. This is the road to East Hendred, 2½ miles/4km to the north. After this junction the Ridgeway is joined by gallops on the right that will stick with the track until the next road junction at the **Bury Down** car parks – the road here goes north to Chilton and south to West Ilsley, about one mile (1.5km) away. Just before the car parks you'll begin to hear the noise of the A34 up ahead. Harwell International Business Centre is clearly visible just over a mile to the north from here. It's perhaps as far back as Swindon since something on this scale has been visible.

When you arrive at the A34 junction (Map 20) you can either use the tunnel underneath or try to cross it. There are paths catering to both these options but it is far safer to use the subway. The track down to it drops steeply and bends to the right then the left. Inside the tunnel, on the right side, are some murals depicting traditional historical scenes from the area and on both sides various amateur graffiti. The floor is littered with empty beer cans and other waste so although people have obviously made an effort with the murals, it's not the kind of place that particularly invites you to linger for a closer look.

Just a few minutes after the tunnel, on the left of the track, almost enclosed by the shrubbery, is a **stone memorial** inscribed with the name of Hugh

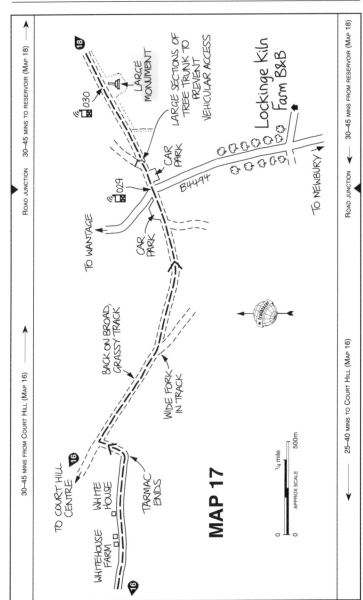

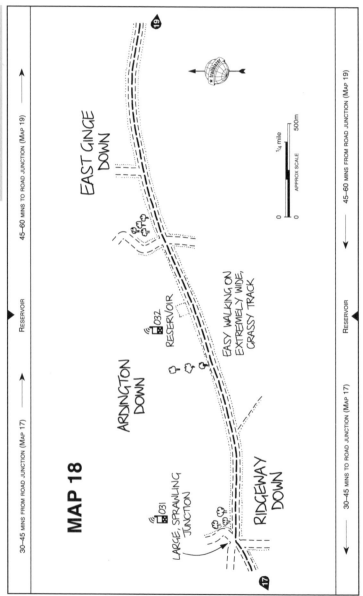

30–45 MINS FROM ROAD JUNCTION (MAP 17)   RESERVOIR   45–60 MINS TO ROAD JUNCTION (MAP 19)

30–45 MINS TO ROAD JUNCTION (MAP 17)   RESERVOIR   45–60 MINS FROM ROAD JUNCTION (MAP 19)

MAP 18

EAST GINGE DOWN

ARDINGTON DOWN

RIDGEWAY DOWN

RESERVOIR

031

032

LARGE, SPRAWLING JUNCTION

EASY WALKING ON EXTREMELY WIDE, GRASSY TRACK

APPROX SCALE
¼ mile
0   500m

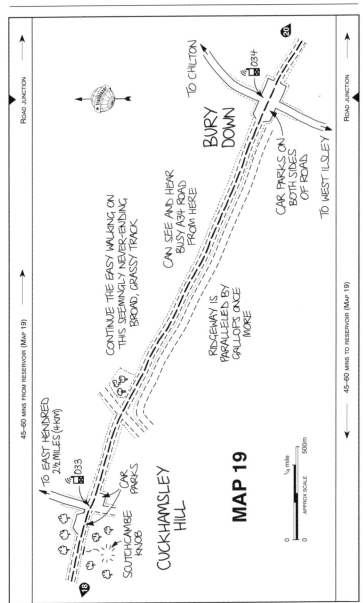

ROAD JUNCTION

45–60 MINS FROM RESERVOIR (MAP 19)

TO CHILTON

034+

BURY
DOWN

CAR PARKS ON
BOTH SIDES
OF ROAD

TO WEST ILSLEY

CAN SEE AND HEAR
BUSY A34 ROAD
FROM HERE

CONTINUE THE EASY WALKING ON
THIS SEEMINGLY NEVER-ENDING,
BROAD, GRASSY TRACK

RIDGEWAY IS
PARALLELED BY
GALLOPS ONCE
MORE

TO EAST HENDRED
2½ MILES (4 KM)

033

CAR
PARKS

SOUTHCOMBE
KNOB

CUCKHAMSLEY
HILL

MAP 19

¼ mile

500m

0

0

APPROX SCALE

ROAD JUNCTION

45–60 MINS TO RESERVOIR (MAP 19)

20

18

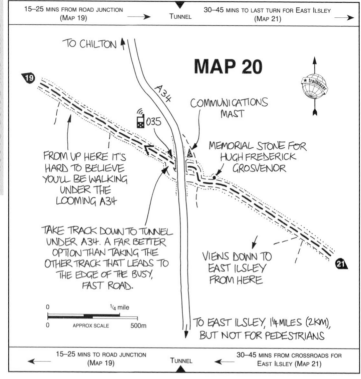

TO CHILTON ↑

MAP 20

★ trailblaze

A34

COMMUNICATIONS MAST

📱 035

MEMORIAL STONE FOR HUGH FREDERICK GROSVENOR

FROM UP HERE IT'S HARD TO BELIEVE YOU'LL BE WALKING UNDER THE LOOMING A34

TAKE TRACK DOWN TO TUNNEL UNDER A34. A FAR BETTER OPTION THAN TAKING THE OTHER TRACK THAT LEADS TO THE EDGE OF THE BUSY, FAST ROAD.

VIEWS DOWN TO EAST ILSLEY FROM HERE

21

0 ¼ mile
0 APPROX SCALE 500m

TO EAST ILSLEY, 1¼ MILES (2KM), BUT NOT FOR PEDESTRIANS

Frederick Grosvenor, a 2nd Lieutenant in the Lifeguards who was killed here in an armoured car accident on 9 April 1947. He was aged just 19.

Look to the south occasionally and soon you'll get a glimpse of East Ilsley – a very welcome sight if you started at Foxhill earlier in the day. There is still the best part of two miles (3km) to go, however, but the path follows the same broad grassy track that has by now become very familiar.

There are four possible ways down into **East Ilsley** from the Ridgeway and they are all less than a mile apart. There's a water tap (disconnected at the time of research) and trough on the path between the second and third turns. If you're visiting the village, the second way is the probably the best choice – it's the most direct with easy walking. However, as the last two leave the Ridgeway that bit later, they give you slightly more of a head-start when you pick it up again. It doesn't really matter though – leaving by any of the tracks you'll have to walk about 1 mile/1.5km into the village.

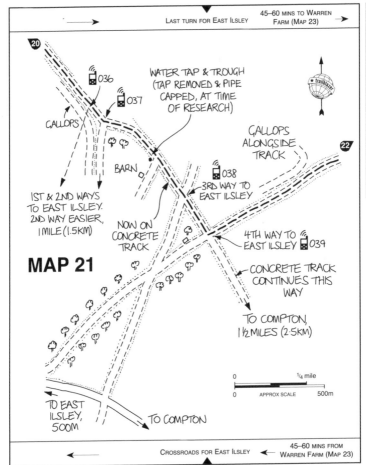

LAST TURN FOR EAST ILSLEY

45–60 MINS TO WARREN FARM (MAP 23)

20

036

037

WATER TAP & TROUGH (TAP REMOVED & PIPE CAPPED, AT TIME OF RESEARCH)

★ trailblazer

GALLOPS

GALLOPS ALONGSIDE TRACK

22

BARN

038

3RD WAY TO EAST ILSLEY

1ST & 2ND WAYS TO EAST ILSLEY. 2ND WAY EASIER, 1 MILE (1.5KM)

NOW ON CONCRETE TRACK

4TH WAY TO EAST ILSLEY 039

MAP 21

CONCRETE TRACK CONTINUES THIS WAY

TO COMPTON, 1½ MILES (2.5KM)

0   ¼ mile
0   APPROX SCALE   500m

TO EAST ILSLEY, 500M

TO COMPTON

CROSSROADS FOR EAST ILSLEY

45–60 MINS FROM WARREN FARM (MAP 23)

EAST ILSLEY

From the 17th century to 1934 East Ilsley was known as a venue for huge sheep markets. At their peak, drovers would descend on the village filling it with up to 70,000 sheep; it has been a lot quieter here since the market stopped. Today it's an attractive-enough place with two pubs, both of which provide food and accommodation, and this makes it a convenient place to break your journey. However, at the time of writing there was no shop or post office but Newbury & District **bus** Nos 6 & 6a serve Newbury, Chievely and Compton on a circular route; see pp42-5.

Where to stay and eat

The *Crown & Horns* (☎ 01635 281545, ⬛ www.crownandhorns.co.uk; 4D/1T/2D, T or F, all en suite, □; 🐾; bar daily 11am-11pm; food Mon-Fri 7-9am, Sat & Sun 8-10am, Mon-Sat noon-3pm & 6-9.30pm, Sun noon-6pm) has a cosy interior – in the colder months there is a welcoming open fire to sit beside – and a shady garden. It's always popular with walkers. The pub has separate dining areas and the walls in the bar are covered with horse-racing memorabilia (see box p96).

The menu includes: pork and leek sausages with mash and onion gravy (£9.95); beer-battered cod (£9.95) and rib-eye steak (£12.99). To wash it down they serve Brakspear's, Doom Bar, Timothy Taylor Landlord and various other beers. The accommodation is in well-kept rooms and costs £50 for one or two sharing and an additional £10 for an extra person. A continental breakfast is £5pp and a full English is £7.95. They also have special deals for weekend Ridgeway walkers: two people sharing a room, two-course evening meal, wine, breakfast and luggage service costs £110/200 for one/two nights. The owner has a dog but welcomes clean dogs.

Opposite is *The Swan* (☎ 01635 281238, 🖥 www.theswaneastilsley.co.uk; 2D/3T en suite, □; bar daily 11am-11pm, food Mon-Sat noon-8.45pm, Sun noon-

2pm), a 16th-century coaching inn in the centre of the village with a pleasant garden that is open all day. From lunchtime until 6pm they serve lunch and 'light-bites'; after 6pm more substantial fare is on offer. On Sundays there is a two-course carvery for £11. B&B here costs £75, or £65 if you are on your own.

You start the Ridgeway again at the crossroads where the last of the four paths to East Ilsley turns off. If you want to go to Compton, 1½ miles/2.5km, it's best to leave the Ridgeway at this point.

COMPTON

The Saxon name given to this village means 'Coombe Town', or, 'town in the valley', but there is evidence of Bronze and Iron Age settlement in the area even before the Saxons were here. Plenty of Roman artefacts, coins in particular, have been found near Compton.

There is a **shop** (☎ 01635 578682; Mon-Fri 7am-6.30pm, Sat 7.30am-6.30pm, Sun 8am-1pm) in the village that stocks a surprisingly large range of groceries; it also contains the local **post office** (Mon-Fri 9.30am-5.30pm, Sat 9.30am-12.30pm).

The *Compton Swan* (☎ 01635 579400, 🖥 www.comptonswan.co.uk; 4D/2D or T, all en suite, □; bar daily 11am-10.30/11pm,

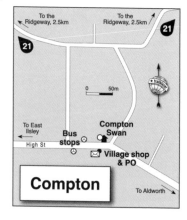

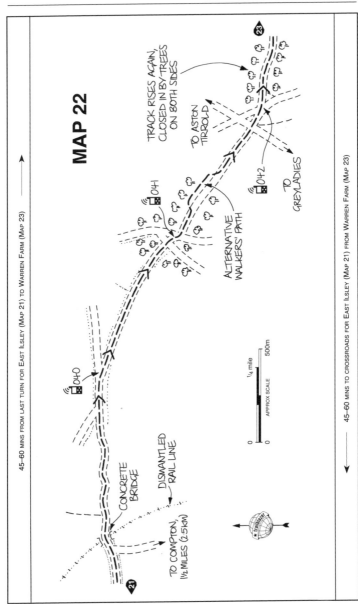

MAP 22

45–60 MINS FROM LAST TURN FOR EAST ILSLEY (MAP 21) TO WARREN FARM (MAP 23)

45–60 MINS TO CROSSROADS FOR EAST ILSLEY (MAP 21) FROM WARREN FARM (MAP 23)

TRACK RISES AGAIN, CLOSED IN BY TREES ON BOTH SIDES

TO ASTON TIRROLD

TO GREYLADIES

ALTERNATIVE WALKERS' PATH

CONCRETE BRIDGE

DISMANTLED RAIL LINE

TO COMPTON, 1½ MILES (2.5KM)

APPROX SCALE

¼ mile

500m

trailblazer

food daily 8am-3pm & Mon-Sat 6-10pm) is a large, white building on the main road through the village. It is often busy with a mixture of locals and visitors and is deservedly a very popular place to eat. Breakfast is served 8am-noon. If you are here for lunch (noon-3pm), try their 'baguette du jour' with chips and salad for £5.50. The stylishly furnished accommodation is £85-95 (no discount for single occupancy). Be sure to book ahead if you want to stay here.

From here you can take a **bus** (Newbury & District Bus Nos 6 or 6a) to Newbury, Chievely and East Ilsley; see pp42-5 for further details.

Follow the broad grass track as it starts a slow descent, paralleled on the left by gallops. To a large extent, this is the last of the really exposed and lonely sections of the Ridgeway. The change isn't abrupt, but over the next few miles it will become obvious. After passing the bridleway from Compton that joins the track from the right, you will cross a **concrete bridge** (Map 22). This takes you over the old, and dismantled, railway that was once the Didcot, Newbury and Southampton Junction Railway. It's been closed since 1962 and the strip where the track once lay is now covered by bushes and trees. The section that you cross lies between the old stations of Churn and Compton. This part of the line was opened in 1882 and owing to its course through remote countryside was given the nickname of the 'Desert Line'.

When you arrive at the slightly **staggered crossroads**, at which the left turning heads north to the wonderfully named Aston Tirrold while the right turning heads for the less enticing Greyladies, you should continue straight ahead for a short distance until the track forks. Make sure you are not daydreaming when you reach here as you need to take the less obvious option, a turn to the left. It's an ascending flinty track, closed in by trees, which bends left after about 200m. It is signposted but if you're not paying attention the natural tendency is to carry straight on. Just after you pass **Warren Farm** (Map 23), on your left, there is a path leading off right, down a 1¼-mile/2km track to Aldworth.

ALDWORTH

The main reason why you might like to detour to this quiet village is to visit *The Bell* (☎ 01635 578272; food Tue-Sat 11am-2.30pm & 6-9pm, Sun noon-2.30pm & 7-9pm). No doubt about it, this is a real country pub. The building dates back to the 15th century and the pub has been in the same family for over 200 years. Take note that the pub is closed in the afternoons (3-6pm) and on Mondays, except Bank Holidays lunchtime only.

A wide selection of filled rolls and ploughman's is served to go with a choice of varied and interesting real ales and farmhouse cider. By the way, in case you need any more encouragement, it's been voted CAMRA (see box pp16-17) 'National Pub of the Year' twice, won the regional award

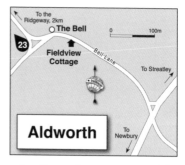

various times and even won an award for being 'the most unspoilt pub in England'. Its high regard amongst real ale drinkers means that it's often very busy despite its quiet location.

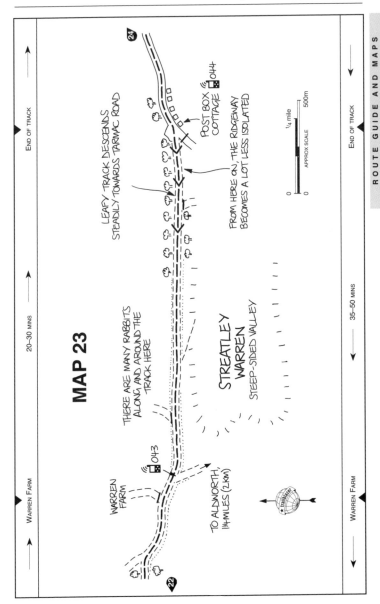

MAP 23

WARREN FARM | 20-30 MINS | END OF TRACK

THERE ARE MANY RABBITS ALONG AND AROUND THE TRACK HERE

WARREN FARM

043

TO ALDWORTH, 1¼ MILES (2km)

LEAFY TRACK DESCENDS STEADILY TOWARDS TARMAC ROAD

STREATLEY WARREN
STEEP-SIDED VALLEY

POST BOX
COTTAGE 044

FROM HERE ON, THE RIDGEWAY BECOMES A LOT LESS ISOLATED

0 ¼ mile
0 APPROX SCALE 500m

WARREN FARM | 35-50 MINS | END OF TRACK

There is no shop, post office or public transport here but if needs be you can stay at the comfortable and quiet *Fieldview Cottage* (☎ 01635 578964, 🖳 haroldhunt@ btinternet.com; 1S/1D/1T, private bath-room, 🗖). The friendly couple who own this place charge £35pp for B&B. So that guests can have a private bathroom only two rooms are let out at the same time unless they are part of a group.

When you arrive at the sealed road by **Post Box Cottage** you have reached the beginning of a new type of Ridgeway. No more windswept wanderings up on grassy tracks 20 metres wide without a building in sight. For the next few miles at least, things are positively urban. You might welcome it after the previous stages, but it certainly lacks a lot of the wild feel. It's picturesque along this road, with each house having its own individuality; this helps to take your mind off the long walk on the tarmac. The final sure symbol that you are about to leave all the tranquillity behind are the 30mph speed limit signs and from here on there are houses on both sides of the road. Just 100m further on you'll come to a T-junction where you join the A417 into the centre of Streatley.

STREATLEY   [MAP 24]

This West Berkshire village is now very much smaller than its neighbour, Goring (see pp132-3), across the river in Oxfordshire, but historically it was the larger of the two. Both places were mentioned in the *Domesday Book* with Streatley being valued higher than its neighbour. Even up until the early 19th century it was larger owing to its location on the road to Reading. For shops, restaurants and other services you should head across the bridge to Goring, just a couple of minutes' walk away. Thames Travel's No 133 and Heyfordian's Nos 134/135 stop here; see pp42-5 for further details.

Where to stay, eat and drink

YHA Streatley (☎ 0845 371 9044, 🖳 www. yha.org.uk; 48 beds – 1T, 3 quads, 2 five beds, 4 six beds) is the main reason to stay in Streatley, rather than in Goring. The hostel is in a large white, Victorian house, just off the road. They provide cooked meals and packed lunches, and have a self-catering kitchen. It's £18.40pp in a dormitory; family rooms cost £30-90 depending on the number of people and time of year.

Other accommodation options include *The Bull* (☎ 01491 872392, 🖳 www.the bullatstreatley.com; 5D/1D, T or F, all en suite, 🗖; 🐾; food Mon-Sat noon-2pm & 6.30-9pm, Sun noon-2pm & 7-8.30pm), a 15th-century former coaching inn where

the spacious bar, closed 3-6pm except summer Sat and Sun, has a relaxed atmosphere. The restaurant here serves a wide variety of food that gets consistently good reviews; the Bull Pie (£8.55) is recommended. The accommodation is in a separate building; B&B costs £75-100 with no discount for single occupancy.

B&B at *3 Icknield Cottages* (☎ 01491 875152; 1S, private bathroom, 🗖) is very good value (£30) if you are walking on your own; it has a good location too. Packed lunches are available on request.

Just before crossing the river to Goring is *The Swan* (Map 25; ☎ 01491 878800, 🖳 www.swanatstreatley.co.uk; 9S/36D or T, all en suite, 🗖; 🐾 £15; restaurant daily 12.30-2.30pm & 6-10pm), an up-market riverside pub/restaurant/hotel. It is right on the bank of the Thames and boasts a spacious riverside terrace: an ideal spot for a break during a long day of walking. Food is available all day in the bar; the 'terrace' menu (available 12.30-2pm & 6-10pm) includes a range of sandwiches (£6.50-11) and dishes such as grilled red mullet (£12). In the afternoon (daily 3-6pm) they serve a traditional cream tea (£9) or a full tea including sandwiches and cakes for £16. A three-course Sunday lunch is from £26.95.

B&B costs £125-200 per night for two sharing and around £115 for a single room.

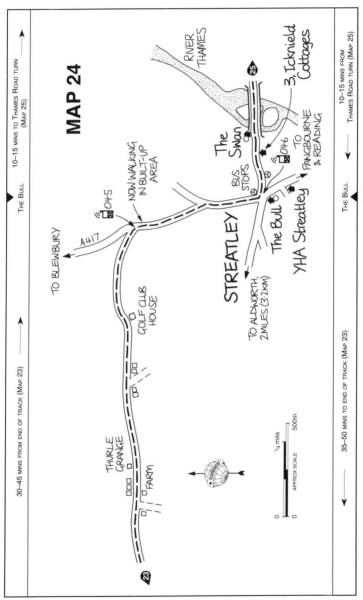

Just a short walk across the double-span bridge from the village of Streatley is the town of Goring where you'll find pretty much everything you could need.

GORING   [MAP 25]

After the Great Western Railway came through here in 1840, the town started to grow larger than its neighbour, Streatley. This growth has continued and as a result nearly all the shops, restaurants and services are located on this side of the river.

Services

There's a Lloyds TSB on the High St, but it doesn't have an ATM. At the time of writing, the HSBC had closed, but the **ATM** remained in operation as the only one in the town. On the High St you'll also find a **chemist** (Mon-Fri 9am-5.30pm, Sat 9am-5pm), **newsagent** (Mon-Sat 6am-10pm, Sun 7am-10pm) which sells most groceries and also houses the **post office** (Mon-Fri 9am-1pm & 2-5.30pm, Sat 9am-12.30pm) and a **grocery** (Mon-Fri 9am-5pm, Sat 8.30am-5pm) which has an interesting selection of locally produced food. The **library** (☎ 01491 873028 ; Mon 9.30am-12.30pm, Tue 9.30am-12.30pm & 2-7pm, Thur & Fri 9.30am-12.30pm & 2-5pm, Sat 9.30am-1pm) has free **internet** access; **tourist information** (☎ 01491 873565, 🖳 www.goring-gap.co.uk, 🖳 goring.info. office@talktalk.net; Easter-Sep Mon-Sat 10am-noon, Oct to Easter Mon-Fri only) is available from the information office in the Community Centre on Station Rd. The office has a lot of leaflets about the area but staff are not able to do accommodation booking, nor do they sell maps or books.

There is also a bicycle shop on the High St called **Trailjunkies** (☎ 01491 871721, 🖳 www.trailjunkies.com; Mon-Fri 9am-6pm, Sat 9am-5.30pm) should you need spares or repairs.

There are **buses** from the railway station to Wallingford via South Stoke and North Stoke (Heyfordian's Nos 134/135) and also to Pangbourne and Reading on Thames Travel's No 133; see pp42-5 for further details. See box p39 for details of **rail** services to Goring & Streatley.

If you need a **taxi** you could try Pangbourne Taxis (☎ 01491 671979); they

are very helpful, but try to book well in advance.

Where to stay

There are two recommended B&Bs: the first is *Melrose Cottage* (☎ 01491 873040, 🖳 rosemary@howarth08.wanadoo.co.uk; 1S/2T, shared bathroom, ▢), a 10-minute walk from the town centre. It is £60 for two sharing and the single costs £35. They also provide packed lunches for £4. Walk straight up Wallingford Rd, looking out for Milldown Rd on your right, but be careful not to confuse this with Milldown Avenue, also on your right. The B&B is at No 36, pretty much at the far end of the road, again on your right. The other, *Southview House* (☎ 01491 872184, ☎ 07957 571620, ☎ 07917 020737, 🖳 goringbnb@rglroberts.com; 1D/1D or T, shared shower room), is at the end of Farm Rd, just a few minutes' walk from the town centre. B&B costs £70-75 (£55-60 for single occupancy). The house was refurbished in 2011 and the friendly owners can supply packed lunches and help with baggage transfers.

You can also stay at one of the inns in town such as *The Miller of Mansfield* (☎ 01491 872829, 🖳 www.millerofmansfield. com; 1S or D/9D/1D or T/2D, T or F, all en suite, ▢; 🐾 deposit required). This lovely 18th-century building, situated right in the town centre, has a collection of striking, individually styled rooms with B&B for £80-175 (single occupancy from £70).

The John Barleycorn (☎ 01491 872509, 🖳 www.thejohnbarleycornpub. co.uk; 3D, all en suite, ▢) is a welcoming place to stay just two minutes' walk from the centre. B&B in the comfortable rooms costs £75-85 (£75 for single occupancy).

Where to eat and drink

If you're in one of the inns enjoying a drink anyway, you could try eating there. *The Miller of Mansfield* (see Where to stay; bar daily all day, food daily noon-9.30pm) serves bar meals (£4.95-11.95) and also has

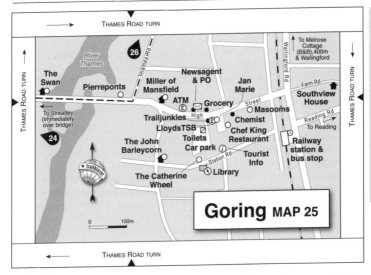

Goring MAP 25

a separate restaurant (daily noon-2.30pm & 6-9.30pm); their interesting menu comprises dishes from around Europe and main courses cost £12.95-18.95. *The John Barleycorn* (see Where to stay; bar daily 11am-11pm, food Mon-Sat noon-2pm & 6.30-9pm, Sun noon-2pm) has a more traditional-style menu with soup and bread (£4.25), beefsteak and ale pie (£9.95), and ham, egg and chips (£9.95). One minute further along the road is *The Catherine Wheel* (☎ 01491 872379, 🖳 www.thecatherinewheelgoring.co.uk; food Mon-Thur noon-3pm & 6-9.30pm, Fri & Sat noon-9.30pm, Sun noon-8pm). This welcoming place is open all day and is probably the most traditional of the pubs in town, serving Brakspear's ales and generous portions of home-cooked food. The baguettes (Mon-Sat only; from £6.10) are ideal for a quick lunch. The menu also includes fish & chips (£11.25) and pies (£10.80-12.50). Booking for an evening meal is recommended.

For lunch or snacks you could try the cheap and cheerful *Jan Marie* (☎ 01491 874264; Mon-Fri 8am-5pm, Sat 9am-3pm), a small café in the centre of town serving cakes, sandwiches and drinks. Alternatively, just before the bridge is *Pierreponts* (☎ 01491 874464; Tue-Fri 8am-4pm, Sat 9am-5pm, Sun 10am-4pm) serving breakfast, lunch and afternoon tea. Their home-made cakes are delicious.

Chef King Restaurant (☎ 01491 872485; daily noon-2pm & 5.30-11pm), in the arcade next to Jan Marie café, is a Chinese restaurant/takeaway; the menu has all the dishes you'd expect, most for around £5-7. *Masooms* (☎ 01491 875078; Sat-Thur noon-2.30pm & daily 5.30-11pm), an Indian restaurant on the High St, has a mouth-watering and varied menu; most main courses cost between £8 and £14. The selection of fish curries is worth a look: the red mullet *biraan* is especially good.

GORING TO WATLINGTON

[MAPS 25-33]

Overview

This stretch of the Ridgeway totals **14½ miles/23km (6½-9hrs)** and is very enjoyable, especially after the previous sections. From the twin towns of

Streatley and Goring the path is easy and follows the Thames for around 5½ miles/9km, sometimes right on its bank, passing through the charming villages of South and North Stoke. Where the path turns east you can head into Wallingford or keep on the Ridgeway, heading along Grim's Ditch (see box p142) for several miles before emerging at Nuffield.

One of the most bizarre sections of the Ridgeway is here – a walk across a golf course – after which you head into woodlands and across open fields for the section to Watlington, passing through Ewelme Park Estate.

Route

Soon after you've crossed the bridge into Goring you need to take a left turn on to Thames Rd. There is a 'Ridgeway' sign on the fence here but it's still possible to miss this turning if you're not looking for it.

You will now be walking parallel to the Thames but won't be able to see it just yet. The Ridgeway follows a succession of roads and paths behind gardens as it gradually gets closer to and level with the Thames. Along here you'll pass a turning down to *The Leatherne Bottel* (Map 26; ☎ 01491 872667, 🖳 www. leathernebottel.co.uk; food Mon-Sat noon-2.15pm & 7-9pm, Sun noon-2.30pm), a riverside restaurant. It's a deservedly popular place serving high-quality food either on the terrace by the river bank or inside the restaurant itself. They offer a set menu (Mon-Sat lunch £15.95/19.50 for two/three courses, Mon-Thur evening two/three courses £19.50/25.50) as well as an à la carte (main courses around £21) and a tasting menu. Booking is recommended. The dress code is smart casual.

Further along the path you veer away from the busy rail line and head diagonally across an open field, towards the village of South Stoke.

SOUTH STOKE   [MAP 26]

This is yet another attractive village on the route. The Ridgeway path follows 'The Street' through the village, lined with a real variety of old, new and renovated houses. You'll pass a primary school and a church, **St Andrew's**, but there are no shops.

The Goring to Wallingford **bus** (Heyfordian's Nos 134/135) stops on the main B4009 road just outside the village; see pp42-5 for further details.

The main place of interest to walkers will be *The Perch & Pike* (☎ 01491 872415, 🖳 www.perchandpike.co.uk; 3D/1T, all en suite, 🛇; bar Mon-Fri 11am-3pm & 5.30-11pm, Sat & Sun 11am-11pm; food Mon-Sat noon-2.30pm & 7-9pm, Sun noon-2.30pm), which is an excellent example of a rare phenomenon – a pub actually on the Ridgeway! For this reason it's a popular stop for many walkers and they are made more than welcome by the owners.

The pub itself is a 17th-century coaching inn that has been tastefully refurbished and has open log fires in the colder months. They serve Brakspear ales, stock a select wine list and have both a lunchtime and a dinner menu. The menus change regularly but may include breast of duck bigarade (£11.65) and parcel of Nile perch (£9.85). The rooms are in a restored barn and cost from £85 per night; there is no discount for single occupancy. One of the rooms even has a Jacuzzi – just the thing after a long day's walk!

The other accommodation option is *The Old Post Office* (☎ 01491 871872, 🖳 www.oakbarn.org; 1D, en suite shower); it has a wonderful self-contained apartment with a sitting area, internet and tea-/coffee-making facilities) in a converted oak barn. B&B costs £50/80 for one/two people.

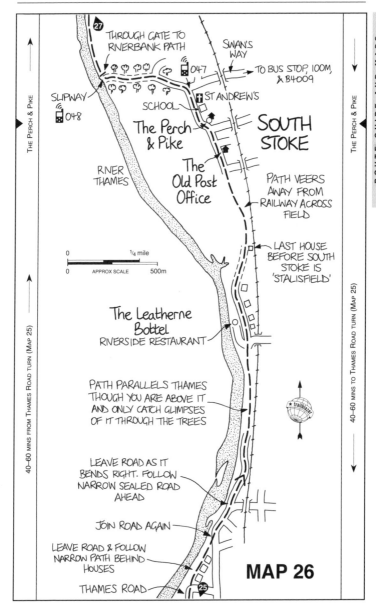

27

THROUGH GATE TO RIVERBANK PATH

SWAN'S WAY

047

TO BUS STOP, 100M, & B4009

SLIPWAY

048

St ANDREW'S

SCHOOL

SOUTH STOKE

The Perch & Pike

RIVER THAMES

The Old Post Office

PATH VEERS AWAY FROM RAILWAY ACROSS FIELD

LAST HOUSE BEFORE SOUTH STOKE IS 'STALISFIELD'

0 — 1/4 mile

0 — 500m
APPROX SCALE

The Leatherne Bottel
RIVERSIDE RESTAURANT

THE PERCH & PIKE

THE PERCH & PIKE

PATH PARALLELS THAMES THOUGH YOU ARE ABOVE IT AND ONLY CATCH GLIMPSES OF IT THROUGH THE TREES

★ trailblazer

LEAVE ROAD AS IT BENDS RIGHT. FOLLOW NARROW SEALED ROAD AHEAD

40–60 MINS FROM THAMES ROAD TURN (MAP 25)

40–60 MINS TO THAMES ROAD TURN (MAP 25)

JOIN ROAD AGAIN

LEAVE ROAD & FOLLOW NARROW PATH BEHIND HOUSES

MAP 26

THAMES ROAD

25

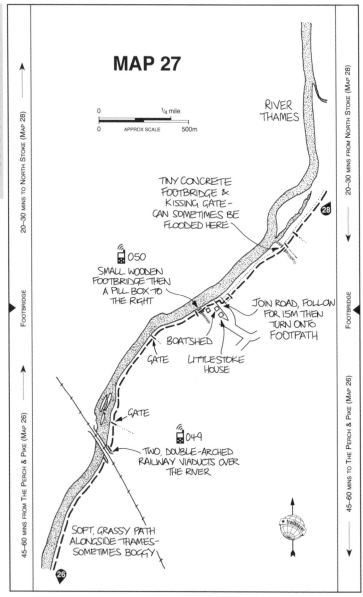

ROUTE GUIDE AND MAPS

MAP 27

0   ¼ mile

0   APPROX SCALE   500m

RIVER THAMES

20–30 MINS TO NORTH STOKE (MAP 28)

20–30 MINS FROM NORTH STOKE (MAP 28)

FOOTBRIDGE

FOOTBRIDGE

45–60 MINS FROM THE PERCH & PIKE (MAP 26)

45–60 MINS TO THE PERCH & PIKE (MAP 26)

TINY CONCRETE FOOTBRIDGE & KISSING GATE – CAN SOMETIMES BE FLOODED HERE

28

050

SMALL WOODEN FOOTBRIDGE THEN A PILL BOX TO THE RIGHT

JOIN ROAD, FOLLOW FOR 15M THEN TURN ONTO FOOTPATH

BOATSHED

GATE

LITTLESTOKE HOUSE

GATE

049

TWO, DOUBLE-ARCHED RAILWAY VIADUCTS OVER THE RIVER

★ trailblazer

SOFT, GRASSY PATH ALONGSIDE THAMES – SOMETIMES BOGGY

26

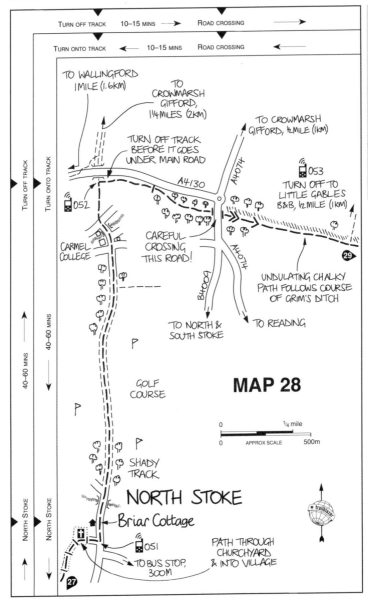

TURN OFF TRACK   10–15 MINS ⟶   ROAD CROSSING   ⟶

TURN ONTO TRACK   ⟵   10–15 MINS   ROAD CROSSING   ⟵

TO WALLINGFORD 1 MILE (1.6KM)

TO CROWMARSH GIFFORD, 1¼ MILES (2KM)

TO CROWMARSH GIFFORD, ½ MILE (1KM)

TURN OFF TRACK BEFORE IT GOES UNDER MAIN ROAD

A4130

053
TURN OFF TO LITTLE GABLES B&B, ½ MILE (1KM)

052

A4074

CARMEL COLLEGE

CAREFUL CROSSING THIS ROAD!

B4009

29

UNDULATING CHALKY PATH FOLLOWS COURSE OF GRIM'S DITCH

A4074

TO NORTH & SOUTH STOKE

TO READING

TURN OFF TRACK

TURN ONTO TRACK

40–60 MINS

40–60 MINS

P

GOLF COURSE

MAP 28

0   ¼ mile
0   APPROX SCALE   500m

P

P

P

SHADY TRACK

NORTH STOKE

Briar Cottage

051

PATH THROUGH CHURCHYARD & INTO VILLAGE

TO BUS STOP, 300M

27

NORTH STOKE

NORTH STOKE

At the end of 'The Street' the Ridgeway branches left and Swan's Way turns right. Swan's Way is a 65-mile (105km), long-distance bridlepath starting in Salcey Forest, on the border with Northamptonshire and finishing at Goring. The Ridgeway crosses it on numerous occasions up ahead.

After leaving South Stoke and following the Thames you'll come to the low, wide **viaduct** (Map 27) that carries the railway over the Thames. From a distance it looks like a standard four-arched viaduct with flattened elliptical arches, as opposed to the semi-circular ones more favoured at the time of its construction. It's only when you get fairly close, and even right under the viaduct, that you see it is really something special. It's not a single viaduct, but two viaducts, built alongside each other with a narrow gap between them. You'll also see that the viaducts are heavily skewed as they cross the Thames on an angle. The red Berkshire brickwork is another interesting feature as the bricks are laid diagonally as opposed to horizontally. The visual effect of this, combined with the skewing of the viaduct, creates a sort of optical illusion as you stand under the arches following the lines of bricks with your eyes. The path keeps alongside the Thames until it reaches **North Stoke** village, after which it starts to turn away from the river.

NORTH STOKE   [MAP 28, p137]

You arrive in this village via the grounds of the 14th-century **church**, the main building of which remains largely unaltered since its construction. Even some of the original stained glass remains in the windows. Once you've had a look at it there isn't much else to do here; the village is much smaller than South Stoke and there are no facilities for the walker. However, *Briar Cottage* (☎

01491 835833, ▭ richardzazie@btinternet. com; 1D, en suite; ✦) offers B&B for £65 (single occupancy £40). It's certainly a peaceful place to spend the night. Evening meals and packed lunches are available if requested in advance.

Heyfordian's Nos 134/135 **bus** service stops on the main B4009 road just outside the village; see pp42-5 for further details.

When you reach the busy A4130 the Ridgeway branches off right, but if you want to visit Wallingford or Crowmarsh Gifford you should continue on the bridleway that goes under the A4130. If heading for Wallingford, soon after you walk under the A4130 take the path on your left to lead you back up onto the road itself. Then follow the road bridge across the River Thames and descend from the bridge to the riverside path which leads straight to Wallingford (1 mile/1.6km). To reach Crowmarsh Gifford from Wallingford you'll have to walk across the **19-arch stone bridge** crossing the Thames. Believe it or not this was the main road crossing of the Thames in this area until the A4130 bypass and new bridge were opened in 1993.

If heading directly for Crowmarsh Gifford (1¼ miles/2km) stay on the bridleway after going under the A4130. The bridleway turns into a road and you pass a farm on your left. On a curve in the road there is a footpath turning off to your left. Take this and stay on it to Crowmarsh Gifford. Alternatively, stay on the Ridgeway for another 500m and then walk to Crowmarsh Gifford on the A4074, though this is a less pleasant route.

WALLINGFORD [see map p141]

This is the largest town you will have come across 'on' the Ridgeway so far which might merit a visit, especially if you need to stock up, or just take some time out.

This historically important town was established by King Alfred in the 10th century and later a fortified castle was built here by William the Conqueror who arrived after the Battle of Hastings in 1066.

The fortifications were added to over the years until it became one of the most important castles in England and remained so for several centuries. It was, however, completely destroyed on the orders of Oliver Cromwell in 1652. You can still visit the **Castle Gardens**, the site of the castle, to the north of town, but there is virtually no evidence of the castle itself.

Although the railway was closed to passengers in 1959, it has since reopened as the **Cholsey and Wallingford Railway**, linking Wallingford, via the old GWR branch line to Cholsey, and the national rail network. Trains run on various weekends and bank holidays during the year and are sometimes pulled by a steam engine. For more information call ☎ 01491 835067 (24-hour recorded message), or go to the railway's website: 🖳 www.cholsey-walling ford-railway.com.

Wallingford Museum (☎ 01491 835065, 🖳 www.wallingfordmuseum.org. uk; Mar-Nov Tue-Fri 2-5pm, Sat 10.30am-5pm, June-Aug Sun 2-5pm; £4 adults, children free if with an adult) traces the history of the town from its Saxon roots to the present day. Agatha Christie lived in the Wallingford area for over 40 years and a new exhibition includes details about her life and her books as well as some of her original letters.

Services

There is a **tourist information centre** (TIC; ☎ 01491 826972, 🖳 wallingfordtic@ btconnect.com; Mon-Fri 10am-12.30pm & 1.30-4pm, Sat 10am-2pm) in the Town Hall, built in 1670. The staff here are helpful and there is a huge amount of information for walkers in the form of free leaflets. They also have some information about accommodation but cannot do bookings.

On the High St the **library** (☎ 01491 837395; Mon, Tue & Fri 9.30am-5.30pm, Thur 9.30am-7pm, Sat 9.30am-1pm) has free **internet access**. The **post office** (Mon-Sat 9am-5.30pm) is on Market Place. On St Mary's St Nationwide, Lloyds TSB and Barclays have **ATMs** as does the NatWest on the High St.

There is a **Lloyds Pharmacy** (Mon-Fri 9am-6pm, Sat 9am-5.30pm) and a branch of **Boots** chemists (Mon-Sat 9am-5.30pm) on Market Place and a **laundrette** (daily 9am-4pm) on the High St. If you need bicycle repairs try **Rides on Air** (☎ 01491 836289, 🖳 www.ridesonair.com; Mon-Fri 9am-5.30pm, Sat 9am-5pm) on St Martin's St. There is a large Waitrose **supermarket** (Mon-Sat 8am-8pm, Sun 10am-4pm) on the corner of St Martin's St and the High St; you'll also find **public toilets** here. There are more public toilets in the car park. There is also a monthly **farmers' market** (see box p15).

Heyfordian's Nos 134/135 **buses** go to Goring via North Stoke and South Stoke; Thames Travel's No 130 operates to Didcot Parkway Railway Station; the No 139 to Huntercombe (Nuffield); and the X39 and X40 to Oxford and Reading. Check you are waiting at the correct bus stop. See pp42-5 for further details. There is a **taxi** rank next to the Town Hall. Hills Taxis (☎ 01491 837022) is also an established local firm.

Where to stay

Right in the centre of the town you could try *The Dolphin* (☎ 01491 837377, 🖳 www. thedolphinwallingford.co.uk; 2T, shared bathroom, ☐) which has accommodation above the pub: it's handy for a drink, but isn't the most peaceful place to stay. B&B costs £60-70 (from £45 if you're on your own) and a hearty breakfast is served downstairs from 8am onwards (see p140).

The *George Hotel* (☎ 01491 836665, 🖳 www.george-hotel-wallingford.com; 9S/19D/2D or F, all en suite, ☐) is a large, upmarket place with a central location. The hotel is in a 16th-century building also incorporating a 'tavern' and a separate restaurant and bar called Wealh's (see p140).

If you can afford the prices, you'll certainly be very comfortable: the rooms start from £110 for two sharing; the singles are from £90. Breakfast is an extra £12.75pp.

Just a couple of minutes' walk from the town centre, at 18 Wood St, is *Huntington House* (☎ 01491 839201, 🖥 www.huntington-house.co.uk; 1S/1D/1D or T; ▢). This friendly place charges from £60 for two sharing and from £45 for the single room. The single room has an en suite toilet and all the rooms share a bathroom.

Where to eat and drink
There are plenty of places to eat in Wallingford and lots of variety, too. All the places listed below are in or around the town centre.

For a quick pizza you could try *The Pizza Café* (daily 10am-2.30pm, Mon-Thur 5.30-10.30pm, Fri & Sat 5.30-11pm), on St Mary's St, which has a large range of pizzas (£6-11) for such a small place. The chain restaurant, *Pizza Express* (☎ 01491 833431; Sun-Thur noon-10.30pm, Fri & Sat noon-11pm) is also on St Mary's St and dishes up various pizzas and pastas for slightly higher prices.

San Sicario (☎ 01491 834078; Mon 6.30-10pm, Tue-Sat 11am-2pm & 6.30-10pm) has been serving pizzas, pasta, risotto and salads for over 20 years. It looks tiny from the outside but has a large dining room seating up to 50 people upstairs. There is another good Italian on the High St: *Avanti* (☎ 01491 835500; Mon-Sat 12.15-2.30pm & 6-10.30pm) serves a range of pasta dishes (£6.50-9.50), plus all the usual pizzas and fresh seafood too.

On the Market Place *The Old Post Office* (☎ 01491 836068, 🖥 www.opowall ingford.co.uk; Mon-Sat 9am-midnight, Sun 9am-11pm) is described as 'a modern interpretation of an original public house'. Food is served all day, starting with cooked breakfasts (9am-noon; £5.40-7.50) and finishing with evening meals such as swordfish steak (£14.95) and duck breast (£16.95).

The best Indian restaurant in town, *Anokhi* (Mon-Sat noon-2.30pm & 5.30-11.30pm, except Fri lunch, Sun noon-3pm & 5.30-11.30pm) is on the High St. They

have an extensive choice of house specialities (£5.95-12.95). Just past Anokhi is *Delhi Brasserie* (Mon-Sat noon-2pm & 5.30-11.30pm, Sun noon-11.30pm). Alternatively try *Wallingford Tandoori* (Mon-Sat noon-2pm & 5.30-11.30pm, Sun noon-11.30pm) which has a standard menu and prices to match.

The only Thai restaurant in Wallingford is *Thai Corner* (Mon-Sat 5.30-11pm); it has an extensive and tasty menu and most main courses cost £6-11.

Hong Kong House (Sun-Thur 5.30-11pm, Fri & Sat 5-11.45pm) and *Welcome Chinese Food* (Sun-Thur 4.30-11.30pm, Fri & Sat noon-1.15pm & 4.30-11.30pm) are both standard Chinese takeaways but you can eat in at *Beijing Diner* (Mon-Thur 6-11pm, Fri-Sun noon-2.30pm & 6-11pm) at the southern end of St Mary's St. Although the menu is fairly standard they do have plenty of vegetarian options and even an indoor fish pond and water feature!

Fast-food options in Wallingford include *Smart's Fish & Chips* (Mon-Sat 11.30am-2pm & 4.30m-11pm, Sun 4-10pm), on the High St, and *USA Chicken & Pizza* (daily noon-11pm), on St Martin's St.

Plenty of pubs here serve food. If the weather is good you should visit the *Coach & Horses* (☎ 01491 825054; food daily noon-2pm, Mon & Wed-Sat 7-9pm) that faces out onto a large grassy park. The food here is good and includes a large ploughman's. They serve a range of cask ales. *The Dolphin* (see Where to stay; food Mon 8am-7pm Tue-Thur 8am-9pm, Fri & Sat 8am-7pm, Sun 8am-2m), nearer the centre of town, has Greene King ales though only has a standard bar menu. From 8am to noon they serve 'full English' breakfasts for £5.75. *The Boathouse* (☎ 01491 834100; food daily noon-9pm) has a large patio area for dining, right on the bank of the Thames. Although the menu is standard pub food it is done well. It can get quite noisy at weekends as they sometimes have live music in the evenings, but you can always sit outside if the weather is warm enough.

Wealh's (food daily 6-9pm, Sun noon-2.30pm) in George Hotel (see Where to

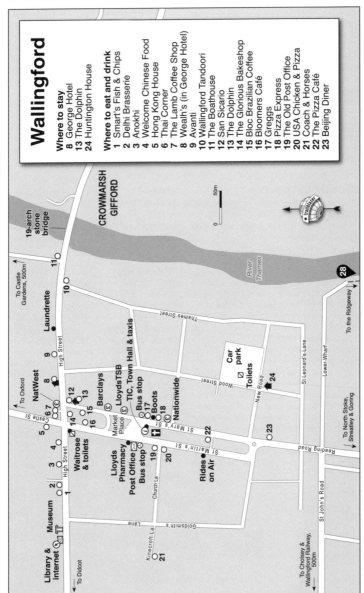

Wallingford

Where to stay
8 George Hotel
13 The Dolphin
24 Huntington House

Where to eat and drink
1 Smart's Fish & Chips
2 Delhi Brasserie
3 Anokhi
4 Welcome Chinese Food
5 Hong Kong House
6 Thai Corner
7 The Lamb Coffee Shop
8 Wealh's (in George Hotel)
9 Avanti
10 Wallingford Tandoori
11 The Boathouse
12 San Sicario
13 The Dolphin
14 The Glorious Bakeshop
15 Bloc Brazilian Coffee
16 Bloomers Café
17 Greggs
18 Pizza Express
19 The Old Post Office
20 USA Chicken & Pizza
21 Coach & Horses
22 The Pizza Café
23 Beijing Diner

stay), has a lovely outdoor eating area in the hotel courtyard; main courses here are £8-15 and may include chicken ballantine (£10.95) and Suffolk pork belly (£12.95).

For lunch you might like to have a look in *The Lamb Coffee Shop* (☎ 01491 826287, 💻 www.thelambcoffeeshop.co.uk; Mon-Sat 9am-4.30pm), tucked away in Lamb Arcade. A full English breakfast costs £6.60 but it is less if you have fewer items; the menu also includes toasted paninis (£5.15-5.35), ham, egg & chips (£7.15) as well as a range of home-made cakes.

For a cup of tea and a fancy cake there is *The Glorious Bakeshop* (☎ 01491 826536; Tue-Thur & Sat 10am-5pm, Fri 9.30am-4.30pm), or if you'd prefer a coffee, head round the corner to *Bloc Brazilian Coffee* (☎ 01491 824256; Mon-Thur 8am-5pm, Fri to 5.30pm, Sat 9am-6pm, Sun 10am-4.30pm).

Bloomers Café (☎ 01491 825465; Mon-Fri 8.30am-4.30pm, Sat 8.30am-5.30pm, Sun 10am-4pm) is a pleasant café that serves a wide range of filling baguettes, sandwiches and rolls from £2.95. *Greggs* (Mon-Sat 8am-5pm) has similar offerings.

CROWMARSH GIFFORD

This town has now become an extension of Wallingford. It's separated from its larger neighbour only by the bridge and, to be honest, most shops and services are located on the other side of the bridge in Wallingford. There are, however, two campsites and a B&B here and it's easy to walk into Wallingford should you need to.

The main claim to fame for this place is that **Jethro Tull** lived here. No, not them, but him, the inventor of the seed drill. You can still see his house on The Street where he lived from 1700 to 1710. It's only a couple of minutes' walk from the bridge, but is not open to the public. It's the middle one of the three terraced Tudor houses.

The seed drill was essentially a device that enabled you to plant three rows of seeds at the same time. He also invented other machines in an effort to improve crop yields. At the time his ideas weren't implemented fully but, looking back, he is now recognised as one of the most important figures in the modernisation of farming methods.

Services

There is a well-stocked **shop** (☎ 01491 837176; Mon-Sat 6.30am-7.30pm, Sun 8am-5pm) on The Street. Thames Travel's **bus** Nos 139, X39 and X40 stop here; see pp42-5 for further details.

Where to stay

There are two very good **campsites** here. On the right as you walk in from the Ridgeway is *Bridge Villa* (☎ 01491 836860, 💻 www.bridgevilla.co.uk; Feb-Dec). They charge £11-13 per night for a tent and two people and advise you to book ahead, especially in the summer months and at weekends. The rate includes use of the toilet and shower facilities. On the banks of the Thames *Riverside Park* (☎ 01491 835232; late May to early Sep) is a very well-run campsite, with heated open-air swimming pools (£2.10; daily 11am-6pm). There are 18 pitches (£13-16 per night per tent) and toilet/shower facilities. It can get busy so you are advised to book ahead.

You could try the excellent B&B at *Little Gables* (☎ 01491 837834, 💻 www.

❑ Grim's ditches

There are many Grim's ditches in England. The reason is that Grim is the Anglo-Saxon word for the devil and his name was often attributed to unnatural features in the landscape. This particular Grim's ditch (see Map 28, p137, but also Map 29 (p144) & Map 30 (p145) was probably built during the Iron Age, probably to mark a boundary as it's not big enough to be a defensive earthwork. 'Probably' being the operative word, as even now little is known about this stretch.

ROUTE GUIDE AND MAPS

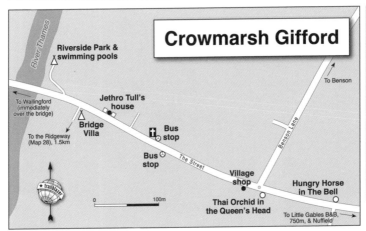

littlegables.co.uk; 1S/1D/2D, T or F; 🐕 £10), at 166 Crowmarsh Hill. The rooms are en suite apart from the toilet for the single room which is separate but next door to the room. Rates are £65/80/105 for a single/double/family room. If arranged in advance they can provide a packed breakfast, a packed lunch (£5-10) and they will also transport your luggage to your next B&B. Little Gables is in a cul-de-sac running parallel to the main road, a couple of hundred metres east of the large roundabout. Although you can walk here from Crowmarsh Gifford, the Ridgeway passes within about half a mile of this place (see Map 28, p137). To get there follow the Grim's ditch and look for a path leading off through a field to your left. Take this path and when it joins a minor road continue on that, in the same direction. You will soon arrive at the cul-de-sac.

Where to eat and drink

There are basically two options but both are places that are part of nationwide chains so the menus are predictable: it just depends whether you prefer standard pub fare or Thai food.

The Bell Inn (☎ 01491 835324; food daily 11am-9pm) on The Street, is a Greene King pub with a Hungry Horse restaurant and lots of facilities – the aim being that it will appeal to anyone who might walk through its doors. The menu is the same in all their branches: burgers with chips, steaks, or vegetable lasagne, but they pride themselves on the large servings and low prices. Most main courses are around £4.50-6, often including a drink. The other place, *Thai Orchid* (☎ 01491 839857; food daily noon-2.30pm & 5.30-10.30pm), in the 13th-century Queen's Head pub, serves authentic Thai food. Since it's part of the group of Thai Orchid restaurants if you've been to one before you'll know what to expect. It's a good idea to go for one of their three-course set meals (between £19.50 and £26.95pp) as they will choose the right dishes to complement each other.

From the junction at the A4130 the section of the Ridgeway almost all the way to Nuffield comprises narrow, undulating paths following the **Grim's ditch** (see box opposite). Sometimes the path is on top of the ditch and sometimes to one side. Most of the way is shaded by trees and you also pass through some attractive woodland. You are much more likely to meet other people, most of whom will be accompanied by a dog or two, on this stretch than on previous ones.

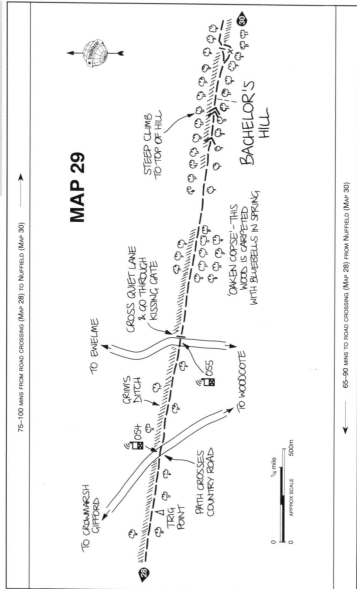

MAP 29

STEEP CLIMB
TO TOP OF HILL

BACHELOR'S
HILL

'OAKEN COPSE' – THIS
WOOD IS CARPETED
WITH BLUEBELLS IN SPRING

CROSS QUIET LANE
& GO THROUGH
KISSING GATE

TO EWELME

GRIM'S
DITCH

054

055

TO WOODCOTE

TO CROWMARSH
GIFFORD

TRIG
POINT

PATH CROSSES
COUNTRY ROAD

¼ mile

APPROX SCALE

500m

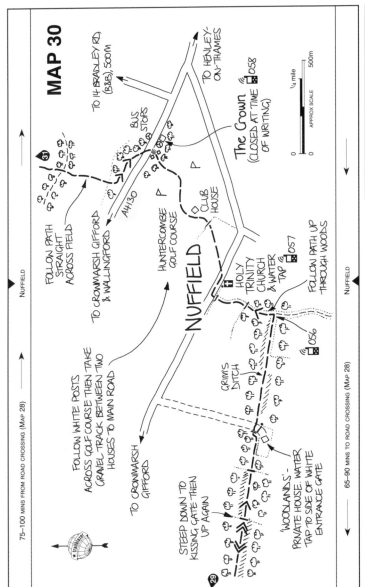

MAP 30

TO 114 BRADLEY RD (B&B), 500M

TO HENLEY-ON-THAMES

058

BUS STOPS

The Crown (CLOSED AT TIME OF WRITING)

FOLLOW PATH STRAIGHT ACROSS FIELD

31

A4130

TO CROWMARSH GIFFORD & WALLINGFORD

HUNTERCOMBE GOLF COURSE

CLUB HOUSE

NUFFIELD

NUFFIELD

057

HOLY TRINITY CHURCH & WATER TAP

FOLLOW PATH UP THROUGH WOODS

FOLLOW WHITE POSTS ACROSS GOLF COURSE THEN TAKE GRAVEL TRACK BETWEEN TWO HOUSES TO MAIN ROAD

056

GRIM'S DITCH

TO CROWMARSH GIFFORD

'WOODLANDS'- PRIVATE HOUSE. WATER TAP TO SIDE OF WHITE ENTRANCE GATE

STEEP DOWN TO KISSING GATE THEN UP AGAIN

29

75-100 MINS FROM ROAD CROSSING (MAP 28)

65-90 MINS TO ROAD CROSSING (MAP 28)

1/4 mile

500m

APPROX SCALE

Several areas of woodland along this section (for example **Oaken Copse**, Map 29) are carpeted with bluebells in the late spring and make for a much-visited and very colourful sight.

Before you can finish this stage you must do something quite unexpected: walk across a golf course. It's called Huntercombe Golf Course (Map 30) and it's in the village of Nuffield. To cross the golf course you'll need to follow the strategically placed wooden posts. You don't skirt round the outside of the course discreetly; you actually have to cross several fairways. Just watch out for the bunkers! Once you've negotiated your way across you enter a small wooded area on a muddy path; this quickly turns into a gravelled track that leads you through a narrow gap between the two houses here, right past their front doors and down their drive. You may feel like a trespasser but this is the correct route. From here, you can see The Crown, the only pub in the village, just a few more steps away. However, sadly at the time of writing it was closed.

NUFFIELD   [MAP 30, p145]

Nuffield is basically a small, quiet village with a church, a pub and a golf course: there is no post office or shop. **Holy Trinity** church, built in 1189, is the final resting place of Viscount William Morris (1877-1963), founder of Morris Motors. He was the Henry Ford of England, starting a mass-production car factory to build the Morris Oxford car.

The Crown was a friendly pub and they were used to Ridgeway walkers dropping in for refreshment but at the time of writing it was closed, though hopefully not for long. The only accommodation is at *14 Bradley Road* (☎ 01491 641359, 🖳 diana

mc@waitrose.com; 2D/1T; 🐾), Hunter-combe Place. B&B costs £30pp; one of the doubles is en suite and the other rooms share facilities. A packed lunch (£2-3) is available if requested in advance; the owner will take guests to Henley-on-Thames for an evening meal if one isn't available in the village. To get here walk past The Crown and take the first left turn. The B&B is at the far end of this road; it's about a ten-minute walk.

Thames Travel's No 139 **bus** (Wallingford to Henley via Crowmarsh Gifford) stops at The Crown (Huntercombe); see pp42-5 for further details.

From The Crown you need to cross the road and head down to where the Ridgeway path disappears into the trees. Once through them you have to walk on a path cutting straight through the middle of a field. In the summer, when the crops are at their highest, the bare trail cutting straight between them can look quite dramatic.

The first buildings you come to after starting from Nuffield are those of the picturesque **Ewelme Park Estate** (Map 31). This estate was formed around 450 years ago from several smaller estates and was an important royal deer park under Henry VIII, Elizabeth I, James I, and Charles I, before being broken up and sold. Nowadays the estate is better known for its pheasants rather than deer, though the finale for both animals is the same. A large cache of Roman coins was also found on the estate, among several other finds in the area. Local schools make trips to the estate to learn about its history and see the archery corridor used by Henry VIII. When you walk through you'll see the beautiful gatehouse and views of the main house itself which, despite its appearance, is

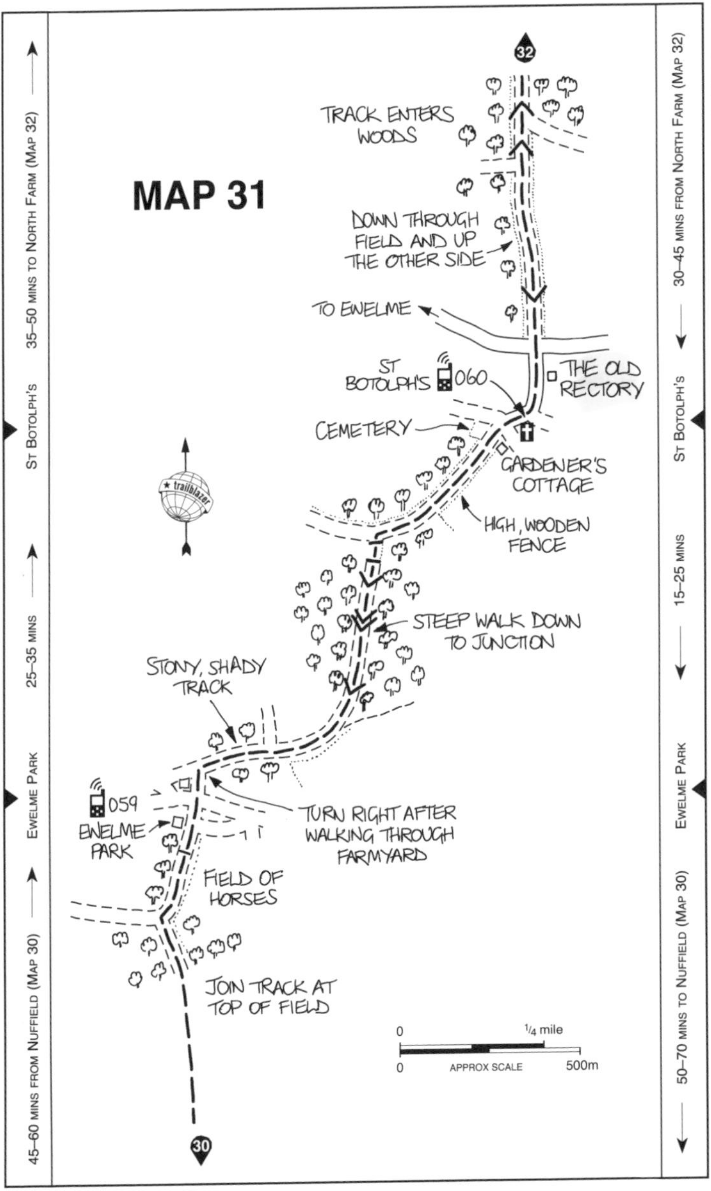

MAP 31

TRACK ENTERS WOODS

DOWN THROUGH FIELD AND UP THE OTHER SIDE

TO EWELME

ST BOTOLPH'S 060

THE OLD RECTORY

CEMETERY

GARDENER'S COTTAGE

HIGH, WOODEN FENCE

STEEP WALK DOWN TO JUNCTION

STONY, SHADY TRACK

059 EWELME PARK

TURN RIGHT AFTER WALKING THROUGH FARMYARD

FIELD OF HORSES

JOIN TRACK AT TOP OF FIELD

trailblazer

32

30

0   ¼ mile

0   APPROX SCALE   500m

35–50 MINS TO NORTH FARM (MAP 32)

ST BOTOLPH'S

25–35 MINS

EWELME PARK

45–60 MINS FROM NUFFIELD (MAP 30)

30–45 MINS FROM NORTH FARM (MAP 32)

ST BOTOLPH'S

15–25 MINS

EWELME PARK

50–70 MINS TO NUFFIELD (MAP 30)

not very old. You may also see some peacocks and will definitely hear several dogs barking, announcing your arrival in the area.

Not much further on is the 11th-century **St Botolph's church**. Considering the remote location it's a large place. The cemetery around the church is full and there is another diagonally across the crossroads. You may recognise the name of the church as it's famous for the carpet of snowdrops that grows around it in early February; so famous, in fact, that there have even been cases of snowdrop-bulb rustling in the churchyard.

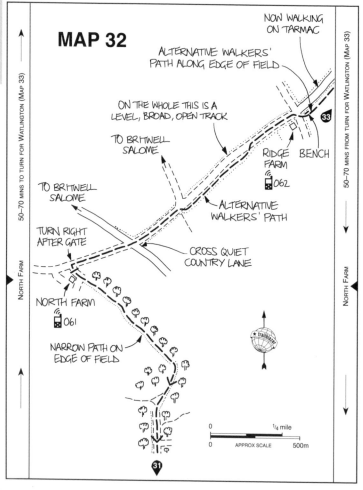

MAP 32

NOW WALKING ON TARMAC

ALTERNATIVE WALKERS' PATH ALONG EDGE OF FIELD

ON THE WHOLE THIS IS A LEVEL, BROAD, OPEN TRACK

TO BRITWELL SALOME

RIDGE FARM
062

BENCH

33

50-70 MINS FROM TURN FOR WATLINGTON (MAP 33)

50-70 MINS TO TURN FOR WATLINGTON (MAP 33)

TO BRITWELL SALOME

ALTERNATIVE WALKERS' PATH

TURN RIGHT AFTER GATE

CROSS QUIET COUNTRY LANE

NORTH FARM
061

NORTH FARM

NORTH FARM

NARROW PATH ON EDGE OF FIELD

0   1/4 mile
0   APPROX SCALE   500m

31

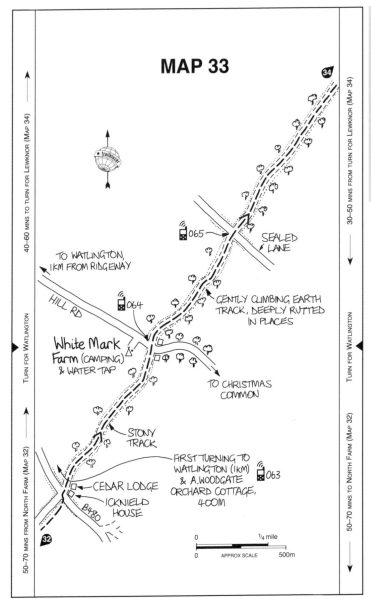

MAP 33

ROUTE GUIDE AND MAPS

34

40–60 MINS TO TURN FOR LEWKNOR (MAP 34)

30–50 MINS FROM TURN FOR LEWKNOR (MAP 34)

065

SEALED LANE

TO WATLINGTON, 1KM FROM RIDGEWAY

HILL RD

064

GENTLY CLIMBING EARTH TRACK, DEEPLY RUTTED IN PLACES

TURN FOR WATLINGTON

TURN FOR WATLINGTON

White Mark Farm (CAMPING) & WATER TAP

TO CHRISTMAS COMMON

STONY TRACK

50–70 MINS FROM NORTH FARM (MAP 32)

FIRST TURNING TO WATLINGTON (1KM) & A. WOODGATE ORCHARD COTTAGE, 400M

063

CEDAR LODGE

ICKNIELD HOUSE

B480

32

0   ¼ mile

0   APPROX SCALE   500m

50–70 MINS TO NORTH FARM (MAP 32)

A good couple of hours after leaving Nuffield you'll get to the two turnings (Map 33) for Watlington. If you're heading for the centre of town it matters little which you take, but if aiming for A.Woodgate Orchard Cottage B&B you'll need the first turning and if aiming for White Mark Farm campsite or Carriers Arms (see below for details of all of these) you'll need the second. Either way it's about half a mile/1km into the town.

WATLINGTON

This is officially the smallest town in England. However, some people, the residents of Manningtree in Essex for instance, might like to take issue with this. For the record the royal charter giving town status to Watlington was issued in 1154.

If you are stopping here for the day most services and shops that you'll need are on one of two streets. The town is pleasant enough and has a few interesting old buildings to look at so it might be nice to relax here for an hour or two over lunch.

Services

There's a **post office** (Mon-Fri 9am-5.30pm, Sat 9am-12.30pm) and **Barclays Bank** (Mon-Fri 10am-3pm) on the High St, though the bank doesn't have an ATM; for that you'll have to go to the Co-op **supermarket** (Mon-Sat 6am-10pm, Sun 6am-9pm), on Couching St, where an **ATM** is located just inside the door. Near the Co-op there is a **chemist** (Mon-Fri 9am-1pm & 2-6pm, Sat 9am-1pm) should you need it.

If you need **internet access** head to the **library** (☎ 01491 612241; Mon 2-7pm, Tue 9.30am-12.30pm & 2-5pm, Thur 2-6pm, Fri 9.30am-12.30pm & 2-5.30pm, Sat 9.30am-1pm), on the High St, where it's free of charge (up to an hour) but they recommend booking in advance. There are **public toilets** at the end of the High St.

Thames Travel's No 106 **bus** goes to Oxford from the stops near the library; see pp42-5 for further details.

Where to stay

Close to the Ridgeway is a B&B at *A.Woodgate Orchard Cottage* (☎ 01491 612675, 🖳 ronnieroper@onetel.com; 1D/2T; shared bathroom, 🛋; 🐾 by arrangement). Rates start at £70, or £45 for single occupancy. The owner can provide packed lunches and luggage transport if booked in

advance. Make sure to book well ahead if you want to stay here as it's very popular, especially with walkers. This place is just 400m from the Ridgeway; the easiest way to get here is to leave the path where it crosses the B480. Icknield House is on this junction. Head down the B480 towards Watlington and the B&B is on your right near the restriction signs.

Another good choice would be *The Fat Fox Inn* (☎ 01491 613040, 🖳 www.foxandhounds-inn.co.uk; 4D/4T/1D or F, all en suite, 🛋; 🐾). This is a delightful old pub near the centre of town. The accommodation here is in a tastefully converted coach barn next to the pub and each room is different. B&B for two people sharing is £79-99 (single occupancy is £69 and three in the family room is £85).

Campers should head for *White Mark Farm* (☎ 01491 612295, 🖳 www.whitemarkfarm.co.uk), just a few minutes' walk from the Ridgeway. There are around 50 pitches on this friendly, well-run campsite and they charge £6pp. The rate includes use of the toilet and shower facilities as well as a microwave oven, kettle and fridge. It's no more than 10 minutes to walk to the centre of town from here. Officially they are closed from the end of October to the beginning of March but if you are walking between November and February and would like to camp here contact them.

Where to eat and drink

At lunchtimes you could try the *Bread Bin* (☎ 01491 613061; Mon-Fri 8am-6pm, Sat 9am-5pm, Sun 10am-4pm) sandwich shop on the High St where you can eat in or takeaway. Food is served till 4pm, coffee is available till they close.

On the way into Watlington, from the second turning off the Ridgeway, is the *Carriers Arms* (☎ 01491 613470; bar Sun-Tue 10am-10.30pm, Wed-Sat 10am to mid-

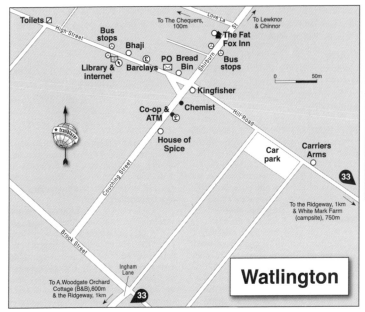

Watlington

night; food Mon-Wed 10am-2pm, Thur-Sat 10am-2pm & 7-9pm, Sun 10am-3pm). Breakfast is served daily till 11.30am and on Sunday they serve a roast from 11.30am-3pm. At other times you can get standard pub grub. This freehouse serves some decent real ales and the location is convenient if you're staying at White Mark Farm Campsite. *The Fat Fox Inn* (see Where to stay; bar daily all day, food daily noon-3pm, Mon-Thur 6.30-9.30pm, Fri & Sat 7-10pm, Sun 7-9pm) offers a more interesting menu which changes regularly and where possible includes locally sourced food; it also serves Brakspear's ales.

The Chequers (☎ 01491 612874, 💻 www.thechequerswatlington.co.uk; bar Sun noon-3pm & 7-10pm, Mon-Sat 11am-3pm & 6-11pm; food Sun & Mon noon-2pm,

Tue-Sat noon-2pm & 7-9pm), a pub on Love Lane, is well known as one of the best places in town for food and it has friendly staff. The menu varies but at lunchtime it may include a sausage and onion baguette (£6.25) and in the evening salmon fillet with lime mayonnaise, new potatoes and vegetables (£10.95).

There are also two Indian restaurants here. At the *House of Spice* (☎ 01491 613552, 💻 www.houseofspice.uk.com; daily noon-2pm & 5.30-11pm), the menu contains all the usual dishes; chicken do-piaza and rice costs £8.50. On the High St is *Bhaji* (☎ 01491 614820; daily 11am-2.30pm & 5.30-10pm) which does much the same thing.

Alternatively *Kingfisher* (☎ 01491 613237; Mon-Sat 11am-2pm & 4-10pm) serves fish & chips and fried chicken.

WATLINGTON TO PRINCES RISBOROUGH   [MAPS 33-39]

Overview

Although this **11-mile/18km (4-5¼hrs)** section of the Ridgeway is pleasant enough, it's fairly uneventful. The walking is easy with few steep sections so you can really slow down, relax and enjoy the scenery. Perhaps take a diversion into Lewknor, Kingston Blount or Chinnor for a drink, or press on and finish early in Princes Risborough.

Route

Continuing on the Ridgeway from the road turn-offs for Watlington it's a long, straight 2¹/₂ miles/4km along shady tracks and through open fields, until you get to the turning for Lewknor. It's about half a mile/0.8km along this minor road to the village.

LEWKNOR   [MAP 34]

Lewknor is a small, picturesque village, much like many others around here. Easy access to the M40, and therefore London, has added to its value on the property market. It's a very quiet place as nearly all the traffic coming through is for the village itself.

The Oxford Tube **bus** stops on the B4009, just off junction 6 of the M40 near Lewknor; see pp40-1 for further details.

At the crossroads in the village, and a good reason to come here, is *Ye Olde Leathern Bottel* (☎ 01844 351482, 🖳 www.theleathernbottle.co.uk; food Mon-Thur noon-2pm & 7-9.30pm, Fri noon-2pm & 6-9.30pm, Sat noon-2.30pm & 6-9.30pm, Sun noon-2.30pm & 7-9.30pm), a pub serving Brakspear ales. It closes in the afternoons, so don't make the trek out here between 2.30pm and 6pm on week-days or 3.30pm and 6pm at weekends. However, when it is open it can get very

busy, especially at weekends, as they don't have a booking policy. You can expect tra-ditional pub food here – sandwiches at lunchtimes and steak and chips, or ham, egg and chips in the evenings. They also have vegetarian options.

Another good reason to visit is for the excellent B&B at *Moorcourt Cottage* (☎ 01844 351419; 1D private bathroom/1T en suite; 🔲). Accommodation in this picture-perfect house is £70, or £45 if you're on your own. The friendly owners will even pick you up from where the Ridgeway joins the road to Lewknor, saving you a fairly tedious stretch of road walking at the end of the day. This is a popular place for walkers to stay so be sure to book well in advance. Packed lunches are available on request, and they will also transport your luggage to your next destination on the Way; a charge is made for both of these.

You'll hear the M40 motorway up ahead long before you see it. There are no two ways about it: this motorway completely dominates the countryside it passes through. The physically elevated status of the M40 at this point only acts to reinforce its dominance over the landscape. Luckily for walkers there is a large tunnel underneath it, albeit without murals, unlike the tunnel under the A34 back near East Ilsley. There was, however, a large pile of horse manure in there last time I passed.

Around 1¹/₂ miles/2.5km after you pass through the tunnel you'll come to a road crossing the path (Map 35). Turn left down this road to get to the village of Kingston Blount, about half a mile/1km away.

KINGSTON BLOUNT [see map p154]

This small village is probably only worth a visit if you're planning to stay for the night. But on the other hand, if you are having an easy day of walking, you could stop at the pub for a long lunch. In times gone by this

place had a number of shops and pubs, a post office, a school and even a telephone exchange, but today just one pub survives. The local people pronounce the 'Blount' part of the village name as 'blunt' – a refer-

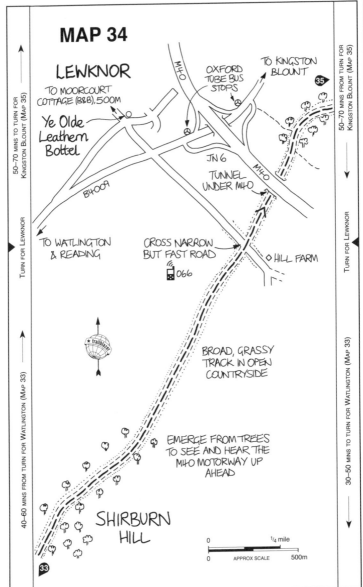

MAP 34

LEWKNOR

TO MOORCOURT
COTTAGE (B&B), 500M

Ye Olde
Leathern
Bottel

B4009

TO WATLINGTON
& READING

MHO

OXFORD
TUBE BUS
STOPS

TO KINGSTON
BLOUNT

35

JN 6

TUNNEL
UNDER MHO

MHO

CROSS NARROW
BUT FAST ROAD
066

◇ HILL FARM

BROAD, GRASSY
TRACK IN OPEN
COUNTRYSIDE

EMERGE FROM TREES
TO SEE AND HEAR THE
MHO MOTORWAY UP
AHEAD

SHIRBURN
HILL

33

50–70 MINS TO TURN FOR KINGSTON BLOUNT (MAP 35)

TURN FOR LEWKNOR

40–60 MINS FROM TURN FOR WATLINGTON (MAP 33)

50–70 MINS FROM TURN FOR KINGSTON BLOUNT (MAP 35)

TURN FOR LEWKNOR

30–50 MINS TO TURN FOR WATLINGTON (MAP 33)

0   ¼ mile

0   APPROX SCALE   500m

ROUTE GUIDE AND MAPS

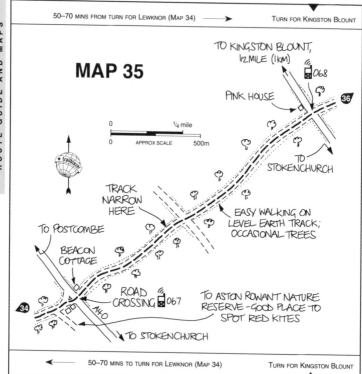

50–70 MINS FROM TURN FOR LEWKNOR (MAP 34) →

TURN FOR KINGSTON BLOUNT

MAP 35

TO KINGSTON BLOUNT, ½ MILE (1KM)

068

PINK HOUSE

36

0   ¼ mile
0   APPROX SCALE   500m

★ trailblaze

TO STOKENCHURCH

TRACK NARROW HERE

EASY WALKING ON LEVEL EARTH TRACK; OCCASIONAL TREES

TO POSTCOMBE

BEACON COTTAGE

34

ROAD CROSSING 067

A40

TO ASTON ROWANT NATURE RESERVE – GOOD PLACE TO SPOT RED KITES

↘ TO STOKENCHURCH

← 50–70 MINS TO TURN FOR LEWKNOR (MAP 34)

TURN FOR KINGSTON BLOUNT

ence to the Le Blunt family who were lords of this area for several hundred years.

Lakeside Town Farm (☎ 01844 352152, 🖥 www.townfarmcottage.co.uk; 2D/1T, all en suite) is a working farm with an old farmhouse that's full of character. The B&B is very-well run: the rooms are £85-95, or £55-60 if you're on your own, and at weekends a minimum stay of two nights is required. They also have a self-catering cabin by the lake (1D) which can be let on a B&B basis (£100). The beautiful gardens encompass lakes and have been featured on the BBC's Gardeners' World programme.

Alternatively, you could stay at *The Cherry Tree Pub* (☎ 01844 352273, 🖥 www .cherrytreepub.net; 3D/1T or D, all en suite,

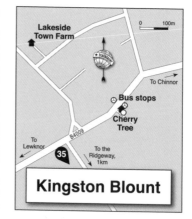

Lakeside Town Farm

0   100m

★ trailblaze

To Chinnor

ⓢ Bus stops

Cherry Tree

To Lewknor

B4009

To the Ridgeway, 1km

35

Kingston Blount

☐; 🐾; food Mon 6.30-9.30pm, Tue-Sat noon-2.30pm & 6.30-9.30pm, Sun noon-3pm); the modern rooms in their converted barn cost £50 including breakfast, or £70 including breakfast and dinner (£60 for single occupancy). The pub itself has a welcoming and contemporary feel and is a popular meeting place for locals. Note that the bar is closed 3-5.30pm. It's well-worth eating here though: main courses range

from £7.50 to £20 and the menu, which changes seasonally, may include sausages, mash and gravy for £7.50. There is also a specials board.

Arriva's No 40 **bus** stops here en route between Thame, Chinnor and High Wycombe; see pp42-5 for further details. If you need a **taxi** you could call Chinnor Cabs (see p156).

The developments (Map 36) at Chinnor stand out for a mile, or two, and not long after you have spotted them the path becomes flanked by the huge pits that are the result of previous activity at the works. Although it's not easy to get a proper view of these, most have water at the bottom. On a sunny day the water

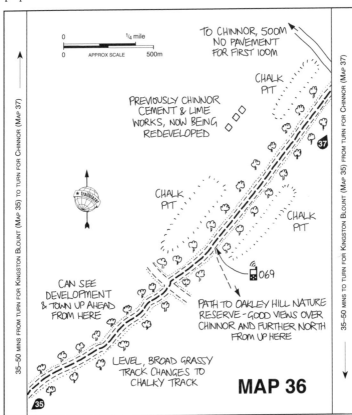

is bright turquoise which contrasts with the brilliant white chalk-pit sides – a bizarre sight in the middle of this countryside.

When you reach the main road that crosses the Ridgeway, turn left and follow it into Chinnor, about a third of a mile/500m. Although Chinnor is a large village there isn't a great deal here, so if you don't want to go on the railway (see below) you might want to keep walking.

CHINNOR

This is the next town in the line of settlements along the Chilterns. In the 19th century this place was well known for producing lace and chair legs. The Chiltern beech forests were the source of wood for the legs. In the early 20th century a cement factory was opened and this steadily expanded as new technology allowed for ever-increasing production levels. The population in the village grew as the works expanded but they were eventually closed in 1999. Part of the land is now being redeveloped as housing.

One thing that has survived is the **Chinnor & Princes Risborough Railway** that runs steam trains along a small section of line from here. By 1961 the line from Watlington to Chinnor had been closed completely, though the section from Chinnor to Princes Risborough was used by the cement factory. In the early '70s Chinnor station and platform were demolished and by the late '80s all traffic on the line from the cement works had ceased.

However, within five years Chinnor & Princes Risborough Railway Association had rebuilt the platform and station and started running a public service. Since then they have extended the line twice and added a loop, enabling the engine to turn around. At the time of writing the round trip was seven miles (11.5km) though plans are afoot to extend the line to Princes Risborough. A steam or diesel engine runs most weekends, but check their talking timetable (☎ 01844 353535) or their website (🖳 www.chinnorrailway.co.uk) before making your way down there.

At the time of writing there was **no accommodation** in the village.

Services

The village is centred on Church Rd where there is a line of shops.

This comprises a Spar **supermarket** (daily 6.30am-9pm), **Lloyds Pharmacy** (Mon-Fri 9am-6pm, Sat 9am-1pm), and a **bakery** (Mon-Fri 6.30am-4.30pm, Sat 7am-2pm).

The **post office** is just around the corner on the High St. The **library** (☎ 01844 351721; Mon & Wed 9.30am-12.30pm & 2-5.30pm, Thur 2-7pm, Fri 2-5.30pm, Sat 9.30am-1pm) offers free **internet** access; booking is recommended especially at peak periods. There is an **ATM** outside the BP filling station on Oakley Rd and also a Co-op supermarket (Mon-Sat 8am-10pm, Sun 10am-10pm) and a **public toilet** here.

Arriva's No 40 **bus** service from High Wycombe to Thame via Kingston Blount stops at the Red Lion and at the other end of the High St. Redline's No 320 to Princes Risborough stops at the Red Lion; see pp42-5 for further details.

If you want a **taxi** call Chinnor Cabs (☎ 01844 353637).

Where to eat and drink

For lunch or a cup of tea you might like to try *Lotte's Kitchen* (☎ 01844 355985, 🖳 www.lotteskitchen.com; Mon-Sat 9am-5pm, Sun 10am-4pm). There is also the *Village Centre* (☎ 01844 353733; Mon-Fri 9.30am-5pm, Sat 9.30am-2.30pm) where the friendly staff serve tea, coffee, all-day breakfasts (£3.90) and toasted sandwiches.

There are two Indian restaurants in the village. *Chinnor Indian Cuisine* (☎ 01844 354843, 🖳 www.chinnorindiancuisine.co.uk; Mon-Sat noon-2.30pm & 6-11.30pm, Sun noon-3pm & 6-11.30pm) is a couple of minutes' walk from the 'centre', but worth it if you like Indian food as this place is good. Most main courses are between £6 and £9. *Coriander Leaf* (☎ 01844 353752; daily 11am-2.30pm & 6-11pm) is also an Indian restaurant. The décor is modern but the food is pretty standard.

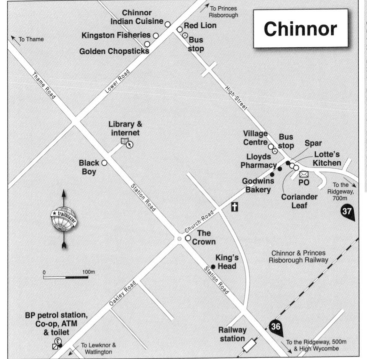

If a Chinese takeaway is more your thing head to *Golden Chopsticks* (☎ 01844 354284; Mon & Wed-Sun 5-10pm). Alternatively, there is the rather grandly named *Kingston Fisheries* (☎ 01844 353874; Tue-Sat noon-1.45pm & 5-9pm, to 10pm on Fri). It's the only fish & chip shop in the village.

As for pubs, there is the *Red Lion* (☎ 01844 353468; bar Mon-Fri noon-2pm & 5-11pm, Sat & Sun noon-11pm; food Mon-Sat noon-2pm & 6-9pm, Sun 12.30-3pm)

serving pub grub including a Sunday roast for £5; *The Crown* (☎ 01844 351244, 🖥 www.thecrownchinnor.co.uk; food Mon-Fri 8.30am-2.30pm & 6-8.30pm, Sat 10am-2.30pm, Sun 10am-3.30pm) on Station Rd; and the *Black Boy* (☎ 01844 350426, 🖥 www.blackboychinnor.co.uk; food daily noon-10pm) at 38 Station Road. The bars at The Crown and the Black Boy are open all day. The **King's Head** was closed at the time of writing but should be reopening with new tenants soon.

Though the Ridgeway and Icknield Way have been sharing the same path since around Watlington, they eventually separate (Map 37) with the Icknield Way taking a straight course to Princes Risborough and the Ridgeway meandering along a much more roundabout route. Depending on how you are feeling at this point in the day, you might decide to take the Icknield Way as it meets up

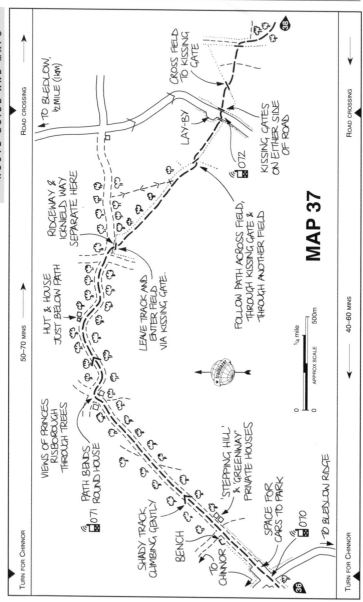

TURN FOR CHINNOR

50–70 MINS

ROAD CROSSING

← TO BLEDLOW, ½ MILE (1KM)

CROSS FIELD TO KISSING GATE

38

RIDGEWAY & ICKNIELD WAY SEPARATE HERE

HUT & HOUSE JUST BELOW PATH

LAY-BY

072

KISSING GATES ON EITHER SIDE OF ROAD

VIEWS OF PRINCES RISBOROUGH THROUGH TREES

LEAVE TRACK AND ENTER FIELD VIA KISSING GATE.

FOLLOW PATH ACROSS FIELD, THROUGH KISSING GATE & THROUGH ANOTHER FIELD

MAP 37

071 PATH BENDS ROUND HOUSE

¼ mile

500m

0

APPROX SCALE

0

SHADY TRACK, CLIMBING GENTLY

BENCH

'STEPPING HILL' & 'GREENWAY' PRIVATE HOUSES

SPACE FOR CARS TO PARK

070

TO CHINNOR

TO BLEDLOW RIDGE

36

TURN FOR CHINNOR

40–60 MINS

ROAD CROSSING

TURN FOR CHINNOR

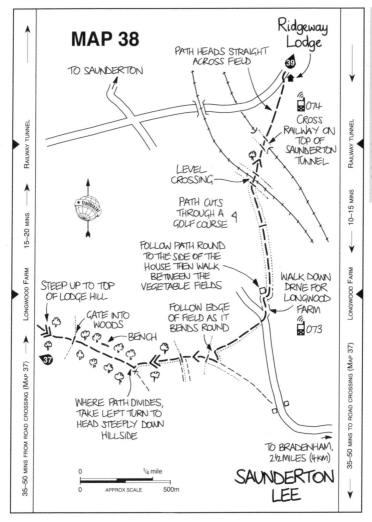

MAP 38

TO SAUNDERTON

PATH HEADS STRAIGHT ACROSS FIELD

Ridgeway Lodge

39

□074

CROSS RAILWAY ON TOP OF SAUNDERTON TUNNEL

LEVEL CROSSING

PATH CUTS THROUGH A GOLF COURSE

FOLLOW PATH ROUND TO THE SIDE OF THE HOUSE THEN WALK BETWEEN THE VEGETABLE FIELDS

WALK DOWN DRIVE FOR LONGWOOD FARM

□073

STEEP UP TO TOP OF LODGE HILL

GATE INTO WOODS

BENCH

37

FOLLOW EDGE OF FIELD AS IT BENDS ROUND

WHERE PATH DIVIDES, TAKE LEFT TURN TO HEAD STEEPLY DOWN HILLSIDE

TO BRADENHAM, 2½ MILES (4KM)

SAUNDERTON LEE

0   ¼ mile
0   APPROX SCALE   500m

RAILWAY TUNNEL

15-20 MINS

LONGWOOD FARM

35-50 MINS FROM ROAD CROSSING (MAP 37)

RAILWAY TUNNEL

10-15 MINS

LONGWOOD FARM

35-50 MINS TO ROAD CROSSING (MAP 37)

again with the Ridgeway before going into Princes Risborough. From where the two paths divide to where they rejoin, the Icknield Way is 1½ miles/2.5km and the Ridgeway is 2¾ miles/4.5km.

Some time later the Ridgeway cuts through a golf course (Map 38), the second so far, and crosses a railway track. It hardly needs to be mentioned to take great care here. A couple of minutes further on there is another railway crossing but this time you are walking on the roof of **Saunderton Tunnel**. As you join the road, you pass Ridgeway Lodge (Map 38; see p159); turn left at Shootacre Corner (Map 39) if staying in Drifter's Lodge (see opposite).

The final part of this section is along the busy A4010; it's as dull as most other walks along fast main roads. The Ridgeway only skirts the town so unless staying at the Poppyseed (see p162), or needing the railway station, the best way to get to the centre is to turn off the A4010 after the Princes Risborough sign (following the Ridgeway path) and then left when New Road crosses the path: it's then about 500m to the centre of town.

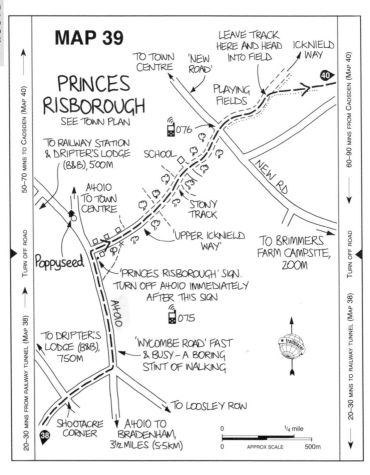

MAP 39

PRINCES RISBOROUGH
SEE TOWN PLAN

TO TOWN CENTRE

'NEW ROAD'

LEAVE TRACK HERE AND HEAD INTO FIELD

ICKNIELD WAY

PLAYING FIELDS

40

076

TO RAILWAY STATION & DRIFTER'S LODGE (B&B), 500M

SCHOOL

NEW RD

A4010 TO TOWN CENTRE

STONY TRACK

'UPPER ICKNIELD WAY'

TO BRIMMERS FARM CAMPSITE, 200M

Poppyseed

'PRINCES RISBOROUGH' SIGN. TURN OFF A4010 IMMEDIATELY AFTER THIS SIGN

075

A4010

TO DRIFTER'S LODGE (B&B), 750M

'WYCOMBE ROAD' FAST & BUSY – A BORING STINT OF WALKING

★ trailblazer

TO LOOSLEY ROW

38

SHOOTACRE CORNER

A4010 TO BRADENHAM, 3½ MILES (5·5KM)

0 .... ¼ mile
0 .... APPROX SCALE 500m

50–70 MINS TO CADSDEN (MAP 40)

20–30 MINS FROM RAILWAY TUNNEL (MAP 38)

TURN OFF ROAD

60–90 MINS FROM CADSDEN (MAP 40)

TURN OFF ROAD

20–30 MINS TO RAILWAY TUNNEL (MAP 38)

ROUTE GUIDE AND MAPS

PRINCES RISBOROUGH
[see map p162]

This is the biggest town you'll have visited so far on the journey. Despite this, the centre is still compact with most of the shops and services occupying the old High St and large supermarkets at either end. As the Ridgeway passes more or less through the town it makes a convenient overnight or lunch stop.

Like many of the towns around here, this one dates back a very long way, possibly to Roman times. The Saxons were certainly here and a couple of hundred years after they arrived there is a mention of this town in the Domesday Book as 'Riseburg'.

Edward, 'The Black Prince', had his palace here in the 14th century, hence the town's name, though the site of the palace is now unfortunately a car park, so not really worth investigating.

The arrival of the railway in 1862 caused the town to grow considerably and by the 1930s the previously separate towns of Princes Risborough and Monks Risborough had merged.

Services

There is a **post office** (Mon-Fri 9am-5.30pm, Sat 9am-12.30pm) in one of the branches of Lloyds Pharmacy (**chemist**) on the High St. On this street you'll also find branches of NatWest, Barclays, Nationwide and Lloyds TSB banks, all with **ATMs**.

Near the roundabout at the bottom of the High St is **Risborough Information Centre** (☎ 01844 274795, 🖳 risborough_office@wycombe.gov.uk; Mon-Wed & Fri 9am-5pm, Thur 10am-5pm, Sat 9am-1pm) which has friendly staff and lots of leaflets. Close by is the **library** (☎ 0845 230 3232; Tue 10am-7pm, Wed 10am-1pm, Thur & Fri 10am-5pm, Sat 10am-4pm) where you can use the **internet** for 30 mins for £1.

Just off the High St is **Risborough Cycles** (☎ 01844 345949, 🖳 www.risboroughcycles.com; Mar-Oct Mon-Tue & Thur-Sat 9.30am-5pm, Oct-Mar Mon-Tue & Fri-Sat 9.30am-5pm), should you need any spares or repairs. There is a **supermarket** at either end of the High St: Tesco (Mon-Sat 6am-midnight, Sun 10am-4pm) at

the top – which has **toilets** – and M&S Simply Food (Mon-Sat 8am-8pm, Sun 10am-4pm) at the bottom; there are also public **toilets** in the car park near by. Next to M&S Simply Food there is a **newsagent** (Mon-Fri 6am-7pm, Sun 8am-2pm) and in the middle of the High St there is a **chemist** (Mon-Fri 9am-6pm, Sat 9am-5.30pm), a branch of Lloyds Pharmacy. There is a **farmers'** **market** once a month (see box p15).

If you need a **taxi** B&V Taxis (☎ 01844 342079) are very helpful but require advance bookings.

Unlike in many of the surrounding towns the railway line is still open; there are regular **trains** to London Marylebone & Birmingham, see box p39. Arriva's No 300 **bus** from High Wycombe to Aylesbury passes through and Redline's No 320 goes to Chinnor. See pp42-5 for further details.

Where to stay

Brimmers Farm (☎ 01844 346171, 🖳 www.brimmersfarm.co.uk; 10 pitches) offers **camping** for £6pp including use of toilet and shower facilities. They sell baskets of logs (£3) and food such as burgers and sausages and there are two BBQs. Booking is recommended at weekends. To reach the campsite you should leave the Ridgeway where it crosses New Road (Map 39) and follow it for 1km. The farm is on your right as you round a sharp corner.

Another good place to stay, which is slightly out of town, is *Drifter's Lodge* (off Map 39; ☎ 01844 274773, 🖳 www.drifterslodge.co.uk; 1D/2T, en suite, 🞏; 🐾) at 60 Picts Lane. The bright and comfortable rooms cost from £65, or from £45 for single occupancy. Packed lunches are available on request and they also provide a luggage transport service; contact them for details.

Also slightly out of town, but directly on the Ridgeway, is *Ridgeway Lodge* (Map 38; ☎ 01844 345438, 🖳 www.ridgewaylodge.co.uk; 1D/1T share facilities/1D or T, en suite; 🞏) which charges £65-85 (from £50 for single occupancy). This is a very well-run B&B in a beautiful location. The owners can provide a packed lunch (£5.50) if given 24hrs' notice. They can also arrange an evening meal for walkers; contact them for details.

Poppyseed (Map 39; ☎ 01844 345569, 🖳 www.the-poppyseed.co.uk; 3S/3D/3T, all en suite, 🖵) is also only a few minutes' walk from the Ridgeway, but further from the town centre. There's an Indian restaurant (see Where to eat) and bar downstairs and well-kept rooms upstairs; B&B costs £39.95 for a single and £49.95-60 for two sharing. To get here follow the Ridgeway as it heads towards the town on the A4010. Where the Ridgeway turns off this main road, you need to simply keep on it for another 200m where the road forks either side of Poppyseed.

Right in the centre of town you could try ***The George & Dragon*** (☎ 01844 343087, 🖳 www.georgeanddragonpr.co.uk; 4D, all en suite). The accommodation at this place was being refurbished at the time of writing but the work was expected to be completed by early 2012. Contact them for further details.

Where to eat and drink

Crumbs Too (☎ 01844 344462; Mon-Sat 8am-5pm) is located at the top of the High St and has an all-day breakfast from £6 and toasted tortilla wraps from £3.50.

At the other end of the street ***Fieldmouse Cheese Store & Deli*** (☎ 01844 344990; Mon-Sat 9am-5pm) has a delicious selection of quiches, ploughman's and sandwiches to eat in or take away. They also serve cream teas (£3.50-5.50) all day. There is a branch of ***Costa*** (Mon-Sat 7.30am-6.30pm, Sun 8.30am-6.30pm) serving the usual range of coffees, teas, cakes and savoury snacks.

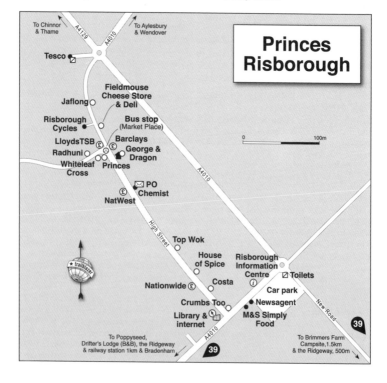

Alternatively, *Top Wok* (☎ 01844 346444; Mon-Sat noon-2pm & 5.30-10.30pm, Sun noon-3pm), on the High St, is a canteen-style Chinese restaurant.

For curry lovers *House of Spice* (☎ 01844 345654, 💻 www.houseofspice.uk. com; daily noon-2pm & 6-11pm), on the High St, is always busy but for a quieter Indian meal try *Jaflong* (☎ 01844 274443; daily 5.30-11pm) further up the road. There is also *Radhuni* (☎ 01844 273741; daily 6-11pm), just off the High St. All of these places have standard Indian restaurant menus as does the restaurant (daily 5.30-11pm) at *Poppyseed* (see Where to stay). Most mains cost £5.50 to £13.95.

Richard's Restaurant at the George & Dragon (see Where to stay; food daily noon-3pm & 6-9pm, to 4pm on Sun) has some well-cooked pub grub: local sausages, yorkshire pudding, bubble & squeak with red onion sauce (£7.90), or home-made pork and chicken pie with fresh salad, apple and home-made pickles (£7.95). The bar (Sun-Thur noon-12.30am, Fri & Sat noon-1.30am) also offers a snack menu.

On the corner of the High St, near Market Place, *Whiteleaf Cross* (☎ 01844 346834; food Mon-Thur 10am-2.30pm & 6-9pm, Fri 10am-2.30pm, Sat 10am-7pm, Sun noon-3pm & 6-9pm) is a friendly pub with a contemporary feel: it's popular with locals and serves standard but filling pub grub. The bar is open all day.

There is also a very busy fish & chip shop on the High St called *Princes* (☎ 01844 343751; Mon & Sat 11.30am-2pm & 4.30-9pm, 11.30am-2pm & 4.30-10pm).

PRINCES RISBOROUGH TO WIGGINTON (& TRING) [MAPS 39-46]

Overview

This section is **12½ miles/20km (6½-8hrs)** but be aware that there are many steep ups and downs to tire you out before the end is in sight. A great deal of the walking is through mature woodlands on good paths and there is plenty of variety. You'll pass by Chequers, the Prime Minister's country house, visit a Boer War monument on top of a hill with stunning views, and pass through the attractive and useful town of Wendover, amongst other things.

If you decide you want to walk right through to Ivinghoe Beacon in one day, be prepared for a tough time. On paper the 17½ miles/28km doesn't sound unreasonable but the steep up and down sections will leave you weary well before you get your first sight of the Beacon. From there it's a strenuous last few miles to the end. Then there is the matter of walking from the Beacon to accommodation or to transport – a walk into Ivinghoe village is entirely possible but that would add another couple of miles. For this reason, starting the last day from somewhere closer, such as Wendover or Wigginton, can make a lot of sense. It'll also mean you'll have some energy left at the end of the day to celebrate finishing the Ridgeway.

Route

The section from Princes Risborough to Wendover is very popular with both day walkers and dog walkers. The Ridgeway and Icknield Way share the same path until they are out of Princes Risborough, then they separate. The Icknield Way continues on the main track and rejoins the Ridgeway later.

At the top of the first steep climb you'll enter **Whiteleaf Nature Reserve** (Map 40). On the west side of the hill, facing Monks Risborough, there is a chalk cross on a triangular base cut into the hill – the **Whiteleaf Cross**. The history of this monument is hazy to say the least, but it was recorded as far back as the mid-1750s. It's probably been enlarged since then and now a concerted effort has been made to restore and maintain it. This nature reserve is also known for its variety of butterflies and wild flowers. Even if you're not looking specifically, you're bound to notice a chalkhill blue butterfly (see opp p65) or two and you'll probably also see the common blue. Flowers that grow well on this chalky soil have wonderful names, such as squinancy wort and viper's bugloss (see p64).

After descending this hill, you come to **Cadsden**, and more importantly a pub, *The Plough* (☎ 01844 343302, 🖳 www.ploughatcadsden.com; 5D or T, all en suite, ☐; Mon-Fri 11am-2.30pm & 5-11pm, Sat 11am-11pm, Sun noon-10pm; food Mon-Sat noon-2pm & 6.30-9.30pm, Sun noon-2.30pm). Some may say this is Lower Cadsden but the pub sign says Cadsden. It's not hard to see why this well-maintained place is extremely popular for food and drink, particularly at weekends: it would be all too easy to get stuck here – especially as they offer accommodation! They charge £65-70 for single occupancy and £95-105 for two sharing, including breakfast. For dogs and walkers (!) there is a **water tap** in the pub's garden on the other side of the road.

Another steep climb will take you through woodlands and you'll eventually catch sight of **Chequers** (Map 41). The dwelling you might be able to see today dates from the 16th century though there has been a house on this site since the 12th century. Over time, Chequers has been modified by its various inhabitants, but a Mr Arthur Lee and his wife Ruth restored the house to its original Tudor glory in the early part of the 20th century. During World War I Chequers was used as a hospital and convalescent home after which it was donated to the then prime minister, David Lloyd George, by the Lees. Since then it has been at the disposal of the current serving Prime Minister, though now it isn't used as much as it previously was. Its isolated position in the middle of the valley floor makes it impossible to miss. Although the route cuts straight across the driveway to Chequers, no other part of the grounds or the house is open to the public. Naturally, security around here is tight: you'll certainly see surveillance cameras and perhaps police on patrol. After Chequers you rejoin the Icknield Way and there is another steep climb back onto high ground followed by some good walking through mature woodland which stays fairly level for some time. There are many paths through here and you'll need to look out for the black 'acorn marker' posts and the occasional Ridgeway signpost, to keep on the right path.

As the path opens out you'll have amazing views to the west before reaching the monument and **trig point** on the north-west corner of Coombe Hill. This is a popular place for day-trippers and after the lonely effort of the last couple of miles it's quite surprising to see so many people up here. The **monument** commemorates those men from Buckinghamshire who were killed in the Boer War. It was completed in 1904 but had to be partially rebuilt in 1939 after being damaged when struck by lightning. In October 2010 major restoration work on the monument was completed.

From here you should be able to see Wendover, the next town on the Ridgeway, down below. It's all downhill (Bacombe Hill, Map 42) to the town but when leaving the monument do not take the obvious gravel path as this does

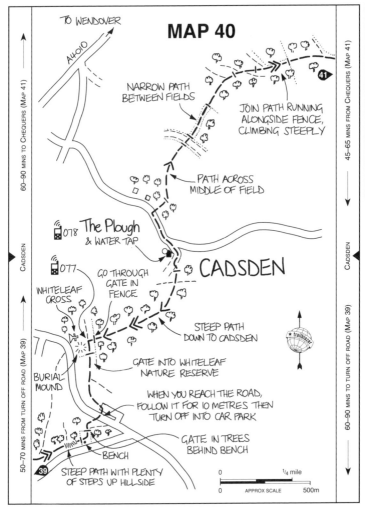

MAP 40

TO WENDOVER

A4010

NARROW PATH
BETWEEN FIELDS

JOIN PATH RUNNING
ALONGSIDE FENCE,
CLIMBING STEEPLY

41

PATH ACROSS
MIDDLE OF FIELD

078 The Plough
& WATER TAP

CADSDEN

077

WHITELEAF
CROSS

GO THROUGH
GATE IN
FENCE

STEEP PATH
DOWN TO CADSDEN

GATE INTO WHITELEAF
NATURE RESERVE

BURIAL
MOUND

WHEN YOU REACH THE ROAD,
FOLLOW IT FOR 10 METRES THEN
TURN OFF INTO CAR PARK

GATE IN TREES
BEHIND BENCH

BENCH

39

STEEP PATH WITH PLENTY
OF STEPS UP HILLSIDE

0   ¼ mile

0
APPROX SCALE   500m

60-90 MINS TO CHEQUERS (MAP 41)

45-65 MINS FROM CHEQUERS (MAP 41)

CADSDEN

CADSDEN

60-90 MINS TO TURN OFF ROAD (MAP 39)

50-70 MINS FROM TURN OFF ROAD (MAP 39)

not lead directly to Wendover. The correct path down the hill eventually joins a surfaced road to take you the last few hundred metres into the town itself.

WENDOVER   [see map p169]

Even if the Ridgeway didn't go straight through the centre of Wendover it would still be a good idea to stop off here. It's an attractive town with a compact centre where all the shops and services are located. This town was mentioned in the Domesday

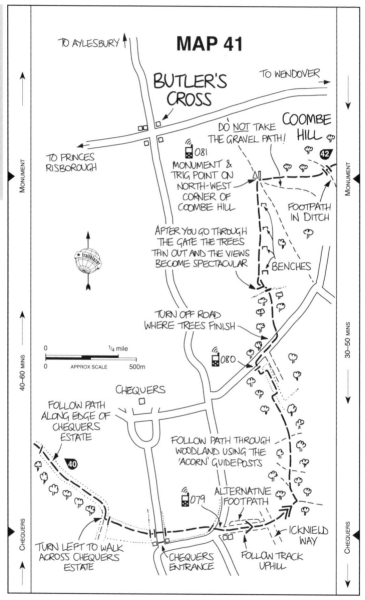

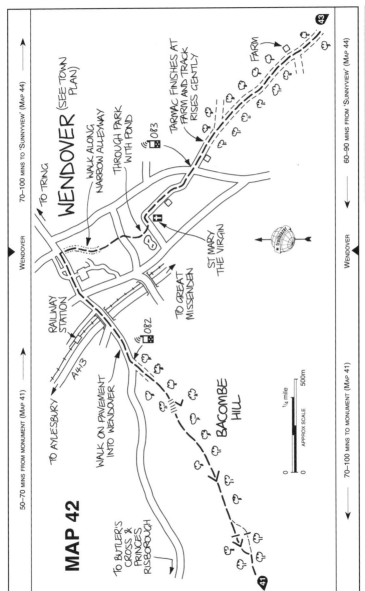

MAP 42

50-70 MINS FROM MONUMENT (MAP 41)

70-100 MINS TO 'SUNNYVIEW' (MAP 44)

60-90 MINS FROM 'SUNNYVIEW' (MAP 44)

70-100 MINS TO MONUMENT (MAP 41)

Wendover

WENDOVER (SEE TOWN PLAN)

TO TRING

WALK ALONG NARROW ALLEYWAY

THROUGH PARK WITH POND

083

TARMAC FINISHES AT FARM AND TRACK RISES GENTLY

FARM

ST MARY THE VIRGIN

TO GREAT MISSENDEN

RAILWAY STATION

A413

TO AYLESBURY

WALK ON PAVEMENT INTO WENDOVER

082

BACOMBE HILL

TO BUTLER'S CROSS & PRINCES RISBOROUGH

¼ mile

APPROX SCALE

500m

43

41

Book but probably dates from a good deal earlier than that. Its position on the road from London to Aylesbury has always ensured it plenty of passing trade and in days gone by it had a large number of inns to cater for weary travellers. There are still some very old pubs to stop off at for a few drinks. Its proximity to London by train also means this is a popular place for city workers to commute from; as a result the town has an air of affluence.

Services

The **post office** (Mon-Fri 9.30am-5.30pm, Sat 9.30am-noon) is on the High St along with a Lloyds TSB **bank** and ATM. Other useful services on this street include a branch of **Lloyds Pharmacy** (Mon-Sat 9am-6.30pm) and a **newsagent** (Mon-Sat 6am-6pm, Sun 7am-1pm). Next to the newsagent is a Budgens **supermarket** (Mon-Sat 6.30am-10pm, Sun 9am-6pm). There's also a monthly **farmers' market** (see box p15).

Wendover **Community and Tourist Office** (☎ 01296 696759, 🖥 www.wendo ver-pc.gov.uk/tourism; Mon-Sat 10am-4pm) is in the clock tower at the bottom of the High St. The staff are very helpful and unless you're careful you'll come out laden with all manner of interesting leaflets about the area. There is also a **library** (☎ 0845 230 3232; Tue & Thur 10am-5pm, Fri 10am-7pm, Sat 10am-4pm) at the back of the car park just off the High St, where you can access the **internet** (£1/30 mins). **Wendover Book Shop** (☎ 01296 696204; approx Mon & Wed-Sat 9.45am-5pm, Tue noon-5pm), on the High St, stocks a range of local interest books. There are **public toilets** in the car park.

Bus services include Arriva's/Redline's No 50 to Tring and Ivinghoe; see pp42-5. There is a **taxi** firm at the railway station called Alexander's (☎ 01296 620888).

Wendover **railway** station is on the Chiltern Line which runs from Aylesbury to London Marylebone; see box p39.

Where to stay

The most atmospheric place in which to stay is **Red Lion Hotel** (☎ 01296 622266,

🖥 www.redlionhotelwendover.co.uk; 2S/16D/3T/2D, T or F, all en suite, ☐). This is a 16th-century coaching inn that used to be the start/end point for coaches to London. The front of the hotel looks as if it has changed little since those days and it really is a place worth stopping off at even if you are not staying here – but if you are you can have a very comfortable single or double room for £89.95 (the twin and family rooms are £99.95). They do get booked up very quickly here so book well in advance.

If you'd prefer something a little cheaper, the B&B at *17 Icknield Close* (☎ 01296 583285, 🖥 grbr.samuels@ntlworld.com; 1S/2T, shared bathroom, ☐) might be just the thing. This friendly place is less than ten minutes' walk from the High St and charges from £35pp. The breakfast is highly recommended. To get there walk up Aylesbury Rd and turn into Wharf Rd which will be on your right. The turning for Icknield Close will then also be on your right.

Where to eat and drink

If you just want something quick you could try *The Bakers Shop* (☎ 01296 624642; Mon, Tue, Thur & Fri 6.30am-3.30pm, Wed 6.30am-3pm, Sat 6.30am-2pm), on Back St, or *Crumbs Café* (☎ 01296 622468; Mon-Sat 8am-5pm, Sun 9am-4pm) where you can get a sandwich and drink. There is also *Whitewaters Deli Café* (☎ 01296 623331, 🖥 www.whitewatersdeli.co.uk; Mon-Sat 9am-6pm) which serves delicious cakes, quiches and salads. *Rumsey's Chocolaterie* (☎ 01296 625060, 🖥 www.rumseys.co.uk; Mon-Sat 8.30am-6pm, Sun 10am-6pm) specialises in handmade chocolates, but also serves tea, coffee and light lunches.

On Pound St the *Shoulder of Mutton* (☎ 01296 623223; food Mon-Sat 11am-10pm, Sun noon-9pm) is a large, old Chef & Brewer establishment serving a decent range of pub grub like gammon & eggs (£7.25) and BBQ pork shanks (£10.95) all day, every day.

The bar at *Red Lion Hotel* (see Where to stay; restaurant Mon-Thur 9am-9.30pm, Fri & Sat 9am-10pm, Sun 10am-9.30pm) serves hot and cold sandwiches and baked potatoes (mostly about £6) throughout the

ROUTE GUIDE AND MAPS

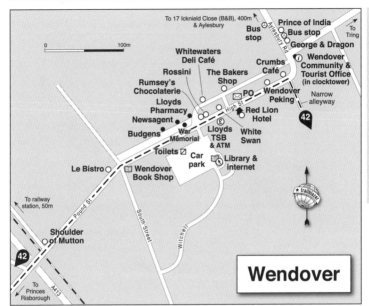

To 17 Icknield Close (B&B), 400m & Aylesbury

Bus stop

Prince of India

Bus stop

To Tring

George & Dragon

Wendover Community & Tourist Office (in clocktower)

Whitewaters Deli Café

Crumbs Café

Rossini

The Bakers Shop

Rumsey's Chocolaterie

PO

Wendover Peking

Narrow alleyway

Lloyds Pharmacy

Red Lion Hotel

Newsagent

High St

42

Budgens

War Memorial

Lloyds TSB & ATM

White Swan

Toilets

Car park

Library & internet

Le Bistro

Wendover Book Shop

To railway station, 50m

Pound St

South Street

Witchell

Shoulder of Mutton

42

To Princes Risborough

A413

Wendover

day and has four real ales that change on a regular basis. The restaurant menu varies but usually includes a pie of the day (£11.85), steaks and burgers (£9.50-15.25) and a specials board.

On the High St you'll find the Mediterranean-styled *Rossini* (☎ 01296 622257, 💻 www.rossinirestaurant.co.uk; Tue-Sat noon-2pm & 7-9.30pm, Sun noon-2pm; closed two weeks late Aug). It's an upmarket place where a set three-course evening meal is £24.95; at lunchtime during the week two/three courses cost £11.95/14.95 and on Sunday it is £17.95/ £21.95. There is also an à la carte menu. The menu varies but may include crabcakes in a herb crust, and spinach and ricotta cannelloni.

Le Bistro (☎ 01296 622092, 💻 www. lebistrowendover.co.uk; Tue-Sat noon-3.30pm & 6-11pm, Sun noon-5.30pm) is a spacious restaurant with an internationally influenced menu. The menu changes but may include chicken schnitzel with spaghetti and spicy tomato and basil sauce

(£11.95) or Persian slow-cooked lamb with saffron-scented rice (£13.95), just two examples from the varied selection of main courses.

Just down from the post office is the only Chinese restaurant in town, *Wendover Peking Restaurant* (☎ 01296 623991; Thur, Fri & Sat noon-2.30pm, Mon-Sat 5-10.30pm, Sun noon-10pm). They serve all the standard Chinese dishes. Inside the *George & Dragon* (☎ 01296 586152; food Tue-Sun noon-2.15pm & Tue-Sat 6-10pm) is a Thai restaurant and takeaway; you can have a starter, main dish and rice for £10 (takeaway). The *Prince of India* (☎ 01296 623233; daily noon-2.30pm & 6-11.30pm), almost next door to the George & Dragon, serves tasty Indian food.

The *White Swan* (Sun-Thur noon-11pm, Fri & Sat noon-midnight) looks small from the outside but has several bar areas inside and is open all day. They do not serve food but appear to make up for that by selling plenty of Fuller's beer.

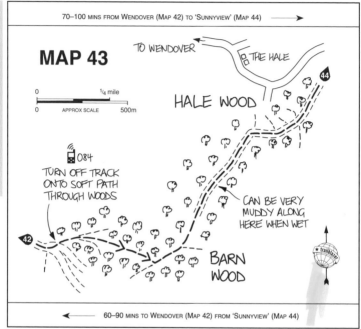

ROUTE GUIDE AND MAPS

MAP 43

TO WENDOVER

THE HALE

HALE WOOD

44

0   ¼ mile
0   APPROX SCALE   500m

084
TURN OFF TRACK
ONTO SOFT PATH
THROUGH WOODS

CAN BE VERY
MUDDY ALONG
HERE WHEN WET

42

BARN
WOOD

★ trailblazer

The path out of Wendover follows a pleasant route between houses and parks before emerging at a T-junction in front of the church of **St Mary the Virgin**. This church was built in the 14th century and was used briefly as a camp by some of Oliver Cromwell's New Model Army troops during the English Civil War. Today it's still well used but for more sedate purposes such as afternoon tea and bellringing practice.

There's another long climb up into woodland that thankfully levels out for some time along the ridge through Barn Wood and the Forestry Commission's **Hale Wood** (Map 43). This is a lovely walk along good paths surrounded by mature woodlands including many conifer trees. Although there are good views back to Wendover from here, the forest blocks them for most of the time.

For many miles now the Ridgeway and Icknield Way have often been following the same route and at times the Icknield Way can provide you with a shortcut if you are in a hurry. For instance, both paths leave Wendover at roughly the same place, but by the time they meet up again Ridgeway walkers have gone 2³⁄₄ miles/4.5km whereas Icknield Way walkers have only gone 1³⁄₄ miles/3km. However, if you're going to walk the Ridgeway, you might as well do it properly. Having said that, up ahead there is a part of the Ridgeway that it might be best not to do properly and I doubt many people do. You'll come to a

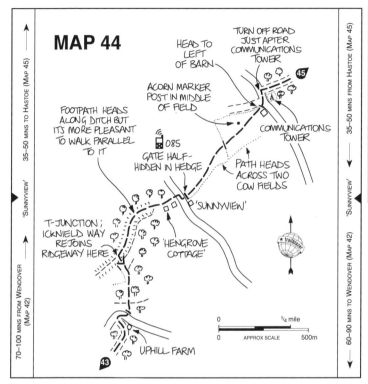

T-junction (Map 44) in woodland (where the Icknield Way rejoins the path) and need to turn right. The official signpost for this is at the bottom of a steep ditch. So, you can either descend into the ditch and follow it up the hill, or simply continue walking on the woodland path parallel to the ditch. Having walked in the ditch I wouldn't recommend it unless you like muddy boots and swarms of flies for company.

After passing through the group of houses and farms collectively known as **Hastoe** (Map 45), you'll enter **Tring Park**, leased to the Woodland Trust (see p56). This park used to be much bigger but in 1974 the A41 was cut straight through the centre of it in an east–west direction. The manor house is now located in the top half, while the Ridgeway passes through the bottom half. It's a really enjoyable section of the walk along decent paths with plenty of wildlife to look out for, including fallow deer.

The next village you come to is Wigginton (Map 46). The Ridgeway passes a few hundred metres from the 'centre' and it's a good place to stay the night if you want a relaxed last day of walking up to Ivinghoe Beacon.

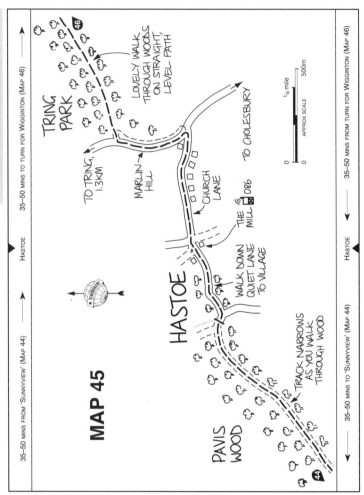

MAP 45

35–50 MINS FROM 'SUNNYVIEW' (MAP 44)

HASTOE

35–50 MINS TO TURN FOR WIGGINTON (MAP 46)

ROUTE GUIDE AND MAPS

TRING PARK

LOVELY WALK THROUGH WOODS ON STRAIGHT, LEVEL PATH

TO TRING, 1.3KM

MARLIN HILL

CHURCH LANE

THE MILL 086

TO CHOLESBURY

HASTOE

WALK DOWN QUIET LANE TO VILLAGE

TRACK NARROWS AS YOU WALK THROUGH WOOD

PAVIS WOOD

¼ mile
500m
APPROX SCALE

35–50 MINS FROM TURN FOR WIGGINTON (MAP 46)

HASTOE

35–50 MINS TO 'SUNNYVIEW' (MAP 44)

WIGGINTON   [MAP 46]

This small village has been here for centuries. It's a sleepy place with little to do, but there is good accommodation in the village pub – a perfect place to wind down after a long day on the Ridgeway. It's probably best known for the exclusive Champneys Health Spa just out of the village on the Chesham Road. There are no shops, nor is there a post office. A **taxi** can be ordered through Diamond Cars (☎ 01442 890303, ⌨ steve.walker@diamondcars.uk.com) which is just as well because Red Rose Travel's No 387 **bus** between Tring and Aldbury is the only service calling here; see pp42-5.

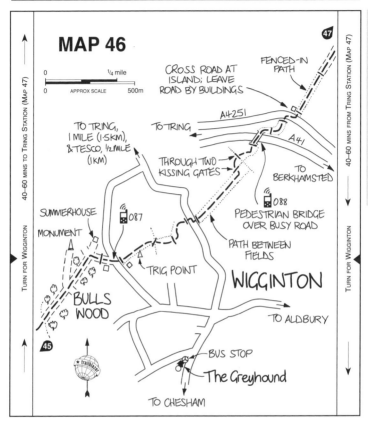

The Greyhound (☎ 01442 824631, 🖳 www.greyhoundtring.co.uk; 1D/1T/1D, T or F, all en suite; 🐾 £50 deposit; bar daily noon-11pm; food Mon-Sat noon-2.30pm & 6.30-9pm, Sun noon-3pm) is the only pub in the village, hence its popularity with the locals. This friendly place has a changing selection of real ales and their menu includes home-made pies and 10oz Aberdeen Angus steaks. It's a deservedly popular place with walkers, so book well ahead if you want to stay here. The rate (£60 for two sharing, £45 single occupancy; £75 for the family room) includes a continental breakfast, a full English breakfast is an extra £7.50.

If you're heading for Tring you'll also need to leave the Ridgeway where the path crosses the roads at Wigginton; either road is fine. It's about 1 mile/1.5km to the centre of Tring from here. The advantage that staying in Tring has over Wigginton is that there are far more facilities, but it's not on the Ridgeway so you'll have to take into account the time and effort of walking there and back.

TRING

This is a large town near the end of the Ridgeway and it would be a good place at which to stop before you tackle the last stretch of walking up to Ivinghoe Beacon, but maybe it would be better to come here after you have finished the Ridgeway as, apart from all the shops and services you might need, there are good public transport links to get you back home. There aren't, however, many places to stay in Tring, so you might prefer to make your visit brief.

Like many of the towns in this chain of settlements along the edge of the Chilterns, there is evidence of Saxon settlement in Tring and it's also mentioned in the Domesday Book.

The town has always been on a natural pathway and when the Grand Junction Canal was cut through here in the late 18th century commerce in the town really started to expand. In the early 19th century a large silk mill was established in Tring and this gave employment to many of the town's women and children. In 1835 a railway was built along the course of the canal which runs to the east of Tring. Although this meant that the railway station was not built in the town it still further improved Tring's accessibility, especially to London.

You might well expect a museum in this town to include some of this history, but in fact its subject is something altogether different. The **Natural History Museum at Tring** (☎ 020 7942 6171, 🖳 www.nhm. ac.uk/tring; entry free; Mon-Sat 10am-5pm, Sun 2-5pm) is at the corner of Akeman St and Park St, just a few minutes' walk from the High St. It comprises about 4000 stuffed animals from Walter Rothschild's personal collection. You'll be able to see anything from a coelacanth to a great auk to a platypus. It really is worth a visit!

Services

The **post office** (Mon-Fri 9am-5.30pm, Sat 9am-12.30pm) can be found on the High St next to the branches of NatWest and HSBC **banks**, both with ATMs. There's also a Barclays with an ATM further along the same street. If you need more local info, **Tring Information Centre** (☎ 01442

823347, 🖳 www.tring.gov.uk/info/infocent. htm; Mon-Fri 9.30am-3pm, Sat 10am-1pm) is conveniently located right in the middle of the High St but the entrance is on Akeman St. It has plenty of literature and advice about Tring and the surrounding area. The **library** (☎ 01438 737333; Mon 9am-6pm, Tue & Wed 2-6pm, Fri 9am-6pm, Sat 9am-4pm), also on the High St, has **internet** access at £1.20 for half an hour, or if you have ID and sign up to be a member you can have an hour's access for free. There is a **newsagent** a minute further along the street.

Dennis's of Tring (Mon-Fri 9am-5.15pm, Sat 9am-5pm), next to the newsagent, should be able to help with some walking-related supplies. There is an M&S Simply Food **supermarket** (Mon-Sat 9am-8pm, Sun 10am-4pm) in a precinct just off the High St and a large branch of Tesco on London Rd. The **farmers' market** (see box p15) is held on the Market Place. There are **public toilets** (Mon-Sat 8am-5pm) in the car park.

A branch of **Lloyds Pharmacy** (Mon-Fri 9am-6pm, Sat 9am-5.30pm) can be found on the High St.

Tring is a stop on London Midland's frequent **rail** service from London Euston to Northampton, see box p39. There is a reasonable number of **bus services** from Tring to nearby villages such as Ivinghoe, Wigginton and places further away such as Aylesbury and Luton. The important thing is to make sure you go to the correct stop: Red Rose Travel's No 387 stops at both the Rose & Crown and the railway station; Arriva's Nos 61 and 500 only stop at the Rose & Crown but their No 30 stops at the station; Redline's No 50 and 164 stop at the Rose & Crown; see pp42-5 for further details.

If you need a **taxi** you should phone John's Taxis (☎ 01442 828828), based at Tring Station (Map 47).

Where to stay

In a great location, right in the town centre is *97 High Street* (☎ 01442 823678, 🖳 scharsachs@aol.com; 2D private bathroom, ❑) which charges £80, or £40-45 if you're

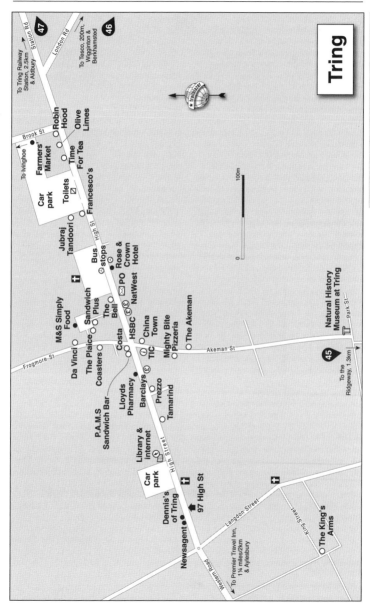

Tring

on your own. Breakfast (with organic ingredients) can either be a full English or continental. Booking is essential.

About 1¼ miles/2km from the town centre there is a *Premier Travel Inn* (☎ 0871 527 9104, 🖳 www.premierinn.com/en/hotel/TRICRO/tring; Tring Hill, HP23 4LD; 30D, en suite, ☐) which has rooms for £56-75 (from £29 if you book online) and a restaurant (daily Mon-Fri 7am-10.30pm & noon-10pm, Sat & Sun 8am-10.30pm, noon-10pm) on site. A full English breakfast costs £7.99 and a continental is £5.25.

You can't beat the location of the Rose & Crown Hotel & Restaurant and it's hard to miss it, too. However, at the time of writing the entire hotel was scheduled to close for about a year for extensive renovations. But *Pendley Manor* (off Map 47; ☎ 01442 891891, 🖳 www.pendley-manor.co.uk; 73 rooms, all en suite, ☐), another hotel in the same group is open and is located near Tring Station. The rooms include doubles (some with four-poster beds), twins and two family rooms. Standard rates for B&B are £150-170 for two sharing and £140 for single occupancy. However, it is always worth looking on their website for their online specials. The rate includes use of their indoor heated pool and other leisure facilities. Food is available throughout the day in their restaurant (smart casual appreciated).

Where to eat and drink

If you fancy a lunchtime sandwich you could head for *P.A.M.S Sandwich Bar* (Mon-Fri 9am-3pm, Sat 9am-2pm), on the High St. They do all the usual sandwiches, baguettes and rolls here including 'giant all-day breakfast rolls'. In the precinct near the M&S, *Sandwich Plus* (Mon-Fri 8.30am-3pm) does much the same thing. Other lunchtime options include the tiny *Time For Tea* (Mon-Fri 8.30am-4pm, Sat 9am-5pm, Sun 9am-3pm), *Coasters* (Mon-Sat 9am-5pm) and *Costa* (Mon-Sat 7.30am-6.30pm, Sun 8am-6pm).

There are several Indian restaurants and among them is the recommended *Jubraj*

Tandoori (daily 12.30-2pm & 6-11.45pm), just off the High St. The *nababi hash* (flame-grilled duck in spices) is well worth £9.95. Other Indian restaurants include *Tamarind* (Sun-Thur 6-11.30pm, Fri & Sat 6pm-midnight) and *Olive Limes* (daily noon-2.30pm & 6-11.30pm) which has a more contemporary feel.

The Italian restaurant and café *Francesco's* (Mon-Sat 10am-3pm & 6-11pm, Sun noon-11pm) is a really popular place, especially in the daytime when the café gets very busy. Authentic pizzas here are priced from £7.50 and lasagne from £8. There's another Italian restaurant on Frogmore St called *Da Vinci* (Mon-Sat 12.30-3pm & 6-10.30pm, Sun noon-10.30pm), which has all the usual pizzas and pasta dishes and a selection of risottos for £8.95. On the High St is a branch of *Prezzo* (daily noon-10.30pm), yet another Italian restaurant. Vegetable fusilli is £7.50 and spaghetti carbonara is £8.95.

Several standard takeaways are dotted around Tring. They include: *China Town* (Wed & Thur noon-1.45pm & 5-11.30pm, Tue & Sun 5-11.30pm, Fri & Sat noon-1.45pm & 5pm-midnight) which serves exactly what you'd expect; *Mighty Bite Pizzeria* (Sun-Thur 5-11pm, Fri & Sat noon-11pm) serving pizzas, burgers and jacket spuds, and *The Plaice* (Mon-Sat 11.30am-2.30pm & 4-9pm), a fish and chip shop.

There are plenty of pubs around town, most of them serving food. The most upmarket is *The Akeman* (☎ 01442 826027, 🖳 www.theakeman.co.uk; bar Mon-Sat 8am-midnight, Sun 8am-11pm, food served daily 8am-10.30pm), a café/pub/restaurant serving Mediterranean-style food. They serve an English-style breakfast (daily 8am-noon; from £5.40) and later on there's a wide choice of Spanish, Italian and Greek dishes ranging from £7 to £15. *The Bell Inn* (food daily 12.30-8.30pm), on the High St, is full of young drinkers and can get quite lively in the evenings. The *Robin Hood* (☎ 01442 824912; bar Mon-Fri 11.30am-3pm & 5.30-11pm, Sat & Sun

---

(Opposite) Following the Ridgeway through Tring Park (see p171), south-west of Tring.

11.30am-11.30pm; food Mon-Sat noon-2.15pm & 6-9.15pm, Sun noon-2.15pm) serves Fullers beer and is far more sedate and really rather quiet.

The most interesting choice is just a short walk away from the western end of the High St; **The King's Arms** (☎ 01442 823318, 💻 www.kingsarmstring.co.uk; bar Mon-Thur noon-2.30pm, Fri & Sat to 3pm, Sun to 4pm, daily 7-11.30pm, food Mon-

Thur noon-2.15pm, Fri & Sat to 2.30pm, Sun to 3pm, daily 7-9.30pm) on King St. This is a friendly freehouse on a suburban street with five real ales and a relaxed atmosphere. It has won various CAMRA (see box p16-17) awards over the years and the food is good too. The menu varies but may include Thai red beef curry (£9.50), and bacon, lentil and spinach soup (£4.50); they also have a specials board.

WIGGINTON TO IVINGHOE BEACON [MAPS 46-48]

Overview

This final **5-mile/8km (2¼-4hrs)** section of the Ridgeway may not seem much of a challenge but as most of this stage is uphill, with a steep climb to the finish itself, it'll probably be enough. From the finish you'll also have to walk at least to the nearest road, or probably to the nearest village, Ivinghoe. This will add around 1½ miles/2.5km to your walk and you don't want to be too tired to celebrate with a drink or two in one of the local pubs at the end.

Route

From Wigginton you'll soon come to the **pedestrian bridge** (Map 46) crossing the crowded A41 that runs from Bicester down to the M25. Next up it's the fast A4251 that you must cross without the aid of a bridge, so take care. Soon after these two road crossings, the Ridgeway crosses the **Grand Union Canal** (Map 47; see box below). After crossing two roads and a canal, next up is a rail line. You pass by **Tring Station**, now a minor stop for trains on the West Coast Main Line to/from London Euston. The large building next to the station used to be a hotel but has closed. There is a taxi company (see p174) in the station car park, but if you're not catching a train here there is little reason to stop. You follow the road for a few more minutes and when you leave it, you can consider yourself to be beginning the last stage of the Ridgeway. If you want to visit Aldbury, don't turn off here, but continue on the road for another half a mile/1km.

❏ **The Grand Union Canal**
This runs from the River Thames in Brentford, up through the Chilterns via many locks, then on to Birmingham where it finishes 137 miles/220km later. Initially this was the Grand Junction Canal, which opened in 1805 and ran only from Brentford, Middlesex, to Braunston, Northamptonshire, to link with the Oxford Canal. In 1929 it was linked to various other branches running up to Birmingham via Warwick and was renamed the Grand Union Canal. Nowadays the main traffic on the canal is boats rented by tourists. The towpath, from the Thames at Brentford to Birmingham, is now also recognised as an official walking path.

(Opposite) Top: St Mary the Virgin church in the centre of Ivinghoe village (see p180). **Bottom**: The trig point atop Ivinghoe Beacon (p181), the end of the Ridgeway.

ROUTE GUIDE AND MAPS

ALDBURY

Aldbury is a picture-perfect English village, complete with duck pond, church and pub. It would be a good alternative to Wigginton if the accommodation there is full. This idyllic village has been captured on film many times: *The Avengers*, *The Dirty Dozen*, *Inspector Morse*, and, more recently, *Bridget Jones's Diary: The Edge of Reason*.

You'll be surprised when you look inside the **village shop** (☎ 01442 851233; Mon, Tue, Thur, Fri 6am-5.30pm, Wed & Sat 6am-7.30pm, Sun 7.30am-4pm). Not only is it very well stocked and much larger than it looks from the outside, but there is a **post office** (Mon, Tue, Thur, Fri 9am-1pm & 2-5.30pm, Wed & Sat 9am-1pm) in here as well as an **ATM** (the charge per withdrawal is £1.95).

Buses leave the village for Tring Station (Arriva's No 30 and Red Rose Travel's No 387) and other destinations; see pp42-5 for further details.

Where to stay and eat

Opposite the duck pond is *The Greyhound Inn* (☎ 01442 851228, 🖳 www.greyhound aldbury.co.uk; 5D/2T or D/1D or F, all en suite, ❑; food Mon-Fri noon-2.30pm & 6.30-9.30pm, Sat noon-9.30pm, Sun noon-7.45pm), a much filmed and photographed place. The food is of a high standard and there is a varied menu: you could try the five-spiced potted duck with hoisin sauce and warm toast (£6.95) for lunch while the evening menu may include Moroccan-spiced lamb tagine (£14.50) and pan-fried

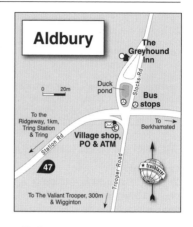

Aldbury

The Greyhound Inn

Duck pond

Bus stops

To the Ridgeway, 1km, Tring Station & Tring

Station Rd

Village shop, PO & ATM

To Berkhamsted

Trooper Road

47

★ trailblazer

To The Valiant Trooper, 300m & Wigginton

0   20m

calf's liver (£15.25). B&B costs £75, £65 if you're on your own and £90 for three in a room.

A good option for food is *The Valiant Trooper* (☎ 01442 851203, 🖳 www.valiant trooper.co.uk; bar Mon-Sat 11am-11pm, Sun noon-10.30pm; food Mon noon-2.30pm, Tue-Fri noon-2.30pm & 6-9pm, Sat noon-9pm, Sun noon-4pm). This pub is less than five minutes' walk from the centre of the village. Being a freehouse, they have a changing selection of real ales to accompany their food choices. The menu itself changes a couple of times a year but includes daily specials as well as standard pub fare such as sausage and mash with onion gravy (£9.95) and 8oz ribeye steak (£16.95).

The path rises through woodland, sometimes level, but more often than not climbing. By now there are only a few miles left and you might think it will all be over soon. Then you'll get your first glimpse of Ivinghoe Beacon, up ahead in the far distance. The word 'far' is appropriate but at least the end is now always in sight. You can admire the increasingly stunning views from up here and plod on.

You can also see, down to your left a large, old **chalk pit**, now filled with water; this is a popular place for relaxing and swimming during the summer. The water takes on a turquoise colour, adding something almost tropical to the atmosphere of the place. If you are plodding your way up to the Beacon on a hot day, just the sight of it can make you want to run down there and dive right in. When you reach the road and car park (Map 48) the Icknield Way puts in an appear-

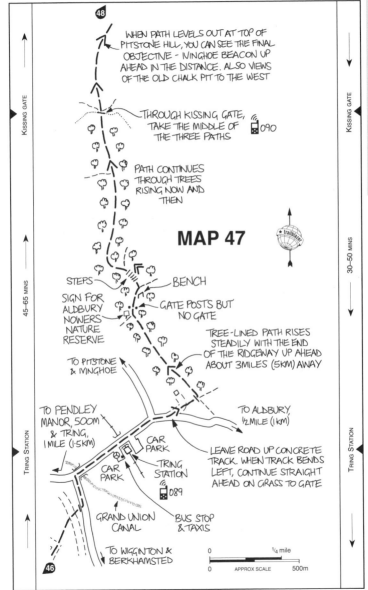

48

WHEN PATH LEVELS OUT AT TOP OF PITSTONE HILL, YOU CAN SEE THE FINAL OBJECTIVE - IVINGHOE BEACON UP AHEAD IN THE DISTANCE. ALSO VIEWS OF THE OLD CHALK PIT TO THE WEST

THROUGH KISSING GATE, TAKE THE MIDDLE OF THE THREE PATHS ☐ 090

KISSING GATE

PATH CONTINUES THROUGH TREES RISING NOW AND THEN

MAP 47

trailblazer

30-50 MINS

KISSING GATE

STEPS

BENCH

45-65 MINS

SIGN FOR ALDBURY NOWERS NATURE RESERVE

GATE POSTS BUT NO GATE

TREE-LINED PATH RISES STEADILY WITH THE END OF THE RIDGEWAY UP AHEAD ABOUT 3 MILES (5KM) AWAY

TO PITSTONE & IVINGHOE

TO ALDBURY, ½ MILE (1KM)

TO PENDLEY MANOR, 500M & TRING, 1 MILE (1.5KM)

CAR PARK

LEAVE ROAD UP CONCRETE TRACK. WHEN TRACK BENDS LEFT, CONTINUE STRAIGHT AHEAD ON GRASS TO GATE

TRING STATION

CAR PARK

TRING STATION ☐ 089

TRING STATION

GRAND UNION CANAL

BUS STOP & TAXIS

TO WIGGINTON & BERKHAMSTED

46

0   ¼ mile

0   APPROX SCALE   500m

ance once more and stays with you all the way to the end of the Ridgeway. Gradually the Beacon gets closer until you are left with just one last climb to the end. This will just about finish you off if you started the day at Princes Risborough.

There is a **Ridgeway information board** and **trig point** at the end of the walk to go with the panoramic views. There are often other people up here but not many who have been on the Ridgeway for the last 87 miles, for sure. Take plenty of time to relax, enjoy the views and reflect on the previous stages. When you are ready to leave the Beacon you have several choices. If you are lucky, someone might be waiting to pick you up from the car park you passed on your way up here. If not, you'll need to walk down to Ivinghoe village. The best way to do this is to follow one of the many paths down the hillside to the main road. Be careful as it's very steep and there are plenty of hidden holes in the ground.

Most paths finish near to the B489 from where it's a boring walk into Ivinghoe. This road is not particularly wide yet people drive very fast along it so be careful. If you get on with it the 1¼-mile/2km walk from the top of Ivinghoe Beacon to Ivinghoe village shouldn't take more than about half an hour.

IVINGHOE

Given its name you'd be right in presuming that this village is the closest to the end of the Ridgeway at Ivinghoe Beacon. This means that most Ridgeway walkers will pass through, or stay here, at some point.

Services

The village **post office** (Mon, Tue, Thur & Fri 9am-1pm & 2-5.30pm, Wed 9am-1pm, Sat 9am-1pm) is located in the **Londis** grocery shop (Mon-Fri 8am-6pm, Sat 8am-4pm, Sun 8am-1pm). The **library** (☎ 0845 230 3232; Tue & Thur 2-5pm, Fri 2-7pm, Sat 10am-1pm) offers **internet access** (£1/30 mins).

A larger shop with longer opening hours, **Mason's Stores** (☎ 01296 660052; Mon-Fri 6.30am-8pm, Sat 7am-8pm, Sun 7.30am-5pm) is on Marsworth Rd in Pitstone village about 10 minutes' walk away. It's also an **off-licence** and **newsagent**.

Arriva's No 61 **bus** and Redline's Nos 164 stop here but the latter is a limited service; see pp42-5 for further details.

Where to stay

An excellent B&B near Ivinghoe is *The Brownlow* (☎ 01296 668787, 🖳 www.the brownlow.com; 4D/1T, all en suite, ☐) about a mile (1km) out of the village where

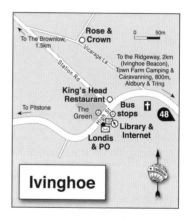

the road crosses the Grand Union canal. Light, spacious rooms are available from £77.50 (from £47.50 if you're on your own). To reach here, head out of the village on Station Rd.

If you want to camp, head for *Town Farm Camping* (☎ 07906 265435, 🖳 www. townfarmcamping.co.uk; 50 pitches) which charges £10pp including use of toilet and shower facilities. Booking is available online.

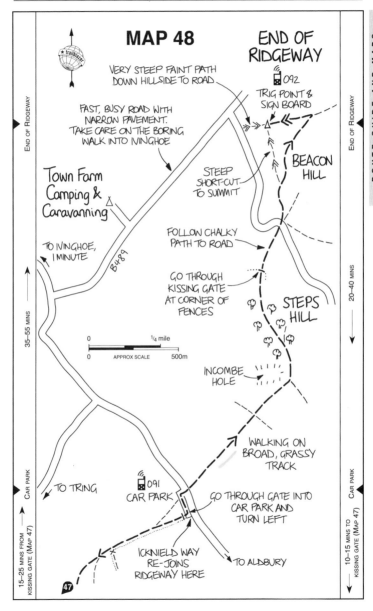

MAP 48

END OF RIDGEWAY

📱 092

TRIG POINT & SIGN BOARD

VERY STEEP FAINT PATH DOWN HILLSIDE TO ROAD

FAST, BUSY ROAD WITH NARROW PAVEMENT. TAKE CARE ON THE BORING WALK INTO IVINGHOE

BEACON HILL

STEEP SHORT-CUT TO SUMMIT

Town Farm Camping & Caravanning

FOLLOW CHALKY PATH TO ROAD

TO IVINGHOE, 1 MINUTE

B489

GO THROUGH KISSING GATE AT CORNER OF FENCES

STEPS HILL

0   ¼ mile
0   APPROX SCALE   500m

INCOMBE HOLE

WALKING ON BROAD, GRASSY TRACK

TO TRING

📱 091
CAR PARK

GO THROUGH GATE INTO CAR PARK AND TURN LEFT

ICKNIELD WAY RE-JOINS RIDGEWAY HERE

TO ALDBURY

47

END OF RIDGEWAY

END OF RIDGEWAY

20–40 MINS

35–55 MINS

CAR PARK

CAR PARK

15–25 MINS FROM KISSING GATE (MAP 47)

10–15 MINS TO KISSING GATE (MAP 47)

Where to eat and drink

Down Vicarage Lane is the cosy *Rose & Crown* (☎ 01296 668472, 🖥 www.roseand crownivinghoe.com; bar Mon-Thur 5-11pm, Fri-Sun noon-11pm; food Tue-Thur 6.30-9.30pm, Fri & Sat noon-2.30pm & 6.30-9.30pm, Sun noon-3pm) which serves real ales and meals such as cod and chips (£10.50), sausages and mash (£8.95), and glazed Aylesbury duck breast (£14.95).

The 17th-century *King's Head Restaurant* (☎ 01296 668388, 🖥 www. kingsheadivinghoe.co.uk; Mon-Sat noon-2.15pm & 6.45-9.30pm, Sun noon-2.15pm), right in the centre of the village, is known for its high-quality cuisine. It's not really

the place for muddy walkers – the dress code is smart, particularly in the evening – and with *entrées* costing from £37.75 to £52.25, you'll probably not find many walkers in there anyway. However, they do a three-course luncheon menu Monday to Saturday for £21.50 which might be worth considering for a celebratory meal.

In **Pitstone** village, next to Mason's Stores, there is a Chinese restaurant and takeaway called *May Fu Peking Restaurant* (☎ 01296 661969; Mon-Sat 5-11pm, Sun noon-11pm). You won't be stuck for choice at this well-liked place where main dishes cost between £5 and £8.

APPENDIX A: MAP KEY

♠ Where to stay	ⓘ Tourist information	☉ Bus stop/station
○ Where to eat & drink	📖 Library/bookstore	Rail line & station
Λ Campsite	Ⓢ Internet	Park
⊠ Post office	🎭 Museum/gallery	CP Car park
Ⓒ Bank/ATM	✝ Church/cathedral	● Other
☐ Building	☒ Public toilet	

Ridgeway	Slope	Fence
Subsidiary path	Steep slope	River
(4WD) track	Stile	Trees/wood
Road	Gate	GPS waypoint
Steps	Bridge	12 Map continuation

APPENDIX B: THE GREATER RIDGEWAY

LYME REGIS TO HUNSTANTON

After you've completed the Ridgeway you might like to consider a stroll along parts of the Greater Ridgeway that link Lyme Regis, in Dorset, with Hunstanton, in Norfolk. The Ridgeway covered in this book comprises just the middle section.

Starting from the popular seaside town of Lyme Regis, you can follow the Wessex Ridgeway 136 miles (219km) up to its finishing point at Marlborough in Wiltshire, crossing the Ridgeway near Avebury. From Lyme Regis the path goes through Beaminster before meandering through open country and numerous small villages and passing within a few miles of Shaftesbury.

You then skirt round the edge of Salisbury Plain taking in the towns of Heytesbury and Warminster. From here you head towards the Westbury White Horse and on to Devizes before arriving in Avebury and finally Marlborough.

From there the Ridgeway in this book takes you up to Ivinghoe Beacon from where you can follow the Icknield Way on to Knettishall Heath in Suffolk, 103 miles (166km) away. The long history of this trail equals that of the Ridgeway and is made evident by the wealth of archaeological remains found along here. The route continues on the high chalky ground visiting numerous towns along the way including Baldock, Royston and Linton. From here the Icknield Way continues to Cheveley and Icklingham before finishing at Knettishall Heath Country Park.

Picking up where the Icknield Way finishes, the Peddars Way, from Knettishall Heath to Hunstanton, clocks in at 46 miles (75km) and provides easy walking to the end of the Greater Ridgeway. This largely straight inland route follows a Roman road in open countryside with few villages en route.

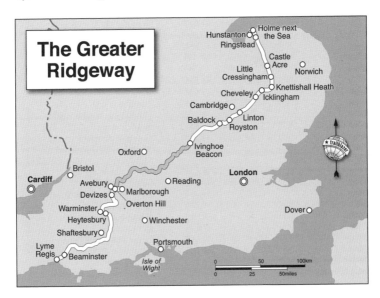

You will pass through Little Cressingham, Castle Acre and Ringstead before reaching the coast at Holme-next-the-Sea. From here you walk along the coast to reach Hunstanton, and the end of the Greater Ridgeway.

Further information
The Wessex Ridgeway, Anthony Burton, Aurum, 1999; *Ancient Trackways of Wessex*, HW Timperley & Edith Brill, Nonsuch, 2005; *The Icknield Way Path: A Walkers' Guide*, Chris James, Icknield Way Association, 2006; *Peddars Way and Norfolk Coast Path*, Alexander Stewart, Trailblazer Publications, 2011

APPENDIX C: GPS WAYPOINTS

Each GPS waypoint below was taken on the route at the reference number marked on the map as below.

MAP	REF	GPS WAYPOINT	DESCRIPTION
Map A	A	N51° 25.712' W01° 51.236'	Red Lion, Avebury
Map B	B	N51° 25.246' W01° 50.749'	Gate to Waden Hill
Map B	C	N51° 25.041' W01° 51.188'	Through gate and follow river
Map B	D	N51° 25.130' W01° 51.336'	Left turn
Map B	E	N51° 24.967' W01° 51.705'	Silbury Hill car park
Map B	F	N51° 24.851' W01° 51.110'	Leave A4 road
Map B	G	N51° 24.732' W01° 51.045'	Turn to the Long Barrow
Map B	H	N51° 24.516' W01° 51.017'	West Kennet Long Barrow
Map B	I	N51° 24.496' W01° 50.096'	Join road into East Kennet
Map B	J	N51° 24.711' W01° 49.834'	Start of the Ridgeway
Map B	K	N51° 25.065' W01° 49.816'	Turn to Avebury
Map A	L	N51° 26.191' W01° 51.236'	Junction with Green Street
Map C	M	N51° 26.234' W01° 48.851'	Cross track
Map C	N	N51° 26.517' W01° 47.638'	Reservoir
Map C	O	N51° 26.597' W01° 47.109'	Junction in path
Map D	P	N51° 26.384' W01° 46.326'	Driveway to Manton House
Map E	Q	N51° 25.957' W01° 44.954'	Road crossing
Map E	R	N51° 25.565' W01° 44.213'	Gate into cemetery
Map E	S	N51° 25.113' W01° 44.031'	Marlborough High Street
Map 1	001	N51° 24.711' W01° 49.834'	Start of the Ridgeway
Map 1	002	N51° 25.065' W01° 49.816'	Turn to Avebury
Map 2	003	N51° 26.191' W01° 51.236'	Junction with Green Street
Map 2	004	N51° 27.312' W01° 49.245'	Kink in path
Map 3	005	N51° 28.294' W01° 48.913'	Hackpen Hill car park
Map 4	006	N51° 29.115' W01° 47.178'	Barbury Castle
Map 4	007	N51° 29.004' W01° 46.469'	Upper Herdswick Farm
Map 5	008	N51° 28.325' W01° 44.461'	Gateway without gate
Map 6	009	N51° 27.752' W01° 43.303'	Turn to Southend
Map 6	010	N51° 27.746' W01° 41.822'	Crossroads

Map 7	011	N51° 28.618' W01° 41.520'	Road crossing
Map 7	012	N51° 29.224' W01° 41.694'	Crossroads by reservoir
Map 8	013	N51° 29.688' W01° 41.640'	Lower/Upper Upham junction
Map 8	014	N51° 30.036' W01° 41.521'	Fork in path
Map 9	015	N51° 30.994' W01° 41.695'	Gate near Liddington Castle
Map 9	016	N51° 31.429' W01° 41.267'	Turn to Foxhill
Map 10	017	N51° 31.803' W01° 40.100'	The Burj, Foxhill
Map 11	018	N51° 32.559' W01° 38.213'	Road junction to Bishopstone
Map 11	019	N51° 33.010' W01° 37.270'	Turn to Idstone
Map 12	020	N51° 33.432' W01° 36.427'	B4000 road crossing
Map 12	021	N51° 33.969' W01° 35.700'	Entrance to Wayland's Smithy
Map 13	022	N51° 34.459' W01° 34.013'	Second gate, Uffington Castle
Map 14	023	N51° 34.452' W01° 32.134'	Turn to Kingston Lisle
Map 14	024	N51° 34.217' W01° 31.436'	Turn Sparsholt/Down Barn Farm
Map 15	025	N51° 33.826' W01° 30.343'	Sparsholt Firs car park
Map 16	026	N51° 33.241' W01° 28.012'	Turn to Letcombe Bassett
Map 16	027	N51° 33.317' W01° 26.871'	Segsbury Farm
Map 16	028	N51° 33.437' W01° 25.960'	A338 road crossing
Map 17	029	N51° 33.266' W01° 23.906'	B4494 road crossing
Map 17	030	N51° 33.411' W01° 23.408'	Large monument
Map 18	031	N51° 33.513' W01° 23.086'	Large, sprawling junction
Map 18	032	N51° 33.648' W01° 22.047'	Reservoir
Map 19	033	N51° 33.737' W01° 20.428'	Turn to East Hendred
Map 19	034	N51° 33.194' W01° 18.598'	Bury Down car park
Map 20	035	N51° 32.880' W01° 17.679'	Tunnel under A34
Map 21	036	N51° 32.373' W01° 16.590'	First turn to East Ilsley
Map 21	037	N51° 32.362' W01° 16.544'	Second turn to East Ilsley
Map 21	038	N51° 32.125' W01° 16.175'	Third turn to East Ilsley
Map 21	039	N51° 32.016' W01° 16.059'	Fourth turn to East Ilsley
Map 22	040	N51° 32.262' W01° 14.490'	Fork in path
Map 22	041	N51° 32.021' W01° 13.844'	Tracks cross
Map 22	042	N51° 31.786' W01° 13.331'	Fork in path
Map 23	043	N51° 31.647' W01° 12.551'	Turn to Aldworth
Map 23	044	N51° 31.639' W01° 11.068'	Post Box Cottage
Map 24	045	N51° 31.726' W01° 09.064'	Path joins A417 road
Map 24	046	N51° 31.363' W01° 08.923'	Streatley crossroads
Map 26	047	N51° 32.929' W01° 08.335'	Turn towards River Thames
Map 26	048	N51° 32.951' W01° 08.701'	Slipway on bank of Thames
Map 27	049	N51° 33.454' W01° 08.544'	Railway viaduct
Map 27	050	N51° 33.862' W01° 08.072'	Small wooden footbridge
Map 28	051	N51° 34.306' W01° 07.271'	North Stoke
Map 28	052	N51° 35.304' W01° 07.232'	Turn before A4130 road
Map 28	053	N51° 35.121' W01° 05.983'	Turn to Little Gables B&B
Map 29	054	N51° 35.069' W01° 05.487'	Road to Crowmarsh Gifford
Map 29	055	N51° 35.012' W01° 05.012'	Road to Ewelme & Woodcote
Map 30	056	N51° 34.716' W01° 02.419'	T-junction in path
Map 30	057	N51° 34.862' W01° 02.281'	Holy Trinity Church, Nuffield
Map 30	058	N51° 35.048' W01° 01.607'	The Crown, Nuffield
Map 31	059	N51° 35.833' W01° 01.732'	Ewelme Park
Map 31	060	N51° 36.393' W01° 00.979'	St Botolph's
Map 32	061	N51° 37.392' W01° 01.316'	North Farm
Map 32	062	N51° 37.831' W01° 00.254'	Ridge Farm

Map 33	063	N51° 38.022'	W00° 59.954'	First turn to Watlington
Map 33	064	N51° 38.413'	W00° 59.528'	Turn to White Mark Farm
Map 33	065	N51° 38.714'	W00° 59.110'	Road crossing
Map 34	066	N51° 39.968'	W00° 57.546'	Narrow but fast road to Lewknor
Map 35	067	N51° 40.404'	W00° 56.903'	A40 road crossing
Map 35	068	N51° 40.908'	W00° 55.741'	Road to Kingston Blount
Map 36	069	N51° 41.309'	W00° 54.704'	Turn to Oakley Hill Nature Reserve
Map 37	070	N51° 41.749'	W00° 54.073'	Road to Chinnor
Map 37	071	N51° 42.264'	W00° 53.218'	Path bends round house
Map 37	072	N51° 41.864'	W00° 51.978'	Road to Bledlow
Map 38	073	N51° 41.741'	W00° 50.531'	Longwood Farm drive
Map 38	074	N51° 42.205'	W00° 50.498'	Saunderton railway tunnel
Map 39	075	N51° 42.930'	W00° 50.118'	Leave A4010 road
Map 39	076	N51° 43.251'	W00° 49.502'	Road crossing
Map 40	077	N51° 43.737'	W00° 48.641'	Turn in path direction
Map 40	078	N51° 43.982'	W00° 48.287'	The Plough, Cadsden
Map 41	079	N51° 44.221'	W00° 46.578'	Leave road for track
Map 41	080	N51° 44.707'	W00° 46.326'	Path joins road
Map 41	081	N51° 45.184'	W00° 46.291'	Monument on Coombe Hill
Map 42	082	N51° 45.545'	W00° 44.999'	Join road into Wendover
Map 42	083	N51° 45.366'	W00° 44.098'	Crossroads
Map 43	084	N51° 44.949'	W00° 43.456'	Path leaves track
Map 44	085	N51° 45.825'	W00° 41.816'	Gate half-hidden in hedge
Map 45	086	N51° 46.532'	W00° 40.269'	The Mill, Hastoe
Map 46	087	N51° 47.138'	W00° 38.777'	Road crossing
Map 46	088	N51° 47.460'	W00° 38.133'	Pedestrian bridge over A41 road
Map 47	089	N51° 48.042'	W00° 37.400'	Tring railway station
Map 47	090	N51° 48.956'	W00° 37.379'	Take middle path
Map 48	091	N51° 49.496'	W00° 36.931'	Car park
Map 48	092	N51° 50.531'	W00° 36.502'	End of the Ridgeway

INDEX

Page references in **bold** type refer to maps

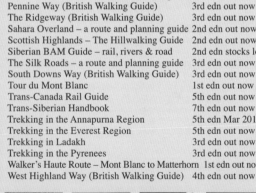

The Inca Trail, Cusco & Machu Picchu
Alexander Stewart, 4th edn, £12.99

ISBN 978-1-905864-15-7, 352pp, 74 maps, 40 colour photos
The Inca Trail, from Cusco to Machu Picchu, is South America's most popular trek. Practical guide including detailed trail maps, plans of Inca sites, plus guides to Cusco and Machu Picchu. Route guides to other trails in the area: the Santa Teresa Trek and the Choquequirao Trek as well as the Vilcabamba Trail plus the routes linking them. This entirely rewalked and rewritten fourth edition includes a new history of the Incas by Hugh Thomson.

New Zealand – The Great Walks
Alexander Stewart, 2nd edn, £12.99

ISBN 978-1-905864-11-9, 272pp, 60 maps, 40 colour photos
New Zealand is a wilderness paradise of incredibly beautiful landscapes. There is no better way to experience it than on one of the nine designated Great Walks, the country's premier walking tracks which provide outstanding hiking opportunities for people at all levels of fitness. Also includes detailed guides to Auckland, Wellington, National Park Village, Taumarunui, Nelson, Queenstown, Te Anau and Oban.

Kilimanjaro – the trekking guide to Africa's highest mountain
Henry Stedman, 3rd edn, £12.99

ISBN 978-1-905864-24-9, 368pp, 40 maps, 30 photos
At 19,340ft the world's tallest freestanding mountain, Kilimanjaro is one of the most popular destinations for hikers visiting Africa. It's possible to walk up to the summit: no technical skills are necessary. Includes town guides to Nairobi and Dar-Es-Salaam, and a colour guide to flora and fauna. Includes Mount Meru.

Nepal Trekking and the Great Himalaya Trail
Robin Boustead, 1st edn, £14.99, ISBN 978-1-905864-31-7

256pp, 8pp colour maps, 40 colour photos
This guide includes the most popular routes in Nepal – the Everest, Annapurna and Langtang regions – as well as the newest trekking areas for true trailblazers. This is the first guide to chart The Great Himalaya Trail, the route which crosses Nepal from east to west. Extensive planning sections.

Trekking in the Everest Region
Jamie McGuinness, 5th edn, £12.99, ISBN 978-1-873756-99-7

320pp, 30 maps, 30 colour photos
Fifth edition of this popular guide to the Everest region, the world's most famous trekking region. Planning, preparation, getting to Nepal; detailed route guides with 30 route maps and 50 village plans; Kathmandu city guide: where to stay, where to eat, what to see.

The Walker's Haute Route – Mt Blanc to the Matterhorn
Alexander Stewart, 1st edn, £12.99

ISBN 978-1-905864-08-9, 256pp, 60 maps, 30 colour photos
From Mont Blanc to the Matterhorn, Chamonix to Zermatt, the 180km (113-mile) Walkers' Haute Route traverses one of the finest stretches of the Pennine Alps – the range between Valais in Switzerland and Piedmont and Aosta Valley in Italy. Includes Chamonix and Zermatt guides.

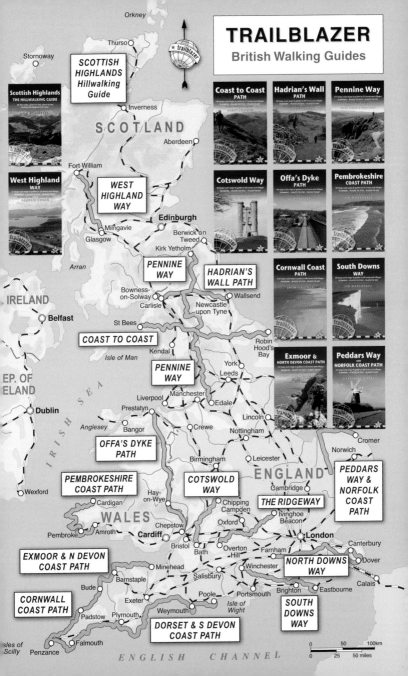

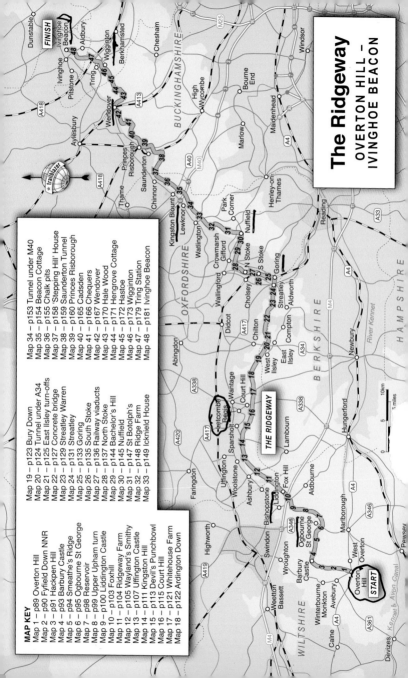

The Ridgeway
OVERTON HILL – IVINGHOE BEACON

THE RIDGEWAY

* trailblazer

START

FINISH